CHRISTOPHER MARLOWE: THE CRITICAL HERITAGE

THE CRITICAL HERITAGE SERIES

General Editor: B. C. Southam

The Critical Heritage series collects together a large body of criticism on major figures in literature. Each volume presents the contemporary responses to a particular writer, enabling the student to follow the formation of critical attitudes to the writer's work and its place within a literary tradition.

The carefully selected sources range from landmark essays in the history of criticism to fragments of contemporary opinion and little published documentary material, such as letters and diaries.

Significant pieces of criticism from later periods are also included in order to demonstrate fluctuations in reputation following the writer's death.

CHRISTOPHER MARLOWE

THE CRITICAL HERITAGE

Edited by

MILLAR MacLURE

LONDON AND NEW YORK

First Published in 1979
Reprinted by Routledge in 1995, 1998

2 Park Square, Milton Park,
Abingdon, Oxon, OX14 4RN
&
270 Madison Ave,
New York NY 10016

Transferred to Digital Printing 2009

British Library Cataloguing in Publication Data

ISBN10: 0–415–13416–1 (hbk)
ISBN10: 0–415–56879–X (pbk)

ISBN13: 978–0–415–13416–3 (hbk)
ISBN13: 978–0–415–56879–1 (pbk)

ISBN 0–415–13415–3 (set)

Publisher's Note
The publisher has gone to great lengths to ensure the quality of this
reprint but points out that some imperfections in the original
may be apparent.

General Editor's Preface

The reception given to a writer by his contemporaries and near-contemporaries is evidence of considerable value to the student of literature. On one side we learn a great deal about the state of criticism at large and in particular about the development of critical attitudes towards a single writer; at the same time, through private comments in letters, journals or marginalia, we gain an insight upon the tastes and literary thought of individual readers of the period. Evidence of this kind helps us to understand the writer's historical situation, the nature of his immediate reading-public, and his response to these pressures.

The separate volumes in the *Critical Heritage Series* present a record of this early criticism. Clearly, for many of the highly productive and lengthily reviewed nineteenth- and twentieth-century writers, there exists an enormous body of material; and in these cases the volume editors have made a selection of the most important views, significant for their intrinsic critical worth or for their representative quality—perhaps even registering incomprehension!

For earlier writers, notably pre-eighteenth century, the materials are much scarcer and the historical period has been extended, sometimes far beyond the writer's lifetime, in order to show the inception and growth of critical views which were initially slow to appear.

In each volume the documents are headed by an Introduction, discussing the material assembled and relating the early stages of the author's reception to what we have come to identify as the critical tradition. The volumes will make available much material which would otherwise be difficult of access and it is hoped that the modern reader will be thereby helped towards an informed understanding of the ways in which literature has been read and judged.

B.C.S.

Contents

vii

CONTENTS

Acknowledgments

This account of Marlowe's reputation and achievements,
extending over three centuries, is inevitably indebted to
S. A. Tannenbaum, 'Marlowe: a Concise Bibliography' (New
York, 1937) and its 'Supplement' (New York, 1947); to
C. F. Tucker Brooke, The Reputation of Christopher
Marlowe, 'Transactions of the Connecticut Academy of Arts
and Sciences', xxv (1922), 347-408; C. F. Tucker Brooke,
'The Life of Marlowe' (1930); F. S. Boas, 'Christopher
Marlowe: A Biographical and Critical Study' (Oxford, 1940;
reprinted 1964). Other obligations to Marlowe scholarship
are indicated in the notes to the Introduction and in the
headnotes to the selections from biography and criticism.

The editor and publishers gratefully acknowledge per-
mission to reproduce copyright material as follows: Ernest
Benn for No. 49; Macmillan, London and Basingstoke, for
Nos 41 and 48; and The Society of Authors on behalf of the
Bernard Shaw Estate for No. 56.

The initial collection and arrangement of documents for
this book was done during a leave of absence (1972-3) from
my College, assisted by a grant from the Canada Council.
Julia Keeler not only found much of the material, but prepared a valuable bibliography of Marlowe criticism beyond
what is reproduced here. I am most grateful to the General Editor of the series, and to Routledge & Kegan Paul,
who have been most helpful in the revival and repair of a
collection which I hope will be useful to students of
Elizabethan drama and nineteenth-century literary journal-
ism.

Chronological Table

1564 26 February. 'Cristofer the sonne of John Marlow'
christened, St George the Martyr, Canterbury.

1578/9 14 January. Entered scholar, King's School,
Canterbury.

1580/1 17 March. Matriculated Corpus Christi College,
Cambridge, on Matthew Parker scholarship.

1583/4 BA.

1587 MA, after reception by the University of a Privy
Council certificate of 29 June.

1589 September–October. Imprisoned in Newgate for
involvement in an affray with Thomas Watson and
William Bradley.

1590 'Tamburlaine the Great.... Divided into two
Tragicall Discourses.... Printed by Richard Ihones'.

1592 Dedication (signed 'C.M.') to Mary, Countess of
Pembroke, of Thomas Watson's 'Amintae Gaudia'.
Epitaph on Sir Roger Manwood, Chief Baron of the
Exchequer.

1593 18 May. Privy Council warrant for Marlowe's
appearance.
30 May. Killed at Eleanor Bull's tavern,
Deptford.
1 June. 'Christopher Marlowe slaine by ffrancis
ffrezar [i.e. Ingram Frizer]' buried, St Nicholas,
Deptford.

1594 'The troublesome raigne and lamentable death of
Edward the second, King of England: with the tragi-
call fall of proud Mortimer.... Written by Chri.
Marlow Gent.... Imprinted... for William Iones'.
'The Tragedie of Dido Queene of Carthage....
Written by Christopher Marlowe, and Thomas Nash.
Gent.... Printed by the Widdowe Orwin, for Thomas
Woodcocke'.

1598 'Hero and Leander. By Christopher Marloe.... Prin-

ted by Adam Islip, for Edward Blunt'.
'Hero and Leander: Begun by Christopher Marloe, and finished by George Chapman.... Printed by Felix Kingston, for Paule Linley'.

ante 1599 'Epigrammes and Elegies. By I.D. and C.M.... At Middleborough'.

ante 1599? 'All Ovids Elegies: 3. Bookes, By. C.M.... At Middlebourgh'.

1599 The Passionate Shepherd to His Love, in 'The Passionate Pilgrim'.

1600 'Lucans First Booke Translated Line for Line, By Chr. Marlowe.... Printed by P. Short... sold by Walter Burre'.

1602? 'The Massacre at Paris: with the Death of the Duke of Guise.... Written by Christopher Marlow.... Printed by E.A. for Edward White'.

1604 'The Tragicall History of D. Faustus.... Written by Ch. Marl.... Printed by V.S. for Thomas Bushell [A-text]'.

1616 'The Tragicall History of the Life and Death of Doctor Faustus. Written by Ch. Marl.... Printed by Iohn Wright [B-text]'.

1633 'The Famous Tragedy of The Rich Jew of Malta.... Written by Christopher Marlo.... Printed by I.B. for Nicholas Vavasour'.

Introduction

This is not a Marlowe 'allusion-book', though it begins
with allusions and some non-literary documents. These,
however well-known from frequent reproduction, are necessary to establish the sources of the Marlowe stereotype
upon which so much of the critical comment depends, down
to the beginning of our own century, and beyond that.
The general pattern of the Marlowe tradition is clear:
a mixed bag of contemporary and early seventeenth-century
references to a powerful personality, a short and brilliant
literary career, and a melodramatic death; then, after the
Restoration, a virtual eclipse both of facts and opinions
about him; the gradual recovery of the texts of his work
and the nature of his milieu by eighteenth- and early
nineteenth-century bibliographers and antiquaries; the
enthusiasm of some Romantic critics and their followers;
the extensive editorial and critical tributes of many
Victorian men of letters and their successors; finally, by
a collaboration of twentieth-century scholarship and the
development of fresh critical assumptions, the emergence
in the learned journals of what can only be called the
Marlowe industry.
   The present collection is intended to carry the reader
barely to the threshold of this last phase; it begins with
the malignant taunts of Robert Greene and the adulatory
remarks of Marlowe's friends and literary associates, and
ends with the abrasive comments of the younger G. B. Shaw
and the rhapsodies of Swinburne. For the twentieth-century
flowering of the critical heritage, one may look to some
important anthologies, 'casebooks', introductions, etc. (1)
   But the pattern will never be complete, for Marlowe is
such a searching and resonant writer that his 'working
words', played in counterpoint to his legend, will always
be reinterpreted, and come home to English-speaking men

1

(and not only those) in ways they can understand in their own frame of time.

I (1588-1642)

The literary world of London in the last decade of the sixteenth century was a small world, focused on the ambitions of theatrical managers and the profits of stationers, in fear always of censorship by the authorities, and sustained by occasional and not always reliable patronage. It was into this 'fringe' society that Marlowe, who had read divinity at Cambridge on an Archbishop Parker scholarship, and had got his MA by special intervention of the Queen's Council (apparently assured that he had been valuable as a secret agent on the Continent), emerged suddenly (1587?) with his 'Tamburlaine', Edward Alleyn in the starring role. And the first important response to this event (so far as we know) came from Robert Greene, Cambridge scholar, playwright, pamphleteer, capable from the beginning of melodramatic exploitation of his own powers and afflictions – though we have to take into account, with him and others, the fact that training in rhetoric could make a minor irritation into a major attack, or a passing approval into a panegyric. Understanding this current idiom helps us to keep in some perspective most of the contemporary references to Marlowe.

'Perimedes the Blacksmith' (1588), a gallimaufry of tales and moral precepts, would be forgotten except by specialists, were it not for the significant reference to Marlowe in the preface 'To the Gentlemen readers' (No. 1a). Greene's envy of Marlowe's 'bragging blank verse' is here a left-handed tribute to the immediate success of 'Tamburlaine', supported, in this mess of oblique allusions, by the pun in 'Merlins race', for 'Marlin' was the form in which Marlowe's name had most frequent occurrence, especially at Cambridge. Here also is the implicit (later explicit) identification of Marlowe's personality and opinions with those of his protagonists, and the charge of 'atheism': atheists, blasphemers and 'epicures' being, not technical terms, but words of abuse for all iconoclasts, loose livers, unorthodox thinkers and, generally, dangerous men.

Greene's last message to the 'University Wits', his address 'to those Gentleman his Quondam acquaintance, that spend their wits in making plays' in his 'Groatsworth of Wit' (1592), is notorious for its attack on Shakespeare as 'the onely Shake-scene in a countrey'; the address to Marlowe (No. 1b), with its obvious reference to the Machiavelli Prologue to 'The Jew of Malta', merely reinforces,

with that histrionic sorrow which overcame him in his last
days, what he had written before, with the added tribute
which he had to give to success. When Henry Chettle edited
this for the press, he was very touchy about Marlowe, while
warm to Shakespeare, yet he did pay tribute to Marlowe's
learning - a theme repeated by others, as we shall see
(No. 2).

This was written late in 1592. On 30 May 1593, Marlowe
was killed at Deptford, and this event, because of the
mysterious circumstances and the man's reputation, was the
subject of ill-informed and heavily moralized comment,
which in time became a 'mirror' for intellectuals and a
staple of journalists. And Marlowe's ghost began at once
to haunt the notorious Thomas Nashe - Gabriel Harvey controversy, which began as the sixteenth-century counterpart
of a 'TLS' correspondence, and ended in pointless scurri-
lity. This is no place to rehearse the course of that
exhilarating exchange, which ended with the burning, in
June 1599, by episcopal authority, of some scurrilous and
libellous publications, including Marlowe's translation of
Ovid's 'Amores' with the 'Epigrams' of Sir John Davies, but
some things come out which are worth notice. We can be
reasonably sure that Nashe wrote an elegy on Marlowe, prefixed to a lost copy of 'The Tragedy of Dido' (1594), (2)
also that his often-quoted attack on 'ideot Art-masters'
who 'think to out-brave better pens with the swelling bum-
bast of bragging blank verse' in his preface to Greene's
'Menaphon' (1589) is not an attack on Marlowe but on
'dramatic writing generally' (as his great editor McKerrow
puts it). We have his word, in 'Have with You To Saffron-
Walden' (1596): 'I never abusd *Marloe, Greene, Chettle* in
my life, nor anie of my friends that usde me like a frend',
and, as we shall see, he paid an especially eloquent and
subtle tribute to Marlowe in a fine phrase. In the second
issue of 'Christs Teares over Ierusalem' (1594), he noted
that Harvey had 'most notoriously & vilely dealt' with
'Maister *Lillie*, poore deceased Kit Marlow' and others:
the reference is to Harvey's 'A New Letter of Notable
Contents', published in late 1593, in which Harvey refers
to Marlowe as 'a Lucian' and, in a set of doggerel verses
at the end, seems to suggest that Marlowe died of the
plague (No. 6).

From Harvey's noisy oblique allusions (he wrote better
in Latin), one turns with grim relief to the most influential of the early contributions to the Marlowe legend, the
Puritan Thomas Beard's 'The Theatre of Gods Iudgements'
(1597). Beard's comments were repeated, paraphrased, ill-
quoted, not so much about the particular (and inaccurate)
account of Marlowe's death, as for putting him in his

place, so to speak, in the scheme of God's providence and
punishments, a pattern that the nineteenth-century critics
could either accept or deny, depending on their way of
thinking about the Elizabethan age, and what they knew
about it, which in some cases was not much. Beard's book
was a translation-compilation of exempla, and in his chap-
ter Of Epicures and Atheists he added to continental mir-
rors of iniquity - for example, Pope Julius II, Rabelais
and Jodelle - Marlowe (No. 8). Francis Meres and William
Vaughan added their variations (Nos 12, 14). And there is
an obvious reference in the obscure William Rankins (No. 9).
   Beard's account, which achieved several editions, is
based on contemporary gossip about Marlowe's atheism.
Thomas Kyd's confessions to the Lord Keeper, Sir John
Puckering, and Richard Baine's 'Note', which are here
placed chronologically among contemporary allusions to
Marlowe, were not public documents (Nos 3, 4). Baines was
often referred to as 'Bame', by a false transcription, and
was first published by Joseph Ritson in 1782 (see below).
(3) The first was written in fear, the second in politic
malice. But there is no reason to suppose that Marlowe did
not say something of what they said he did: he was a Deist
before Deism, a Higher Critic before the Higher Criticism,
all this apart from incidental blasphemy, uttered in drink,
perhaps, or just to shock. He was a pretty rough character, to tell the truth. But it is now proper to turn to
the testimonies of other contemporaries and successors who
professed letters: publishers, fellow dramatists, custo-
dians of the house of fame.
   The only work of Marlowe published in his lifetime, the
two parts of 'Tamburlaine' (1590), was prefaced by an
address 'To the Gentlemen Readers' by the printer Richard
Jones, in which he explains that he has left out 'some
fond and friuolous Iestures ... far unmeet for the matter'
used on the stage but not fitting for 'the eloquence of
the Authour'. Marlowe's name did not appear on the title
page, but the authorship was no secret. The tribute to
learning, to *eloquentia*, comes out, with reservations or
not, time and again.(4) For example, in George Peele's
catalogue of 1593 (No. 5), Marlowe is able to give words
to the 'strengthless dead', as Homer was to Achilles in
'Odyssey', XI; this is a tribute to Marlowe as a primal,
a first poet, echoed by Nashe as preface to his comical
and affectionate parody of the story of Hero and Leander
in his 'Lenten Stuffe' (1599): 'Hath any bodie in Yarmouth
heard of Leander and Hero, of whom diuine *Musaeus* sung,
and a diuiner Muse than him, *Kit Marlow*?'(5) The point of
the posthumous compliment is that Musaeus, 'the Grammarian', was taken by Marlowe's contemporaries, including

George Chapman, as one of the triad of 'makers', the others
being Homer and Orpheus. Chapman's characteristically
solemn and powerful gesture in Marlowe's direction, early
in his completion of 'Hero and Leander' (No. 11), supports
this; so does the epigrammatic verdict of the Cambridge
scholars, with their 'wit lent from heaven' and its hellish
counterpart (No. 13); even the casual bumblings of Henry
Petowe, one of the most minor of minor versifiers, who
attempted a continuation of 'Hero and Leander' in a pseudo-
Italianate manner in 1598, pay tribute to an 'admired
Poet'.(6) The whole tradition is summed up in the often-
quoted verses of Michael Drayton, written before 1627
(No. 15).

Marlowe's words were all air and fire; the baser elements were left to his enemies, though he had friends too,
notable among them the printer Edward Blunt (No. 10); and
Thomas Thorpe, the publisher of Shakespeare's 'Sonnets',
dedicating to Blunt Marlowe's translation of the first book
of Lucan's 'Civil Wars', in 1600, refers to 'that pure
elemental wit' whose memory was good for both friends and
stationers.(7)

It is impossible here to reproduce or even refer to many
of the great number of allusions, incidental tributes, and
parodies, which were collected by Tucker Brooke from the
period before the closing of the theatres in 1642.(8) Some
are especially significant, and a majority have to do with
'Hero and Leander' and 'Tamburlaine', both treasuries of
familiar quotations.

No one matched the condensed allusiveness of Shakespeare,
in whose shadow, for later generations, Marlowe was eclip-
sed. When, in III, iii of 'As You Like It' (1598), Touch-
stone says: 'When a man's verses cannot be understood, nor
a man's good wit seconded with the forward child, understanding, it strikes a man more dead than a great reckoning
in a little room', he manages to get into a few words, with
the help of a mention of 'the most capricious poet, honest
Ovid ... among the Goths' just before, not only references
to Marlowe's translation of Ovid's 'Amores', and to the
most famous line from the first scene of 'The Jew of
Malta', but, apparently, to the actual wording of the
Queen's coroner's verdict on Marlowe's death, in a quarrel
over 'le recknynge', discovered for us by Professor Hotson
in 1925.(9) When he was writing 'As You Like It', Shakespeare certainly had 'Hero and Leander' in his mind, for
Phebe says (in III, v):

Dead Shepherd, now I find thy saw of might,
'Who ever loved that loved not at first sight?'

The Passionate Shepherd was the most popular song of the
time, 'that smooth song which was made by Kit Marlow, now
at least fifty years ago', says Izaak Walton in 'The Compleat Angler' (1653, 1655).

Parody and burlesque, from whatever motives directed,
are tributes to the power of the original words. All
depend on recognition. They are also reductive, because
they separate the most popular and exposed parts from the
total composition. So (to have done with 'As You Like
It'), Rosalind says gaily that Leander 'being taken with
the cramp was drownd' and adds the final anti-romantic
sentiment: 'Men have died from time to time, and worms
have eaten them, but not for love' ('AYL', IV, i, 99-103);
Jonson makes 'Hero and Leander' the staple of a poetaster
in 'Every Man in His Humour' (1598; IV, i), but in the
prelude to the parody in 'Bartholomew Fair' (1614), as in
the report of his remarks about Marlowe in the preface to
William Bosworth's 'The Chast and Lost Lovers' (1651) –
'examples fitter for admiration than for parallel' – we
find one side of his balanced judgment on Marlowe and his
influence, as we find the other in his well-known comment
on the 'Tamburlaine-style' in his 'Timber' (No. 18), and,
perhaps, in his competitive translation of Ovid's 'Amores',
I, xv, incorporated in 'The Poetaster' (1601).(10). The
famous phrase, 'Marlowe's mighty line', is a generous dis-
missal from the presence chamber of the immortals.

'Hero and Leander' (seven editions, 1606-37) was a bedside book, though its popularity owed nothing to Chapman's completion of 'that partly excellent Poem of Maister
Marloes', as he called it in his preface to his translation of Musaeus (1616). One of Thomas Middleton's topical
characters refers to it, with 'Venus and Adonis', as 'two
luscious marrow-bone pies for a young married wife'.(11)
But the stage is not familiar but public, and the count-
less reminiscences of striking lines and scenes from the
plays, during this period, testify not only to the memor-
ability of Marlowe's verse, but to the power of a style in
the public theatres, a style which inflates the purple
passage or the scene-concluding couplet, where the comic
exchanges are conducted unintelligibly full-voice with
horseplay and special effects (as in 'Doctor Faustus'),
and the narrative and descriptive parts are done at speed.
Edward Alleyn is not dead yet. But when Thomas Heywood
revived 'The Famous Tragedy of the Rich Jew of Malta' at
Court and the Cockpit in 1632, having apparently tampered
a bit with whatever text he had, in his rather elaborate
preliminary matter he felt obliged to divide the honours
between the learned poet and the actor, who forty years
before had held the stage (No. 17). The 'high astounding

terms' of Tamburlaine, when badly imitated, could slide all
too easily into rant, 'Graced with huf-cap termes, and
thundring threats', in the words of Joseph Hall's satiric
description,(12) and offered a generous invitation to
parody. Bajazet in his cage, Tamburlaine drawn by the
'pampered jades of Asia', were favourite episodes for such
treatment.(13)

Apart from very numerous echoes and imitations of conspicuous passages, such as the apostrophe to Helen, 'Doctor
Faustus' 'made the greatest noise with its Devils and such
like Tragical sport'. For example John Melton, in 'The
Astrologaster' (1620), tells how 'shaggehayr'd Deuills
runne roaring ouer the Stage with Squibs in theire mouthes,
while Drummers make Thunder in the Tyring-house', and
William Prynne reports a horrific legend of a particular
performance, also current in Germany, where the play was
carried by touring companies (No. 16). Among these allusions, it is notable that there seems to be little or no
reference to the central tragedy of the play; rather Faustus and Mephistophilis, like Barabas in 'The Jew of Malta',
become stock types unconnected with their creator. This
did not happen with 'Edward II', 'Dido', or 'The Massacre
at Paris', presumably because they did not enjoy such a
theatrical notoriety, at least not after the 1590s.

II (1660-1781)

It may seem that I have given a disproportionate amount of
attention to these bits and pieces, none of them critical
comment in a sense we can allow to the later researches of
antiquaries and bibliophiles, to the essays of the Romantic
and Victorian men of letters, many of whom seemed to regard
sixteenth-century literature as the production of a lively
but semi-civilized colony in time, or to the modern sett-
lers in that time, who bring their own critical techniques
with them to achieve 'growth' in literary criticism. But
it is upon these fugitive allusions, often light-hearted,
often prejudiced, that so much of the heritage depends.
Though there were successive reprints of 'Hero and Leander'
and 'Doctor Faustus' into the 1630s, and all the plays
appear in booksellers' catalogues at least until 1671,(14)
we find little or no attention given to the text of Marlowe
in the century after the Restoration, either in the study
or the theatre. Instead we have a set of errors or professions of ignorance, clichés of biography, and snap judgments which make poor reading.

Like others who have considered this break in the Marlowe tradition (notably Tucker Brooke and Boas), I have no

easy explanation for this virtual eclipse. Some obvious
reasons come to mind: the re-establishment of the London
theatres under different managerial arrangements, with
different audiences and partly different theatrical traditions; the influence of the Puritan calumnies; the
scarcity of texts which confined them to the casual interest of collectors and the curiosity of antiquaries, and
helped to make Marlowe a 'chamber' dramatist, and, above
all, an assumption of 'period', of the remoteness of every-
body but Shakespeare. Marlowe was of an age, and often
lost even to that.

Any survey of Marlowe's fate in the Restoration period
must begin with Samuel Pepys's account, when he went with
his wife to the Red Bull on 26 May 1662, and they saw
'Doctor Faustus' 'so wretchedly and poorly done, that we
were sick of it'. This was the version printed in 1663,
much mutilated, 'with several New Scenes', including reference to the plot of the 'The Jew of Malta'. The little
left of Marlowe virtually disappears from the stage with
William Mountford's 'The Life and Death of Doctor Faustus,
with the Humours of Harlequin and Scaramouch', acted at
Dorset Garden c. 1686 (1697). When Charles Saunders published his 'Tamerlane the Great. As it is Acted by their
Majesties Servants at the Theatre Royal' in 1681, a play
which he claimed had 'received some rules of correction
from Mr. Dryden himself', he affirmed against some cap-
tious critics:(15)

> I never heard of any Play on the same Subject, untill my
> own was Acted, though it hath been told me, there is a
> Cock Pit Play, going under the name of the 'Scythian
> Shepherd', or 'Tamberlain the Great', which how good it
> is, anyone may Judge by its obscurity.... I drew the
> design of this Play, from a late Novell, call'd
> 'Tamerlane and Asteria'.

The silence on the stage was echoed from the study.
Marlowe does not appear in Thomas Fuller's 'Worthies of
England' (1662), and he is not mentioned by Dryden, of all
people. (It is perhaps proper to mention in this place the
continuing disappearance of Marlowe among the literary
journalists: in an unsigned notice in the 'Monthly Review'
(September-December 1820, xciii, 59-67) Marlowe appears as
'a borrowed designation of the great Shakespeare' and his
murder is considered 'allegorically true'.) The compilers
of literary history after the Restoration are spare, inaccurate, and tend naturally to repeat the mistakes and
emphases of their predecessors. So Edward Phillips (No.
19), whom one finds cited often in biographical

dictionaries and the like, partly no doubt because of the tradition that his uncle, John Milton, had a hand in his 'Theatrum Poetarum'; so William Winstanley (No. 20), and Gerard Langbaine (No. 21); so Anthony à Wood, with some flourishes (No. 22). The canon was uncertain: 'Tamburlaine' was excluded (by Phillips) and then restored; 'Lust's Dominion' keeps cropping up. The dates of birth and death were either vague or altogether mistaken: for example, the antiquary William Oldys, in his marginalia on a copy of Langbaine, writes, incredibly, that Marlowe 'was born about the former part of Edwd. VI', and John Aubrey jotted down in his notes on Ben Jonson that he had it from Sir 'Ed. Shirburn' that Jonson killed 'Marlow ye Poet on Bunhill, comeing from the Green-curtain playhouse'. Marlowe meant so little that he could be confused with Gabriel Spencer.

In 1744, Robert Dodsley published his first 'Selection of Old Plays', including 'Edward II', a series which continued to go under his name; the prefatory material adds nothing new: Marlowe was actor as well as poet, Beard and the 'Return from Parnassus' are quoted, 'Lust's Dominion' is in the canon (116-17). Tucker Brooke marks this as the beginning of the rediscovery of Marlowe, with 'The Jew of Malta' in the second edition of 1780. But the catalogues continue to reproduce the old stuff: 'The Poetical Register' (1723) has nothing to add to Phillips; nor has 'A Compleat List of all the English Dramatic Poets' (1747); W. R. Chetwood, in his 'General History of the Stage' (1749), believes that Marlowe wrote the preface to 'The Jew of Malta' at the Cockpit in 1633. Chetwood was for twenty years prompter at the Theatre Royal. Theophilus Cibber (No. 23) follows Phillips and Wood, and reproduces the usual canon, but has an interesting reservation about Marlowe's atheism: he can hardly believe that Marlowe was not a good Anglican, 'the best and most amiable system of Religion that ever was'. The allusion to The Passionate Shepherd in Bishop Percy's 'Reliques of Ancient English Poetry' (1767) means very little, and the notes of John Berkenhout in his 'Biographia Literaria' (1777), which mentions Petowe as the continuator of 'Hero and Leander', without any mention of Chapman (so Bishop Tanner in his 'Bibliotheca Britannico-Hibernica' of 1748), provide no new information save for one fragment of opinion: 'Posterity will hardly believe, that there ever was a time when *free-thinking* was deemed criminal.' Berkenhout also produced or copied a forged letter from George Peele, which could never have managed publication in a better informed time.(16) Dr Johnson's famous 'Preface to his Edition of Shakespear's Plays' (1765), though it does not mention

Marlowe, reflects current opinion in a memorable way:(17)

> This however is certain that [Shakespeare] is the first
> who taught either tragedy or comedy to please, there
> being no theatrical piece of any older writer, of which
> the name is known, except to antiquaries and collectors
> of books, which are sought because they are scarce and
> would not have been scarce, had they been much esteemed.

Elsewhere in the 'Preface' he speaks of the barbarity of
that age: 'The publick was gross and dark.... Whatever is
remote from common appearances is always welcome to vulgar,
as to childish credulity.' And he notes that 'other dramatists can only gain attention by hyperbolical or aggravated
characters, by fabulous and unexampled excellence or de-
pravity'. This could serve as a representative pre-
Romantic comment on Marlowe.

Thomas Warton's discussion of Marlowe in his 'History of
English Poetry' (1774-81, No. 24) is a convenient landmark;
even his inaccuracies and snap judgments provided starting-
points for other scholars, and his extenuating comment on
Marlowe's character provoked Joseph Ritson to publish the
Baines 'Note' (No. 25).

III (1782-1896)

Of the great Shakespearean scholars of the late eighteenth
century who did so much to collect, preserve and annotate
Elizabethan literary texts (for example, Reed, Steevens and
Malone) it was Edmund Malone (1741-1812), friend of Johnson
and Reynolds and editor of Shakespeare (1790), who did most
for Marlowe. He made up a volume of the works by putting
together early editions of individual pieces, supplemented
by manuscript transcriptions where the originals were not
available, and adding valuable and interesting marginalia
and annotations. This book, which is now in the Bodleian
Library (Mal. 133), cost him five guineas, including the
binding. In his notes he disposes of the legend that Marlowe was an actor, gets the birth date right within a year,
transcribes the Baines libel in full, cites the usual
authorities and contemporary testimonies. But he made mistakes: he included 'Lust's Dominion' (1657) in the canon
and, by a misinterpretation of two ambiguous documents,
attributed 'Tamburlaine' first to Nashe, and later to
Nicholas Breton.(18) Malone dealt with facts and objects
rather than *aperçus*, but his sensibility was refined, so
that he can write of 'Hero and Leander' that 'many of the
lines remind one of Dryden'.

The outpouring of reprints of Marlowe's plays and poems
in the first quarter of the nineteenth century(19) was not
generally accompanied by much advance in bibliographical
investigation or inventive criticism. The painful discoveries and speculations could not be exploited by popular
compilers, among whom there is nothing worth mentioning
between D. E. Baker's 'Biographica Dramatica' (2nd ed.,
1782) and the first collected edition of 1826, edited by
one George Robinson, full of 'the grossest errors' (Dyce)
and valuable to us for the MS. notes of James Broughton (in
the British Museum copy; for Broughton, see below), though
Robinson used Malone's notes, did not accept 'Lust's
Dominion', and summed up the early allusions with a nice
antithesis: Marlowe was 'the favorite of the learned and
witty, and the horror of the precise and religious'. Nor
were the reprints received with constant approbation of
their quality. A reviewer of the republication of 'The Jew
of Malta' in the series 'The Ancient British Drama' (I,
1810) cannot see any obvious reason for it:(20)

> It is one of the most extravagant of the old plays in
> plot and conduct: though as to conduct indeed there is
> none in it, - for events of the utmost consequence ...
> follow one another even without the division of acts
> ... and whatever abstract notion besides there may be,
> most incapable of dramatic accomodation, are here drag-
> ged neck and heels into the service of the stage.

The editor of 'Doctor Faustus', C. W. Dilke (in his 'Old
English Plays' (1814, I, 8-9)), is apologetic: 'This singular evidence of "the credulous ignorance" which then prevailed, is by no means a favourable specimen of the plays
to be submitted to the public in this work.' Henry Maitland found the play 'exceedingly imperfect and dispropor-
tioned' while recognizing its lofty and magnificent passages; he thought 'Edward II' has 'more propriety'.
Francis Jeffrey compared 'Faustus' unfavourably with
Byron's 'Manfred':

> There is nothing to be found in 'Faustus' of the pride,
> the abstraction, the heartrooted misery in which that
> originality consists.... The style, too, of Marlow,
> though elegant and scholarlike, is weak and childish
> compared with the depth and force of much of what we
> have quoted from Lord Byron.

Byron himself wrote to John Murray: 'As to the "Faustus"
of Marlow, I never read, never saw, nor heard of it.....
I deny Marlow and his progeny.'(21)

There is persistent evidence of ignorance and incomprehension, for example in an article on Marlowe and his principal writings in the 'European Magazine' of April-May 1821 (liiix, 309-15, 413-18); among his comments the author ('J.T.M.'), after reproducing the usual 'memoir', interprets Drayton's 'fine madness' as meaning that the author was insane. We may pass over this stuff, and note that even among the most pedestrian references to Marlowe during the Romantic period there is an increasing emphasis upon the great poet and the imperfect dramatist, the two in one, the one exalted, the other accommodated to contemporary tastes. The Romantic idea of Marlowe begins to emerge, and even if it does not continue without reservations through the Victorian age, the vocabulary is there, and often repeated; and indeed this way of considering Marlowe is a 'translation' both of the plays and poems and the earlier allusions and judgments into tentative and sometimes abortive theories of the progress of literature and of the stage. Marlowe ceases to be provincial in time and place, becomes, by way of 'Faustus', European, by way of the cult of the *artist*, universal.

The incidental comments about 'Doctor Faustus' by Scott ('Christopher Marlowe's "Tragicall History of Dr. Faustus" - a very remarkable thing. Grand subject - end grand') and, later, by Goethe ('I mentioned Marlowe's "Faust". He burst out into an exclamation of praise. "How greatly is it all planned!" He had thought of translating it. He was fully aware that Shakespeare did not stand alone'), (22) though ritually reproduced by most editors, are unhelpful. In the inevitable comparison of Marlowe's and Goethe's treatments of the ancient legend, Marlowe often suffers from his lack of great thoughts, great ideas, sublimity, cloudy abstraction. In retrospect, the tribute of the young Irish poet Thomas Dermody, in his The Pursuit of Patronage, A Poetical Epistle, is perhaps more significant, not only because he exploits the Meres account of Marlowe's end, but because he has some empathy with a lost young poet of another age (No. 26). Charles Lamb's brief comments in his 'Specimens', first published in 1808 (No. 27), were most influential for future estimates of Marlowe; in them, amazement alternates with easy perceptiveness, and, as Lamb was to write later, the selections are 'scenes of passion, sometimes of the deepest quality ... that which is more nearly allied to poetry than to wit, and to tragic rather than to comic poetry ... to illustrate what may be called the moral sense of our ancestors'. This anthologizing of 'purple passages' excludes the stage from the bedside book, and in effect seeks to make contemporary an idiom which, in its own frame of reference, was so different.

Lamb's brief but pregnant observations were succeeded by others displaying more or less enthusiasm. Sir Egerton Brydges, for example, reprinting 'Hero and Leander' in his 'Restituta' (1815), notes 'that fervency of language, that copiousness of natural and beautiful imagery, which breathe the soul of the genuine child of the Muse, bathed in the living waters of the Pierian spring' (ii, 320), and contrasts Marlowe's poems, including the translation of Lucan, with other productions of that age 'that are only valuable as curiosities'. 'Shakespeare and His Times' (1817) by Nathan Drake, MD, 'a religious and truly excellent man', finds Marlowe 'egregiously misled ... by bad models, and his want of taste has condemned him, as a writer for the stage, to an obscurity from which he is not likely to emerge'. Of 'Tamburlaine', Drake observes: 'whilst a few passages indicate talents of no common order, the residue is a tissue of unmingled rant, absurdity, and fustian' (ii, 245), though he found 'truth, simplicity, and moral feeling' in 'Edward II', and echoed Lamb's famous tribute to the death-scene. William Oxberry, 'a comedian of no great note', in his prefatory remarks to his edition of 'The Jew of Malta' (1818), writes of Marlowe as 'a genius that is inferior only to Shakespeare', deplores the paucity of biographical materials, and wonders how a man 'of such exalted genius' could have fallen into the error of atheism. Thomas Campbell, the editor of 'Specimens of the British Poets' (1819, 7 vols), observes that Marlowe 'had powers of no ordinary class, and even ventured a few steps into the pathless sublime. But his pathos is dreary, and the terrors of his Muse remind us more of Minerva's gorgon than of her countenance' (i, 145).

Drake's predicted curtain of obscurity for Marlowe's plays was lifted for a short time by Edmund Kean's revival of 'The Jew of Malta' in the spring of 1818, at Drury Lane (No. 28). I have reproduced two reviews and a later account unabridged: any performance of a Marlowe play between the seventeenth and the twentieth centuries has a special importance, and the 'Blackwood's' notice in particular confirms our impression of the inevitably ambiguous attitude to Marlowe at that time. Kean and Penley did not take the play as it was; neither did Heywood before them; it is, after all, what we now call a black comedy. The production at Drury Lane in 1825 of George Soane's 'Faustus: A Romantic Drama', recalled by a contributor to 'All the Year Round' (28 June, 1879, 42) as 'a curious mixture of Marlowe's and Goethe's work, with a strong infusion of Der Freischutz and Don Giovanni', would not deserve our attention, except to note that the Faust subject offered itself from the beginning as an opportunity for the makers of harlequinades and buffoonery.

We have noted the silence of Dryden, to one reader at least inexplicable because Marlowe (like Chapman after him) obviously anticipated the 'heroic play', the serene and imprecise remarks of Johnson; we may note also the casual references from Coleridge, who attributed 'Titus Andronicus' to Marlowe because it was like 'The Jew of Malta', said he was 'familiar enough' with Marlowe's 'Faustus' and planned a 'Faust' of his own.(23) The first of the major critics to write expansively on Marlowe is Hazlitt (No. 29).

Hazlitt had a 'quotation-memory', and that sort of recall, like Lamb's, tends to dissociate the 'striking parts' from the whole, and so is untheatrical, in the sense that a play, like an heroic poem, begins with a plan. He also subscribes to the notion that the Elizabethans were ignorant and barbarous, and that their productions were the fruits of nature and not of art. He presents 'the scattered fragments and broken images' of those dramatists with judicial enthusiasm. We must remember that his comments were public, adapted to his audiences; when Thomas Lovell Beddoes wrote of them as ghosts - 'the worm is in their pages' - he was expressing the private view that there could be a new Elizabethan, 'a bold trampling fellow', like himself.(24) Hazlitt's influential description of Marlowe, 'there is a lust of power in his writings, a hunger and thirst after unrighteousness, a glow of the imagination, unhallowed by any thing but its own energies', is no less interesting than his ignoring 'Tamburlaine' and undervaluing 'Edward II'; it is the 'fierce glow of passion' which moves him to admiration.

The early Collier (No. 30) is level-headed and simple, like one writing a firm letter of recommendation, but in his 'The Poetical Decameron' (Edinburgh, 1820, II, 274) he, like Hazlitt, produced a memorable characterization of Marlowe: 'The very Tom Paine of the age of Elizabeth; nothing short of it.' Such was the current avatar of the Baines 'Note'. When in his 'History of English Dramatic Poetry' (1832, III, 107) he observes that Marlowe 'made great sacrifices, as a poet, to promote' the success of 'Tamburlaine', and uses such expressions as 'fervid and exalted genius', he anticipates Leigh Hunt's opinion (No. 32) that Marlowe condescended 'to write fustian for the town'. Condemned to be a 'chamber dramatist', Marlowe was left to such fuzzy eulogies as 'a born poet' or 'the first of our poets who perceived the beauty of words'. These sentiments belong to a school of lecturing on the poets, the 'God! gentlemen, that's wonderful' style, of which I

have had some experience. It is not to be despised, nor
is R. H. Horne's 'The Death of Marlowe' (1837), which
Bullen reprinted in 1885. It is absurd, of course, but
what Horne tried to do was to bring together some of those
'poor, poor dumb names' that Hazlitt recalled, and make a
little story. Marlowe is the protagonist in a play written by one who, in the words of the encyclopedist, 'took
up literature'.

After all this nonsense, we may return to James
Broughton, walking in the easy steps of Malone. There was
no 'Times Literary Supplement' then, with its communica-
tions, and it seems that in spite of 'Blackwood's', the
'Gentleman's', the 'Edinburgh Review', the men of letters
skated easily over such information as was gradually
brought to bear upon Marlowe, and not without repetition
preserved him in Hazlitt's disguise. Broughton's articles
in the 'Gentleman's Magazine' (1830) are concerned to
review and correct the current estimate of Marlowe's life
and work. He writes without prejudice and with a
scholar's care, and is the best authority between Malone
and Dyce (No. 31). Meanwhile the references to Marlowe
preserved their usual routine: a translation of Schlegel's
'A Course of Lectures on Dramatic Art and Literature'
(1846) reports that Marlowe's 'verses are flowing, but
without energy', a curious remark; there is little to
interest us in an early American view, Thomas B. Shaw's
'Outlines of English Literature' (Philadelphia, 1858),
except that there Marlowe is called 'the Aeschylus of the
English stage' and one whose life was as 'wild and irregular as his genius'. 'Titus Andronicus' was for Isaac
Disraeli in his 'Amenities of Literature' (1859) 'evidently one of Marlowe's gigantic pieces'. Robert
Cartwright, in his 'Footsteps of Shakspere' (1862),
attributed The Passionate Shepherd to Shakespeare, and
added the interesting note, in the light of the tradition,
that Marlowe's life was not of dissipation, 'but that of
an artist devoted to his profession'.

Such compilers and writers of surveys as these operate
on a very different level from the scholar-editors.
Alexander Dyce's edition of the 'Works' (1850, 3 vols;
revised ed., 1858) remains an important landmark. As the
extracts from his introduction here reproduced show (No.
33), Dyce made no creative break-through as an interpreter, but he had a passion for the Elizabethan drama - 'it
became for us the embodiment of that Renaissance which had
given sculpture, painting, architecture and a gorgeous
undergrowth of highly-coloured poetry to the Italians'
(I, xvii) - and for him the worm is not in their pages.

In spite of time and neglect, in spite of the fire of
London, in spite of Warburton's too-celebrated cook,
in spite of maimed editions and atrocious printers'
errors, in spite lastly of Puritanical animosity, we
still have at our disposal documents for building up
the English drama as a whole (I, xxiii).

In his account of Marlowe's career Dyce clears up some
points, for example the firm attribution of 'Tamburlaine'
to Marlowe, but follows his predecessors in accepting the
tradition that he began as an actor; he prints in an
appendix the 'ballad' 'The Atheist's Tragedy', and also a
bowdlerized version of the Baines document. It is
instructive to compare his information, and his tentative
treatment of some of it, with the account of Marlowe in
C.H. and T. Cooper, 'Athenae Cantabrigienses' (1861),
which sets out to assemble rather than to evaluate the
elements of the tradition, and to list works written or
ascribed together. The authors, however, exorcise the
canon of 'Lust's Dominion'.
    In 1888, when Edward Dowden's 'Transcripts and Studies'
appeared, he noted that his essay on Marlowe (No. 35) had
been written 'before the literary cult of Marlowe's genius
had become the mode'; it was first published in the
'Fortnightly' in January 1870. Indeed there is much mis-
cellaneous stuff between the editions of Dyce and Bullen
(1885), but some of it at least should not be passed over.
The 'Faustus' makes the see-saw of comparison between
Marlowe and Goethe. On the light side, we have Arthur
Houston, Professor of Political Economy at Trinity
College, Dublin: 'Any one accustomed to the plot as constructed by Goethe, will sadly miss the sweet face of
Marguerite from the group drawn by Marlowe in his
"Faustus".... The play, I think, grows weaker as it
proceeds.'(25) (Houston, by the way, excuses the excesses
of 'Tamburlaine' for the reason that 'the principal
characters are Eastern barbarians, proverbially prone to
the extremes of passion, and addicted to the use of
hyperbolical expressions. Marlowe in my opinion has been
rather under-rated'. On the heavy side, we have
G. H. Lewes (No. 34), who finds Marlowe's play, in spite
of many magnificent passages, 'wearisome, vulgar and ill-
conceived'. This he blames in part on a literal-minded
audience - the Renaissance habit of allegory was out of
his view. Marlowe, he says, does not give the legend a
'philosophical treatment'; Dowden, on the other hand,
remarks that 'the starting-point of Marlowe ... is something abstract, a passion or an idea'. And it is Dowden
who is right. The Introductory Notice to Francis

Cunningham's edition of the 'Works' (1870) is completely
derivative, but an unsigned review in the 'Eclectic Magazine' (February 1871, lxxvi, 241-3) returns to this theme:
'His characters are not so much men as types of humanity,
the animated mould of human thought and passion which include, each one of them, a thousand individuals.' The
latent insights in such readings are unconsciously paro-
died in such judgments as this:(26)

He plunged into the haunts of wild and profligate men,
lighting up their murky caves with his poetical torch,
and gaining nothing from them but the renewed power of
scorning the unspiritual things of our being, without
the resolution to seek for wisdom in the daylight track
which every man may tread.

After these humid phrases, Dowden is cool and clear.
He finds Marlowe a 'subjective poet', like Schiller, but
'Satanic': he is 'great, ardent, aspiring', but the critic
recognizes an imaginative control working there.
Two New England voices, sharing the same assumptions
but reaching quite different conclusions, according to
their qualities, belong here. Edwin P. Whipple (1819-86),
born in Gloucester, Mass., Hazlitt's counterpart in what
we now call 'adult education', gave a series of lectures
in the Lowell Institute, published first in the 'Atlantic
Monthly' (1867-8) and later as 'The Literature of the Age
of Elizabeth' (Boston, Mass., 1869). For him Marlowe was
'this stormy, irregular genius, compound of Alsatian ruf-
fian and Arcadian singer'; he shared with his Faustus some
'intimate business' with the Evil One; he was 'the proud-
est and fiercest of intellectual aristocrats'; in 'Tamburlaine', 'the writer seems to say, with his truculent hero,
"This is my mind, and I will have it so."' H. N. Hudson,
who also finds Marlowe making a big archaic noise - which
he, like his contemporaries, had never heard on the stage
- anticipates in his comments the critical vehicle which
makes Marlowe one ancestor of the 'heroic play' (No. 37).
'Make it new' was not a direction for the mid-Victorian
critics of Marlowe, or indeed their successors to the end
of the century. They repeat each other, and they return
to a few reverberant figures. The translation of H. A.
Taine's 'Histoire de la littérature Anglaise' (1972), in
which the author examines the *faculté maîtresse* of a man's
work in terms of his milieu, seems to have had some influence: in that florid prose, Marlowe appears as a Bohemian
sceptic, 'a primitive and genuine man ... the slave of his
passions ... moulded by his lusts', and all that (No. 36).
Poor 'G.B.S.', in the 'Cornhill Magazine' (September 1874,

xxx, 329-49) spends some time over the apocryphal portrait, has some reservations about the Taine stereotype,
but decides that Marlowe is 'a superb Byron', feels more
at home with 'Doctor Faustus' than with 'Faust', and anticipates later comments by observing that, as for the
poet's theological views, 'they were not more greatly
unorthodox than those of many intellectual men and
advanced thinkers of the present day'. He refers
obliquely to Bishop Colenso. 'His face is in shadow',
'G.B.S.' says; he is 'the illustrious pioneer'. *Passion*
is the key. So William Minto, who makes it a *leitmotif*
(No. 38); so Charles Grant, in The Two Fausts 'Contemporary Review', July 1881), 'concentrated passion rather than
objective insight and just appreciation of the comparative
value of the various elements of human life'. 'Wantonness
of imagination', writes Henry J. Nicholl, in his 'Land-
marks of English Literature' (New York, 1883, 71),
'characteristic of a hot and fevered youth unrestrained by
law, and of a mind ill at ease yet conscious of and aspiring after better things.'
    A. W. Ward returns us once again to sobriety, in his
comments on 'Edward II', and in the only sensible explanation I have read from a scholar rather than an actor or
director of what blank verse is supposed to do (No. 39).
But Ward says finally of Marlowe that 'the element in
which as a poet he lived was passion'. In fact, continued
reading in these 'appreciations' by Victorian men of
letters can be a numbing experience. These writers have
not seen performances of the plays, however deformed; and
they have not read the text with attention to how the
words work. Their comments are summary and expansive, and
though they may choose different elements in the oeuvre
for emphasis, they remain for the most part within the
limits of the tradition and delight in repeating the
aperçus of their predecessors. Occasionally there is
relief from the over-riding vocabulary: the author of
Faust on the Stage (No. 40), for example, making the
inevitable comparison of 'Faustus' with 'Faust', comments
on the persistence of superstition, and on the literalness
of Marlowe; his play 'is the outcome of an undoubting
mind'.
    The illustrious A. C. Bradley is in the mainstream of
interpretation, but his range of reference, his incisive-
ness and his enthusiasm make his essay the most satisfying
we have so far considered (No. 41). Like other critics,
he chooses dominant motifs, 'lift upward', for example,
but he will not accept Hazlitt's 'hunger and thirst after
unrighteousness', and his comments on 'Hero and Leander'
are eulogistic without being soppy. The comparison and

contrast with 'Endymion' is not just a gesture. J. A.
Symonds's eighty-seven-page essay on Marlowe, some of the
more influential parts of which are reproduced here (No.
42), deals very briefly with the biographical material,
more at length with the techniques of dramatic blank
verse, and gives us 'the sculptor-poet of Colossi', who
dramatizes ideal conceptions infused with 'the blood of
his own untamable heart'. In a phrase as often quoted as
Hazlitt's 'hunger and thirst', Symonds finds the 'leading
motive' to be 'L'Amour de l'Impossible'.
     The Symonds essay was read by A. H. Bullen before
publication, but Bullen, in the introduction to his edition of the 'Works' (1885) writes, as an editor should,
with more detachment, so that while one may catch a phrase
from Symonds one gets an established doctrine from Bullen
(No. 43). But some of his incidental comments show a
finer sensibility informing scholarly balance. He refers
to Greene's 'Groatsworth of Wit' as 'that crazy death-bed
wail of a weak and malignant spirit'; he recognizes how
important Lucan was for Elizabethans, and praises
Marlowe's verse in his translation of the 'Civil Wars', I;
and he puts Marlowe's 'atheism' in its historical setting,
adding, 'If Marlowe had been a man of such abandoned principles as his enemies represented, I strongly doubt
whether Chapman, who was distinguished for strictness of
life, would have cherished his memory with such affection
and respect' (I, lxix). Marlowe's life and opinions are
seen through the perspective glass of a nineteenth-
century 'free-thinker' in the pages of the magazine 'Progress' (No. 46). Bullen's reviewer in the 'Nation' is
eloquent, detached, amusing and important (No. 44).
     I have noted earlier in this introduction that it is
necessary to distinguish the 'higher criticism' of
Marlowe, the work of scholars and sages, from other allusions and comments, which, however uninspiring or uninven-
tive, at least demonstrate Bullen's prediction that the
study of Marlowe's works would no longer be restricted to
antiquaries and bibliophiles. There was little influence
exerted from the first development upon the second. When
H. C. Beeching, in a review of Bullen's edition, observed
that 'the idea that under cover of Tamburlaine and
Faustus, and Barabas, Marlowe was venting his own unholy
lusts is ludicrous. The way in which his Mephistophilis
is conceived ought to acquit him of that charge forever,'
(27) he went against the simplistic view of Faustus as
Marlowe's 'twin-spirit'.(28) And Henry Arthur Jones's
dramatic solution of the problem of religion in 'Faustus'
is too sophisticated for the moralists (No. 45).
     Marlowe was indeed 'taken up' by the literary societies

in the 1880s, and the records of their sessions, of which
I give two examples (Nos 50, 51), should not be treated
with condescension; Frederick Rogers's paper on 'Tamburlaine', for example, has more interest than some more
academic discussions of the play. At another meeting of
the Clifton Shakspere Society, in 1893, one speaker found
Milton's 'simple, sensuous and passionate' an appropriate
description of 'Hero and Leander', thought it a pity that
Chapman finished the poem, and added: 'Keats would have
been the ideal man ... to have finished the work, because
he also was capable of fixing his mind merely upon the
beauty of a story, without giving it a bearing upon conduct - a rare gift.'(29) Henry Morley anticipated some
twentieth-century opinions about Marlowe's orthodoxy:(30)

> Thus Marlowe in his first two plays set forth the ruin
> of a human pride that turns away from God. 'Blaspheming
> Tamburlaine' was not the work of a blaspheming poet.
> It was a picture of the pride of self-dependent fleshly
> power and its vanity, as Faustus was a picture of the
> pride of self-dependent intellect, commending in its
> epiloque a simple trust in God. Depths of religious
> feeling were stirred when this was the new play, and
> the last great event in the real world had been the
> defeat of the Spanish Armada.

But the stormy, truculent, humourless, titanic being, who
in Edward Meyer's words 'had studied Machiavelli with a
vengeance', remains to the end of the century the favourite portrait.
     A nice example of the contrast I have noted between two
levels of critical appreciation may be found by considering together two American scholars writing about the same
time, Denton J. Snider and James Russell Lowell. Snider
(1841-1925) was a graduate of Oberlin College, Ohio, pro-
minent in the 'St Louis Movement' of popular education, a
prolific author and lecturer on the 'great books', or, as
he termed them, 'the Literary Bibles of the Occident'.
Treating of the Faust legend, he notes that in the Renaissance 'the mythus of Faust will ... become all-embracing,
the gigantesque image of the time', and that the Faust of
Marlowe is 'a Protestant, tragic, the Devil gets him'.
Faust (here he means the Faust mythos) (31)

> finds his completest possibility, if not his completest
> fulfilment, in the Anglo-Saxon man of today. The
> latter is wrestling with untamed continents, and is
> conquering Nature in terms quite unheard of hitherto;
> the limits of the physical world seem no boundary to

him...but the spiritual striving is not present in so
high a degree, nor is the spiritual victory.

Snider looks west; Lowell, on whose intellectual distinction, sensibility and influence no comment is needed,
looks east, back to the roots of the language, and the
roots of his own passion for literature (No. 47). His
response to Marlowe's language is itself moving, and the
inevitable comparison with Shakespeare is conducted with
propriety.
Marlowe's effects seem to him sometimes like those of
'an imaginative child'. George Saintsbury returns to this
analogy in his account of the 'romantic genius', and ends
with the description of 'Marlowe and his crew' as dis-
ordered Titans (No. 48). Havelock Ellis's introduction
(No. 49) is of importance not for its florid eulogy but
because it inaugurated a popular series and was widely
read. (As I recall, it was the first thing I ever read
about Marlowe.)
What is one to say about the rhapsodies of Swinburne?
Out of fashion now, though some strains of the old music
were heard when Dylan Thomas died. The source of such
tributes is at the beginnings of our culture: the god is
in the poet. Of the three pieces reprinted here (No. 52),
the essay from 'The Age of Shakespeare', hyperbolical
though it is, gives us Swinburne's summing up.
Two other critics of the 1890s decide, regretfully,
that Marlowe will never take his place among the immortals. He is wonderful, but he won't do. So a critic of
'Doctor Faustus', very appreciative though deploring lack
of 'fun' in Marlowe, writes that 'it is impossible that
Marlowe will ever receive just recognition'; he is
quenched by Shakespeare (No. 54); and W. J. Courthope
finds the dramatist lacking in Conscience (No. 55). 'A
just instinct has told us', wrote William Archer,(32)

that the great mass of Elizabethan, Restoration and
Eighteenth-century plays have nothing to say to the
modern audience because they exemplify primitive and
transitional types of art, portray, with much exaggeration, gross and unpleasing manners, and call for forms
of virtuosity in representation which are well nigh
extinct on the modern stage.

A brief account of two public occasions, very different
in their intentions and effects, closes this survey. On
16 September, 1891, Henry Irving, who had played Mephistophilis in W. G. Wills's adaptation of 'Faustus' at the
Lyceum in 1885, unveiled a memorial to Marlowe at

Canterbury. The money was raised by public subscription,
and one J. G. Lewis issued 'Christopher Marlowe: Outlines
of his Life and Works' (Canterbury, 1891) to awaken local
(and other) interest in the project. He confesses that he
'was amazed at the ignorance, apathy, or positive hostility displayed with reference to Marlowe'. In the course
of the pamphlet, Lewis associates Marlowe's early death
with those of Shelley and Keats, touches lightly on the
atheism bogey - 'we live in a more tolerant age' - and
explains how the dramatist wrote for robust audiences,
full of beef and beer, 'men well-nigh as ardent as himself'. The speeches at the Commemoration (No. 53) were
full of the usual platitudes, but it was noted that Irving
'was very guarded in expressing his opinion of the dramatic qualities of Marlowe's plays'.

The revival of 'Doctor Faustus' by the Elizabethan
Stage Society at St George's Hall, on a stage after the
model of the Fortune Playhouse, on 2 and 4 July 1896, was
produced by William Poel. Swinburne's Prologue (No. 52b)
was recited by Edmund Gosse. In his programme note, Poel
noted that (33)

> the greater seriousness which marked the age of the
> Reformation gives a tragic dignity to the conception
> of the revolt of a human being against his god, and
> invests the spirit of such a defiance with what has
> been truly called a titanic character.

Bernard Shaw's review (No. 56), with its vivid description
of the production, and its enthusiastic attack on the
Elizabethan dramatists, returns us by a circuitous path to
near where we began, with Robert Greene's scorn for those
who 'set the end of scollerisme in English blancke verse'.
(34)

IV

In the quatercentenary year, 1964, the 'Tulane Drama
Review' devoted its summer issue to articles on Marlowe.
Of these the most relevant here is Irving Ribner's Marlowe
and the Critics. Ribner reviews succinctly much of the
matter reproduced in the present book, and notes how
twentieth-century critics have been supported by the
important biographical and bibliographical discoveries of
contemporary scholars, in their revaluations of Marlowe's
place in the thought and dramatic experience of his own
age and of his significance for ours. He concludes that
Marlowe 'in a real sense belongs to the twentieth century

... only in the last fifty years have either the man or
his works come to be seen for what they really were'.(35)
In another place, I have made the same point, though in a
less provocative way,(36) for I do not share Ribner's
dismissive approach to the mass of Romantic-Victorian
criticism, nor the assurance in the explicit 'what they
really were'. Still less is it possible to accept such a
superficial version of our vested interest in Marlowe as
this: that he is 'singularly relevant to the twentieth
century' because like us he 'is fascinated by power' and
saw 'the ancient moral and religious limitations giving
way'.(37)

But it is true that the critical tools have been sharp-
ened, made more numerous and subtle by accretions from
other disciplines, and this process has effectively under-
cut that prevailing and stultifying nineteenth-century
assumption that the plays and poems are wholly expressions
of the personality of their maker. We have seen how this
assumption limits both a free reading of Marlowe and free
experiment in the critic's own imagination, so that he
ascends to rhapsody or descends to speculation. This
approach did not disappear with Ellis and Swinburne; my
rather arbitrary cut-off of selections disguises its continuity. Ribner cites various examples; it appears in its
most extreme expression in A. L. Rowse's 'Marlowe'.(38)
On the other side, to detach the poet so thoroughly from
his work that it is possible to analyse it almost purely
in terms of Elizabethan literary conventions and techniques, to explicate his text as if he were Donne or his
ideas as if he were Hooker, is, as Robert Burton would
say, all out as bad as the other extreme.

Marlowe comes through so strongly that a *via media* is
possible only for bibliography - or students' notes.
What is possible in interpretation is a kind of emphasis
which reflects, however modestly, the reader's collaboration with his author. For most of the authors of this
earlier part of the critical heritage Marlowe exists in
the shadow of Shakespeare, either as precursor or as inferior, but something else can be made of the comparison,
and a few of them made it. In Harry Levin's words,
'Marlowe is always himself - as opposed to the "negative
capability" of Shakespeare'.(39) To this we may add the
immensely sensible judgment of J. B. Steane: 'It is not
sentimental or romantic to see the man in his work to a
greater extent than is true of most artists; it is natural
and reasonable.'(40)

What is unreasonable and unsatisfying in the older
criticism is the custom of dealing with the works seria-
tim, without for the most part taking into account the

relations of the parts to the whole oeuvre, or the significance of the classical sources. The influence of Ovid's
'Amores' on 'Hero and Leander' goes unmentioned, nor is
there any serious suggestion that Lucan must have contributed to Marlowe's imagination of the superman; the
reflections of the university curriculum in 'Faustus' are
not related to the form of the 'prolusion' in 'Hero and
Leander', I, 199 ff., and the implications of the poet's
fascinated interest in geography ('the great globe
itself'), which also owes something to Lucan as well as to
old maps, are hardly considered at all.

But this is cavilling: their intuition of power, expan-
siveness and denseness of texture in Marlowe's writing was
not only congenial to their age, but right, like the conception of him as a *first* poet - Drayton's word - so that
these writings I have collected make a 'fruitful plot of
scholarism' too.

NOTES

Place of publication for works cited is London, unless
otherwise indicated.

1   See 'Marlowe: A Collection of Critical Essays', ed.
    Clifford Leech (Twentieth Century Views, Englewood
    Cliffs, NJ, 1964); 'Tulane Drama Review' (summer 1964),
    viii, no. 4; 'Christopher Marlowe', ed. Brian Norris
    (Mermaid Critical Commentaries, 1968); 'Critics on
    Marlowe', ed. Judith O'Neill (Readings in Literary
    Criticism, IV, 1969); among 'casebooks ' and other
    aids to study, I am especially indebted to 'Marlowe:
    Doctor Faustus: A Casebook', ed. John Jump (1969).
2   Thomas Nashe, 'Works', ed. R. B. McKerrow (Oxford,
    1904), II, 335-7.
3   Another reference to Marlowe's atheism may be found in
    Simon Aldrich's remarks to Henry Oxinden, how he
    'wrote a book against the Scriptures'. Aldrich matric-
    ulated at Trinity College, Cambridge, in 1593. See
    F. S. Boas, 'Christopher Marlowe: A Biographical and
    Critical Study' (Oxford, 1940), 19, 110.
4   Cf. Oxinden: 'Mr. Aldrich saies that Marloe ... was a
    rare scholar and made excellent verses in Latin.' The
    only Latin verses we have that can be attributed to
    Marlowe is the epitaph on Sir Roger Manwood; see 'The
    Poems', ed. Millar MacLure (London, 1968), xxxviii,
    259.
5   'Nashes Lenten Stuffe' (Scolar Press Facsimiles, 1971),
    sig. G1v.

6   'The Second Part of Hero and Leander. Conteyning
    their further Fortunes' (1598), sig. Bij.
7   For the complicated copyright arrangements, see
    'Poems', xxiv-xxv, xxxiv.
8   C. F. Tucker Brooke, The Reputation of Christopher
    Marlowe, 'Transactions of the Connecticut Academy of
    Arts and Sciences', (1922), 359-82.
9   J. L. Hotson, 'The Death of Christopher Marlowe'
    (London, 1925).
10 I, i, 43-84; Marlowe's 'Poems', ed. cit., 141-2.
11 Ibid., xxvi.
12 Joseph Hall, 'Virgidemiarum' (1597), I, iii.
13 Tucker Brooke, Reputation, 367-72.
14 Boas 'Marlowe', 298-9.
15 C. Saunders, 'Tamerlane the Great' (1681), The
    Preface.
16 Tucker Brooke, Reputation, 391.
17 Scolar Press Facsimiles (1969), xliii.
18 'Tamburlaine the Great', ed. U. M. Ellis-Fermor
    (1930), 14.
19 Boas, 'Marlowe', 301-2.
20 'Monthly Review' (April 1812), lvi, 434.
21 Henry Maitland, Marlowe's Tragical History of the Life
    and Death of Doctor Faustus, 'Blackwood's Edinburgh
    Magazine' (April 1917), i, 393; Analytical Essays on
    the Early English Dramatists (October 1817), ii,
    21-30; (December 1817) ii, 260-6; Francis Jeffrey,
    review of 'Manfred', 'Edinburgh Review' (1817),
    xxviii, 430; 'Works of Lord Byron, Letters and
    Journals' (reprinted Octagon Books, New York, 1966),
    IV, 175.
22 Scott's private notebooks, 26 May 1797, in J. G.
    Lockhart, 'Memoirs of the Life of Sir Walter Scott'
    (18-37-8), I, 264; 'Diary, Reminiscences, &c. of Henry
    Crabb Robinson' (1869), II, 434.
23 See 'Coleridge's Shakespeare Criticism', ed. T. M.
    Raysor (Harvard, Mass., 1930).
24 From a letter to T. F. Kelsall, 11 January 1825,
    quoted in Edmund Gosse, 'Critical Kit-Kats' (1913),
    38.
25 'The Afternoon Lectures in English Literature' (1863),
    151.
26 Charles Knight, 'Studies in Shakspere' (1868), 31.
27 In the 'Academy' (15 November 1884), xxvi, 316.
28 See Alfred H. Welsh, 'The Development of English
    Literature and Language' (Chicago, 1886), I, 318.
29 In the 'Academy' (30 December 1893), xliv, 592.
30 'Spenser and His Time' (1892), 259.
31 'Goethe's Faust. First Part. A Commentary on the

Literary Bibles of the Occident' (Boston, Mass., 1886), I, 27, 39, 41.

32 'The Old Drama and the New' (Boston, Mass., 1923), 19.

33 Robert Speaight, 'William Poel and the Elizabethan Revival' (1954), 113.

34 No attempt has been made in this survey to give proper representation to Continental editions of and comments on Marlowe, where the emphasis, at least at first, is inevitably on 'Doctor Faustus'. Tucker Brooke (Reputation, 406-7) lists the important titles. Here, in addition to Taine, (No. 36), we may note the first German translation of 'Faustus', by Wilhelm Muller (Berlin, 1818); the French translation by François-Victor Hugo (Paris, 1858) – 'Marlowe, ce poete de l'Angleterre calviniste'; Hermann Ulrici's 'Shakespeare's Dramatic Art' (trans. 1876), which helped to establish the stereotype of the *titanic* Marlowe; and the excellent edition of 'Edward II' by Wilhelm Wagner (Hamburg, 1871).

35 'Tulane Drama Review' (summer 1964), viii, no. 4, 211.

36 'Poems', xliii.

37 R. E. Knoll, 'Christopher Marlowe', Twayne English Authors Series (New York, 1969), 8.

38 A. L. Rowse, 'Christopher Marlowe: A Biography' (1964), especially 29, 32, 58.

39 'Tulane Drama Review', viii, no. 4, 26.

40 'The Complete Plays of Christopher Marlowe', ed. J. B. Steane (Penguin English Library, 1969), 16.

Note on the Text

The text for Marlowe's plays, poems and translations used
throughout is 'The Works and Life of Christopher Marlowe',
General Editor R. H. Case (1930-3, 6 vols, reprinted
Gordian Press, 1966). The place of publication for works
cited in the headnotes to the selections is London, unless
otherwise indicated.

In the notes following the documents, original notes
are indicated by *, †, etc., and editor's notes are numbered.

I
1588-1642

1. ROBERT GREENE

1588, 1592

Robert Greene (1560?-92), romancer and playwright, was
educated at Cambridge and thereafter lived by his pen in
London, according to his own and other accounts, a dissi-
pated existence. His best known play is 'The Honorable
Historie of Friar Bacon and Friar Bungay' (acted 1594).
He exploited his knowledge of the Elizabethan underworld
in the Cony-Catching pamphlets. 'A Groatsworth of Wit'
was his dying testament, and is chiefly remembered for
the attack on Shakespeare as 'the onely Shake-scene in a
countrey'.

(a) From 'Perimedes the Blacksmith' (1588), sigs A3-A3v.

To the Gentlemen readers, *Health*

I keepe my old course, to palter vp some thing in Prose,
vsing mine old poesie still ... although latelye two
Gentlemen Poets, made my two mad men of Rome beate it out
of their paper bucklers: & had it in derision, for that I
could not make my verses iet vpon the stage in tragicall
buskins, euerie worde filling the mouthe like the fubarden
of Bo-Bell, daring God out of heauen with that Atheist
Tamburlan, or blaspheming with the mad priest of the
sonne: but let me rather openly pocket vp the Asse at
Diogenes hand: then wantonlye set out such impious

instances of intollerable poetrie, such mad and scoffing
poets, that haue propheticall spirits as bold as Merlins
race, if there be anye in England that set the end of
scollerisme in English blancke verse, I thinke either it
is the humor of a nouice that tickles them with selfe-
loue, or to much frequenting the hot house ... hath swet
out all the greatest part of their wits.

(b) From 'A Groatsworth of Wit bought with a Million of
Repentance' (1592), sigs E4v-F1.

Wonder not, (for with thee wil I first begin), thou
famous gracer of Tragedians, that *Greene*, who hath said
with thee (like the foole in his heart), There is no God,
should now giue glorie vnto his greatnes: for penetrating
is his power, his hand lyes heauie vpon me, hee hath
spoken vnto me with a voice of thunder, and I haue felt he
is a God that can punish enemies. Why should thy excellent wit, his gift, bee so blinded, that thou shouldst
giue no glorie to the giuer? Is it pestilent Machiuilian
pollicy that thou hast studied? O peeuish follie! What
are his rules but meere confused mockeries, able to extir-
pate in small time, the generation of mankind. For if
Sic volo, sic iubeo,(1) hold in those that are able to
commaund: and if it be lawfull *Fas & nefas* (2) to doe any
thing that is beneficiall, onely Tyrants should possesse
the earth, and they striuing to exceed in tyrannie, should
each to other be a slaughter man; till the mightiest out-
liuing all, one stroke were lefte for Death, that in one
age mans life should end. The brocher of this Diabolicall
Atheisme is dead, and in his life had neuer the felicitie
hee aymed at: but as he began in craft, liued in feare,
and ended in despaire. *Quam inscrutabilia sunt Dei
iudicia?* (3) This murderer of many brethren, had his conscience seared like *Caine*: this betrayer of him that gaue
his life for him, inherited the portion of *Iudas*: this
Apostata perished as ill as *Iulian*: and wilt thou my
friend be his disciple? Looke but to me, by him perswaded
to that libertie, and thou shalt find it an infernall bondage. I knowe the least of my demerits merit this miser-
able death, but wilfull striuing against knowne truth,
exceedeth all the terrors of my soule. Defer not (with
me) till this last point of extremitie; for little knowst
thou how in the end thou shat be visited.

NOTES

1 If I wish it so, I order it so.
2 Right and wrong.
3 How inscrutable are the judgments of God!

2. HENRY CHETTLE

1592

Henry Chettle (d. 1607) was connected with the printing
trade, and was an industrious minor collaborator with
other dramatists in many plays produced by Philip
Henslowe.
    From 'Kind-Harts Dreame' (1592), sigs A3v-A4.

'To the Gentlemen Readers'

About three moneths since died *M. Robert Greene*, leauing
many papers in sundry Booke sellers hands, among other
his Groatsworth of wit, in which a letter written to
divers playmakers, is offensively by one or two of them
taken, and because on the dead they cannot be avenged,
they wilfully forge in their conceites a liuing Author:
and after tossing it two and fro, no remedy, but it must
light on me. How I haue all the time of my conuersing
hindred the bitter inueying against schollers, it hath
been very well knowne, and how in that I dealt I can sufficiently prooue. With neither of them that take offence
was I acquainted, and with one of them I care not if I
neuer be: The other, whome at that time I did not so much
spare, and since I wish I had, for that I haue moderate
the heate of liuing writers, and might haue usde my owne
discretion (especially in such a case) the Author beeing
dead, that I did not, I am as sory, as if the originall
fault had beene my fault, because my selfe haue seene his
demeanor no lesse ciuill than he excelent in the qualitie
he professes.... For the first, whose learning I
reuerence, and at the perusing of *Greenes* Booke, strooke
out what then in my conscience I thought he in some dis-
pleasure writ: or had it beene time, yet to publish it,
was intollerable: him I would wish to use me no worse than
I deserue.

3. THOMAS KYD

1593

In the spring of 1593, the authorities were anxious to
find, under a general warrant, persons suspected of libel
or sedition, or just 'unsafe' opinions. The Privy Council
issued a warrant for Marlowe's arrest on 18 May, with
instructions to seek him at Scadbury in Kent, Sir Thomas
Walsingham's house. On 12 May they arrested Thomas Kyd,
the author of 'The Spanish Tragedy' (1558?-94?), then a
conspicuous playwright, apparently tortured him, and
secured a document from him in two letters to the Lord
Keeper, Sir John Puckering. It must be remembered that
Kyd wrote in fear.
    From BM Harl. MS 6849, f. 218, Harl. 6848, f. 218,
reproduced from C. F. Tucker Brooke, 'The Life of Christopher Marlowe' (1930), apps XI, XII.

I

At my last being with your Lordship to entreate some
        speaches from you in my favor
to my Lorde, whoe (though J thinke he rest not doubtfull
        of myne inocence) hath yet
in his discreeter iudgment feared to offende in his
        reteyning me, without your honours
former pryvitie; so is it nowe Right honourable that the
        denyall of that favour (to my
thought resonable) hath mov'de me to coniecture some
        suspicion, that your Lordship holdes me
in, concerning Atheisme, a deadlie thing which J was
        vndeserved chargd withall, &
therfore have J thought it requisite, aswell in duetie to
        your Lordship, & the Lawes, as
also in the feare of god, & freedom of my conscience,
        therein to satisfie the
world and you:
    The first and most (thoughe insufficient surmize) that
        euer as therein
might be raisde of me, grewe thus. When J was first
        suspected for that
Libell that concern'd the state, amongst those waste and
        idle papers (which J carde
not for) & which vnaskt J did deliuer vp, were founde some

fragmentes of a
disputation toching that opinion affirmed by Marlowe to be
his, and shufled
with some of myne (vnknown to me) by some occasion of our
wrytinge in one
chamber twoe yeares synce
My first acquaintance with this Marlowe, rose vpon his
bearing name to
serve my Lord although his Lordship never knewe his
service, but in writing for
his plaiers, ffor never cold my Lord endure his name, or
sight, when he had heard
of his conditions, nor wold in deed the forme of devyne
praier vsed duelie in his
Lordships house, haue quadred with such reprobates.
That J shold loue or be familer frend, with one so
irreligious, were verie rare,
when Tullie saith Digni sunt amicitia quibus in ipsis
inest causa cur diligantur
which neither was in him, for person, quallities, or
honestie, besides he was
intemperate & of a cruel hart, the verie contraries to
which, my greatest enemies
will saie by me.
It is not to be nombred amongst the best conditions of
men, to taxe or to
opbraide the deade Quia mortui non mordent, But thus
muche haue J with your
Lordships favour, dared in the greatest cause, which is to
cleere my self of being
thought an Atheist, which some will sweare he was.
Ffor more assurance that J was not of that vile
opinion, Lett it but
please your Lordship to enquire of such as he conversd
withall, that is (as J am
geven to vnderstand) with Harriot, Warner, Royden, and
some stationers
in Paules churchyard, whom J in no sort can accuse nor
will excuse
by reson of his companie, of whose consent if J had been,
no question but
J also shold haue been of their consort, for ex minimo
vestigio artifex agnoscit
artificem.
Of my religion & Life J haue alredie geven some
instance to the Late comissioners
& of my revered meaning to the state, although perhaps my
paines and
vndeserved tortures felt by some, wold haue engendred more

impatience
when Lesse by farr hath dryven so manye imo extra caulas
    which it shall
never do with me.
    But whatsoeuer J haue felt Right honourable this is my
    request not for reward but
in regard of my trewe inocence that it wold please your
    Lordships so to [use] the same
& me, as J maie still reteyne the favours of my Lord, whom
    J haue servd almost
theis vj yeres nowe, in credit vntill nowe, & nowe am
    vtterlie vndon without
herein be somewhat donn for my recoverie. ffor J do knowe
    his Lordship holdes
your honours & the state in that dewe reverence, as he
    wold no waie move the
Leste suspicion of his Loves and cares both towardes hir
    sacred Majestie your Lordships
and the Lawes whereof when tyme shall serve J shall geue
    greater instance which
J haue observed.
    As for the Libel Laide vnto my chardg J am resolued
    with receyving of ye sacrament
to satisfie your Lordships & the Wold that J was neither
    agent nor consenting therevnto
Howebeit if some outcast Jsmael for want or of his owne
    dispose to lewdnes haue
with pretext of duetie or religion, or to reduce himself
    to that he was not borne
vnto by enie waie incensd your Lordships to suspect me,
    J shall besech in all humillitie
& in the feare of god that it will please your Lordships
    but to censure me as J shall
prove my self, and to repute them as they ar in deed Cum
    totius iniustitiae
nulla capitalior sit quam eorum, qui tum cum maxime
    fallunt id agunt vt viri
boni esse videantur ffor doubtles even then your
    Lordships shalbe sure to breake
[up] their Lewde designes and see in to the truthe, when
    but their Lyues that
herein haue accused me shalbe examined & rypped vp
    effectyally, soe
maie J chaunce with paul to Liue & shake the vpyer of my
    hand into the
fier for which the ignorant suspect me guiltie of the
    former shipwrack.
And thus (for nowe J feare me I growe teadious) assuring
    your good Lordship

that if J knewe eny whom J cold iustlie accuse of that
    damnable offence to
the awefull Majestie of god or of that other mutinous
    sedition towrd the state
J wold as willinglie reveale them as J wold request your
    Lordships better thoughtes of
me that never haue offended you
        Your Lordships most humble in all duties
                           Th. Kydde

II

Pleaseth it your honourable Lordship toching marlowes
    monstruous opinions as J
cannot but with an agreved conscience think on him or
    them so can J but particulariz
fewe in the respect of them that kept him greater com-
    pany, Howbeit in
discharg of dutie both towardes god your Lordships &
    the world thus much haue J thought
good breiflie to discover in all humblenes
ffirst it was his custom when J knewe him first & as
    J heare saie he
contynewd it in table talk or otherwise to iest at the
    devine scriptures
gybe at praiers, & stryve in argument to frustrate &
    confute what hath byn
spoke or wrytt by prophets & such holie men.
1 He wold report St John to be our saviour Christes
    Alexis J cover it with reverence
and trembling that is that Christ did loue him with an
    extraordinary loue.
2 That for me to wryte a poem of St paules conversion as
    J was determined
he said wold be as if J shold go wryte a book of fast &
    loose, esteming
paul a Jugler.
3 That the prodigall Childes portion was but fower nobles
    he held his
purse so neere the bottom in all pictures, and that it
    either was a iest
or els fower nobles then was thought a great patrimony
    not thinking it a parable.
4 That things esteemed to be donn by devine power might
    haue aswell been don
by observation of men all which he wold so sodenlie
    take slight occasion to
    slyp out as J & many others in regard of his other

rashnes in attempting
soden pryvie iniuries to men did ouerslypp though often
reprehend him for it
& for which god is my witnes aswell by my lordes com-
aundment as in hatred
of his Life & thoughts J left & did refraine his companie
He wold perswade with men of quallitie to goe vnto the
k of Scotts whether
K heare Royden is gon and where if he had liud he told
me when J
sawe him last he meant to be.

4. RICHARD BAINES

1593

Richard Baines (b. 1566?) has been identified with some
assurance by Brooke and Boas as a member of the Middle
Temple, a shady character who appears here as an informer
(see F. S. Boas, 'Christopher Marlowe', Oxford, 1940,
245-50). He seems to have sent his note to the council
about the time of Marlowe's death; a copy was sent to the
queen on 2 June. The most useful discussion of Marlowe's
'atheism', his possible connection with the circle of
free-thinking intellectuals about Sir Walter Ralegh,
including Thomas Harriot the distinguished mathematician,
and, with other connections, one Richard Chomley, is in
Boas, chs xiv and xv.
   Text in BM Harl. MS 6848, ff. 185-6; reproduced here
from C. F. Tucker Brooke, 'The Life of Christopher
Marlowe' (1930), app. IX. words in square brackets have
been scored through in the original.

A note Containing the opinion of on Christopher Marly
Concerning his damnable [opini] Judgment of Religion, and
scorn of Gods word.
   That the Jndians and many Authors of antiquity haue
assuredly writen of aboue 16 thousand yeares agone wheras
[Moyses] Adam is [said] proued to haue lived within 6
thowsand yeares.
   He affirmeth that Moyses was but a Jugler & that one

Heriots being Sir W Raleighs man Can do more then he.
That Moyses made the Jewes to travell xl yeares in the
wildernes, (which Jorney might haue bin done in lesse then
one yeare) ere they Came to the promised land to thintent
that those who were privy to most of his subtilties might
perish and so an everlasting superstition Remain in the
hartes of the people.
That the first beginning of Religioun was only to keep
men in awe.
That it was an easy matter for Moyses being brought vp
in all the artes of the Egiptians to abuse the Jewes being
a rude & grosse people.
That Christ was a bastard and his mother dishonest.
That he was the sonne of a Carpenter, and that if the
Jewes among whome he was borne did Crucify him theie best
knew him and whence he Came.
That Crist deserved better to dy then Barrabas and that
the Jewes made a good Choise, though Barrabas were both a
thief and a murtherer.
That if there be any god or any good Religion, then it
is in the papistes because the service of god is performed
with more Cerimonies, as Elevation of the mass, organs,
singing men, Shaven Crownes & cta. That all protestantes
are Hypocriticall asses.
That if he were put to write a new Religion, he would
vndertake both a more Exellent and Admirable methode and
that all the new testament is filthily written.
That the woman of Samaria & her sister were whores &
that Christ knew them dishonestly.
That St John the Evangelist was bedfellow to Christ and
leaned alwaies in his bosome, that he vsed him as the
sinners of Sodoma.
That all they that loue not Tobacco & Boies were
fooles.
That all the apostles were fishermen and base fellowes
neyther of wit nor worth, that Paull only had wit but he
was a timerous fellow in bidding men to be subject to
magistrates against his Conscience.
That he has as good Right to Coine as the Queen of
England, and that he was aquainted with one Poole a prisoner in Newgate who hath greate Skill in mixture of
mettals and hauing learned some thinges of him he ment
through help of a Cunninge stamp maker to Coin ffrench
Crownes pistoletes and English shillinges.
That if Christ would haue instituted the sacrament with
more Ceremoniall Reverence it would haue bin had in more
admiration, that it would haue bin much better being
administred in a Tobacco pipe.
That the Angell Gabriell was baud to the holy ghost,

because he brought the salutation to Mary.

That on Ric Cholmley [hath Cholmley] hath Confessed
that he was perswaded by Marloe's Reasons to become an
Atheist.

These thinges, with many other shall by good & honest
witnes be aproved to be his opinions and Comon Speeches
and that this Marlow doth not only hould them himself, but
almost into every Company he Cometh he perswades men to
Atheism willing them not to be afeard of bugbeares and
hobgoblins, and vtterly scorning both god and his minis-
ters as J Richard Baines will Justify & approue both by
mine oth and the testimony of many honest men, and almost
al men with whome he hath Conversed any time will testify
the same, and as J think all men in Cristianity ought to
indevor that the mouth of so dangerous a member may be
stopped, he saith likewise that he hath quoted a number of
Contrarieties oute of the Scripture which he hath giuen to
some great men who in Convenient time shalbe named. When
these thinges shalbe Called in question the witnes shalbe
produced.

Richard Baines

5.   GEORGE PEELE

1593

George Peele (1558?-97?) was another of the 'University
[in his case Oxford] Wits', 'driven (as my selfe) to
extreme shifts', as Greene puts it in his 'Groatsworth
of Wit' (sig. Flv). His finest play is 'The Old Wives
Tale' (1595), a fascinating romantic piece. 'The Honour
of the Garter' is an occasional poem, directed to the Earl
of Northumberland on his installation as a knight of that
order, 26 June 1593. In the Prologus, Marlowe, who was
four weeks dead, is commemorated after Sidney, Sir Francis
Walsingham and others.

   From 'The Honour of the Garter', in 'The Life and Minor
Works of George Peele', ed. D. H. Horne (New Haven, Conn.,
1963), 246.

                        And after thee
Why hie they not, unhappy in thine end,
Marley, the Muses darling for thy verse;
Fitte to write passions for the soules below,
If any wretched soules in passion speake?

6. GABRIEL HARVEY

1593

Gabriel Harvey (c.1550-1631) was a frustrated academic
politician, at once an ornament to Cambridge as a
rhetorician, and an embarrassment as a personality. The
friend and promoter of Spenser, in an evil hour he became
involved in pamphlet controversy with the Elizabethan
Juvenal, Thomas Nashe. The piece reproduced below is
obscure: it may just possibly not refer to Marlowe at all.
    From 'A New Letter of Notable Contents' (1593), sigs
D3v-D4.

                      SONET.

Slumbring I lay in melancholy bed,
Before the dawning of the sanguin light:
When Eccho shrill, or some Familiar Spright
Buzzed an Epitaph into my hed.

Magnifique Mindes, bred of Gargantuas race,
In grisly weedes His Obsequies waiment,
Whose Corps on Powles, whose mind triumph'd on Kent,
Scorning to bate Sir Rodomont an ace.

I mus'd awhile: and hauing mus'd awhile,
Iesu, (quoth I) is that Gargantua minde
Conquerd, and left no Scanderbeg behinde?
Vowed he not to Powles A Second bile?

What bile, or kibe? (quoth that same early Spright)
Haue you forgot the Scanderbegging wight?

GLOSSE

Is it a Dreame? or is the Highest minde,
That euer haunted Powles, or hunted winde,
Bereaft of that same sky-surmounting breath,
That breath, that taught the Timpany to swell?

He, and the Plague contended for the game:
The hawty man extolles his hideous thoughtes,
And gloriously insultes vpon poore soules,
That plague themselues: for faint harts plague them-
selues.

The tyrant Sicknesse of base-minded slaues
Oh how it dominer's in Coward Lane?
So Surquidry rang-out his larum bell,
When he had girn'd at many a dolefull knell.
The graund Dissease disdain'd his toade Conceit,
And smiling at his tamberlaine contempt,
Sternely struck-home the peremptory stroke.
He that nor feared God, nor dreaded Diu'll,
Nor ought admired, but his wondrous selfe:
Like Iunos gawdy Bird, that prowdly stares
On glittering fan of his triumphant taile:
Or like the vgly Bugg, that scorn'd to dy,
And mountes of Glory rear'd in towring witt:
Alas: but Babell Pride must kisse the pitt.

7. JOSEPH HALL

1597-8

Joseph Hall (1574-1656) published 'Virgidemiarum' (six
books of 'Tooth-lesse' and 'Byting' satires) when he was a
Fellow of Emmanuel College, Cambridge. The first group
includes much comment on the accepted literary genres,
and incidental reference to a number of popular contemporary writers. Hall later became a conspicuous churchman,
Bishop of Exeter and Norwich, and engaged in a pamphlet
war with Milton. 'Virg.', I, iii is concerned with
tragedy.
From 'Virgidemiarum' (1597-8), I, iii, in 'The Collected Poems of Joseph Hall', ed. A. Davenport (Liverpool,
1949), 14.

One higher pitch'd doth set his soaring thought
On crowned kings that Fortune hath low brought:
Or some upreared, high-aspiring swaine
As it might be the Turkish *Tamberlaine*.
Then weeneth he his base drink-drowned spright,
Rapt to the threefold loft of heavens hight,
When he conceives upon his fained stage
The stalking steps of his great personage,
Graced with huf-cap termes and thundring threats
That his poor hearers hayre quite upright sets.
Such soone, as some brave-minded hungry youth,
Sees fitly frame to his wide-strained mouth,
He vaunts his voyce upon an hyred stage,
With high-set steps, and princely carriage:
Now soouping in side robes of Royaltie,
That earst did skrub in Lowsie brokerie.
There if he can with termes Italianate,
Big-sounding sentences, and words of state,
Faire patch me up his pure *Iambick* verse,
He ravishes the gazing Scaffolders.

8. THOMAS BEARD

1597

Thomas Beard (d. 1632) had the distinction of being
Oliver Cromwell's schoolmaster at Huntingdon. 'The
Theatre of Gods Iudgements' was his first book of many,
including a proof that the Pope is Antichrist (1625), like
all his work utterly unoriginal.
      From 'The Theatre of Gods Iudgements' (1597), ch. xxv.

Not inferiour to any of the former in Atheisme & impiety,
and equall to all in maner of punishment was one of our
own nation, of fresh and late memory, called *Marlin* [mar-
ginal note: *Marlow*], by profession a scholler, brought vp
from his youth in the Vniuersitie of Cambridge, but by
practise a playmaker, and a Poet of scurrilitie, who by
giuing too large a swinge to his owne wit, and suffering
his lust to haue the full raines, fell (not without iust
desert) to that outrage and extremitie, that hee denied
God and his sonne Christ, and not only in word blasphemed

the trinitie, but also (as it is credibly reported) wrote
bookes against it, affirming our Sauiour to be but a
deceiuer, and Moses to be but a coniurer and seducer of
the people, and the holy Bible to be but vaine and idle
stories, and all religion but a deuice of pollicie. But
see what a hooke the Lord put in the nosthrils of this
barking dogge: It so fell out, that in London streets as
he purposed to stab one whome hee ought a grudge vnto with
his dagger, the other party perceiuing so auoided the
stroke, that withall catching hold of his wrest, he
stabbed his owne dagger into his owne head, in such sort,
that notwithstanding all the meanes of surgerie that could
be wrought, hee shortly after died thereof. The manner of
his death being so terrible (for hee euen cursed and blasphemed to his last gaspe, and togither with his breath an
oath flew out of his mouth) that it was not only a manifest signe of Gods iudgement, but also an horrible and
fearefull terrour to all that beheld him. But herein did
the iustice of God most notably appeare, in that hee compelled his owne hand which had written those blasphemies
to be the instrument to punish him, and that in his
braine, which had deuised the same. I would to God (and I
pray it from my heart) that all Atheists in this realme,
and in all the world beside, would by the remembrance and
consideration of this example, either forsake their horrible impietie, or that they might in like manner come to
destruction: and so that abominable sinne which so flour-
isheth amongst men of greatest name, might either be quite
extinguished and rooted out, or at least smothered and
kept vnder, that it durst not shew it head any more in the
worlds eye.

9. WILLIAM RANKINS

1598

_____

Little is known of Rankins. He wrote a book against
stage-plays, 'A Mirrour of Monsters' (1587), and, probably, 'The English Ape' (1588), listing the vices Englishmen have taken over from foreign nations; he may also be
the 'Rankens' who worked on plays for Philip Henslowe.
The passage reproduced almost certainly refers to Marlowe.
    From 'Seauen Satyres' (1598), ed. A. Davenport (Liver-
pool, 1948), 15.

_____

> For for a while I must associate them [i.e. the melan-
> choly, Saturnian types]
> That reaching Polliticians will be nam'd,
> And what is done in countryes far do ken,
> Vrging that nature all the world hath fram'd,
> Affirming God in things is needlesse nam'd:
> But that the influence of the hauen effects
> Our good or bad still grac'te by all respects.
> That take a pride in damned *Machiauile*,
> And study his disciples to be thought:
> Allowing all deedes be they neu'r so vile.
> Such as haue hell-borne Atheisme taught,
> Accounting scripture customes that are naught.
> Such as are earnest Turks, where is a Turke,
> And call the *Alchoran* a godly worke.

10. EDWARD BLUNT

1598

Edward Blunt or Blount (1564-1632) was one of the most
important printers and publishers of the period. He
published Florio's 'Montaigne' (1603) and Shelton's
'Don Quixote' (1612, 1615), and shared in the printing of
the Shakespeare First Folio (1623).
 From the dedication to Sir Thomas Walsingham of 'Hero
and Leander by Christopher Marloe' (the first known edition: Marlowe's part of the poem, incomplete).

To the Right Worshipfull, Sir Thomas Walsingham, Knight.:

Sir, wee think not our selues discharged of the dutie wee
owe to our friend, when we haue brought the breathless
bodie to the earth: for albeit the eye there taketh his
euer farwell of that beloued obiect, yet the impression of
the man, that hath beene deare vnto us, liuing an after
life in our memory, there putteth vs in mind of farther
obsequies due vnto the deceased. And namely of the performance of whatsoeuer we may iudge shal make to his
liuing credit, and to the effecting of his determinations
preuented by the stroke of death. By these meditations
(as by an intellectual will) I suppose my selfe executor

to the vnhappily deceased author of this Poem, vpon whom
knowing that in his life time you bestowed many kind
fauors, entertaining the parts of reckoning and woorth
which you found in him, with good countenance and liberall
affection: I cannot but see so far into the will of him
dead, that whatsoeuer issue of his brain should chance to
come abroad, that the first breath it should take might be
the gentle aire of your liking: for since his selfe had
been accustomed therevnto, it would prooue more agreeable
& thriuing to his right children, than any other foster
countenance whatsoeuer.

11. GEORGE CHAPMAN

1598

_____

George Chapman (1559-1634), the translator of Homer,
Hesiod and Musaeus, was also an important innovating
dramatist in both tragedy and comedy, and a learned, eloquent, if often obscure poet.
    From 'Hero and Leander: Begun by Christopher Marlowe:
and finished by George Chapman' (1598).

_____

(a) From the dedication to Lady Walsingham.

I present your Ladiship with the last affections of the
first two Louers that euer _Muse_ shrinde in the Temple of
Memorie; being drawne by strange instigation to employ
some of my serious time in so trifeling a subiect, which
yet made the first Author, diuine _Musaeus_, eternall. And
were it not that wee must subiect our accounts of these
common receiued conceits to seruile custome; it goes much
against my hand to signe that for a trifling subiect, on
which more worthines of soule hath been shewed, and weight
of diuine wit, than can vouchsafe residence in the leaden
grauitie of any _Mony-Monger;_ in whose profession all serious subiects are concluded.

(b) From the Third Sestyad, ll. 1-10, 183-98.

New light gives new directions, Fortunes new
To fashion our indeuours that ensue,
More harsh (at lest more hard) more graue and hie
Our subiect runs, and our sterne *Muse* must flie,
Loues edge is taken off, and that light flame,
Those thoughts, ioyes, longings, that before became
High vnexperienst blood, and maids sharp plights
Must now grow staid, and censure the delights,
That being enioyd aske iudgement; now we praise,
As hauing parted: Euenings crowne the daies....
Then thou most strangely-intellectual fire,
That proper to my soule has power t'inspire
Her burning faculties, and with the wings
Of thy vnspheared flame visitst the springs
Of spirits immortall; Now (as swift as Time
Doth follow Motion) finde th'eternall Clime
Of his free soule, whose liuing subiect stood
Vp to the chin in the Pyerean flood,
And drunke to me halfe this Musean storie,
Inscribing it to deathles Memorie;
Confer with it, and make my pledge as deepe,
That neithers draught be consecrate to sleepe.
Tell it how much his late desires I tender,
(If yet it know not) and to light surrender
My soules darke ofspring, willing it should die
To loues, to passions, and societie.

12.   FRANCIS MERES

1598

Francis Meres (1565-1647), an amateur of literature, was
educated at Pembroke College, Cambridge (Spenser's college). 'Palladis Tamia' was the continuation of a work
published the previous year; it is useful to scholars
chiefly for its list of Shakespeare's works known to the
author in 1598. Boas observes that Meres's' obsession
with parallels ... works more mischief than Beard's theological fanaticism'.
    From 'Palladis Tamia, Wits Treasury, Being the Second
Part of Wits Commonwealth' (1598); text from Scholars'
Facsimiles and Reprints (New York, 1938), 286v and 287r.

As Iodelle, a French tragicall poet being an Epicure, and
an Atheist, made a pitifull end: so our tragicall poet
Marlow for his Epicurisme and Atheisme had a tragicall
death; you may read of this *Marlow* more at large in the
'Theatre of God's Judgment'.... As the poet Lycophron was
shot to death by a certain rival of his: so *Christopher
Marlow* was stabbed to death by a bawdy serving man, a
rivall of his in his lewde love.

13. 'THE PARNASSUS PLAYS'

1598-1601

This trilogy, produced by the students of St John's
College, Cambridge, contains a number of allusions to
recently conspicuous literary figures. In the first,
'The Pilgrimage to Parnassus', there is a timely imitation
of Marlowe's aside on the poverty of scholars ('Hero and
Leander', I, 471-2), and in 'The Second Part of the
Return from Parnassus' a summing-up.
From 'The Three Parnassus Plays', ed. J. B. Leishman
(1949), 242-3.

Ingenioso	*Christopher Marlowe*
Iudicio	*Marlowe* was happy in his buskind muse,
	Alas unhappy in his life and end.
	Pitty it is that wit so ill should dwell,
	Wit lent from heaven, but vices sent from hell.
Ingenioso	Our *Theater* hath lost, *Pluto* hath got,
	A Tragick penman for a driery plot.

14. WILLIAM VAUGHAN

1600

William Vaughan (1577-1641), educated at Jesus College,

Oxford, was a deeply religious person of the Puritan per-
suasion, a very minor poet in Latin and English, and one
of the early 'planters' of Newfoundland.
From 'The Golden-grove, moralized in three bookes'
(1600), I, iii (Of Atheists).

Not inferiour to these was one Christopher Marlow by profession a play-maker, who, as is reported, about 7. yeeres
a-goe wrote a booke against the Trinitie: but see the
effects of Gods iustice; it so hapned, that at Detford, a
little village about three miles distant from London, as
he meant to stab with his ponyard one named Ingram, that
had inuited him thither to a feast, and was then playing
at tables, he quickely perceyving it, so auoyded the
thrust, that withall drawing out his dagger for his def-
ence, hee stabd this Marlow into the eye, in such sort,
that his braines comming out at the daggers point, hee
shortlie after dyed.

15. MICHAEL DRAYTON

1627

Michael Drayton (1563-1631) wrote successfully in most of
the genres, from the pastoral eclogue to the historical
narrative poem. His most ambitious works were 'The
Barrons Wars' (1603) and the immense topographical poem
on England, 'Polyolbion' (1622).
From To my Most Dearely-Loved Friend Henry Reynolds,
Esquire, of Poets and Poesie (1627), in 'Works', ed.
J. W. Hebel et al. (Oxford, 1931-41), 228.

Next *Marlow* bathed in the *Thespian* springs
Had in him those brave translunary things,
That the first Poets had, his raptures were,
All Ayre, and fire, which made his verses cleere,
For that fine madnes still he did retaine,
Which rightly should possesse a Poets braine.

16. WILLIAM PRYNNE

1633

William Prynne (1600-69) was an immensely prolific and savage Puritan pamphleteer. 'Histrio-Mastix' is the most conspicuous attack on the stage between Stephen Gosson's 'Schoole of Abuse' (1579) and Jeremy Collier's 'Short View of the Immorality and Profaneness of the English Stage' (1698). Another version of the fabricated tale reproduced below was 'reported' from Exeter; see E. K. Chambers, 'The Elizabethan Stage' (1923), III, 424.
From 'Histrio-Mastix' (1633), fol. 556.

Not to relate the various tragicall ends of many, who in my remembrance at London, have beene slaine in Playhouses, or upon quarrels there commenced ... together with the *visible apparition of the Devill on the Stage at the Belsavage Play-house, in Queene* Elizabeths *dayes, (to the great amazement both of the Actors and Spectators) whiles they were there prophanely playing the History of* Faustus (the truth of which I have heard from many now alive, who well remember it).

17. THOMAS HEYWOOD

1633

Thomas Heywood (1574?-1641) was a man of the theatre for over thirty years; students of the drama remember him especially for 'A Woman Kilde with Kindness' (1607). His revival of 'The Jew of Malta' in 1632, with probable additions and adaptations by himself or others gives us the only extant first version of the play.
From 'The Famous Tragedy of the Rich Jew of Malta As it was Playd before the King and Queene, in His Majesties Theatre at White-Hall, by her Majesties Servants at the Cock-pit. Written by Christopher Marlo' (1633), sigs A3, A4, A4v.

(a) From To my Worthy Friend, Mr. Thomas Hammon, of Grayes
Inne, &c.

This Play, composed by so worthy an Authour as Mr. *Marlo*;
and the part of the Jew presented by so unimitable an
Actor as Mr. *Allin*, being in this later Age commended to
the Stage: As I usher'd it unto the Court, and presented
it to the Cock-pit, with these Prologues and Epilogues
here inserted, so now being newly brought to the Presse,
I was loath it should be published without the ornament
of an Epistle....

(b) From The Prologue spoken at Court:

> Gracious and Great, that we so boldly dare,
> ('Mongst other Playes that now in fashion are)
> To present this; writ many yeares agone,
> And in that age, thought second unto none;
> We humbly craue your pardon....

(c) From The Prologue to the Stage, at the Cocke-pit:

>   We know not how our Play may passe this Stage,
> Marlo. But by the best of Poets in that age
>   The 'Malta Jew' had being, and was made;
> Allin. And He, then by the best of Actors play'd:
>   In 'Hero and Leander', one did gaine
>   A lasting memorie: in 'Tamberlaine',
>   This *Jew*, with others many: th'other wan
>   The Attribute of peerelesse, being a man
>   Whom we may ranke with (doing no one wrong)
>   *Proteus* for shapes, and *Roscius* for a tongue,
>   So could be speake, so vary....

18. BEN JONSON

1640

Ben Jonson (1572-1637), poet and playwright, in his references to Marlowe, as otherwise, was a passing-point between the old rhetoric and the new, and self-consciously a
maker of literary history.

From 'Timber, or Discoveries', text from the 1640
folio, in 'Ben Jonson', ed. C. H. Herford and P. Simpson
(Oxford, 1925-52), VIII, 587.

The true Artificer will not run away from nature, as hee
were afraid of her; or depart from life, and the likenesse
of Truth; but speake to the capacity of his hearers, and
though his language differ from the vulgar somewhat; it
shall not fly from all humanity, with the *Tamerlanes*, and
Tamer-Chams of the late Age, which had nothing in them but
the *scenicall* strutting, and furious vociferation, to warrant them to the ignorant gapers.

II

1660-1782

19. EDWARD PHILLIPS

1675

Edward Phillips (1630-96) was Milton's nephew, and educated by him. He was a hack writer and compiler; his 'New World of Words' (1658), a philological dictionary, was very popular. He tutored the son of John Evelyn, the diarist and dilettante; Evelyn wrote of him, 'a sober, silent, and most harmless person, a little versatile in his studies'.

From 'Theatrum Poetarum Anglicanorum.... First published 1675, and now enlarged' (1800), 113-4.

Christopher Marlow, a kind of second Shakesphear (whose contemporary he was) not only because like him he rose from an actor to be a maker of plays, though inferior both in fame, and merit; but also because in his begun poem of 'Hero and Leander', he seems to have a resemblance of that clean, and unsophisticated Wit, which is natural to that incomparable poet; this poem being left unfinished by Marlow, who in some riotous fray came to an untimely and violent end, was thought worthy of the finishing hand of Chapman; in the performance whereon nevertheless he fell short of the spirit and invention with which it was begun. Of all that he hath written to the stage his 'Dr. Faustus' hath made the greatest noise with its Devils, and such like tragical sport, nor are his other two tragedies to be forgotten, namely, his 'Edward the Second' and 'Massacre at Paris', besides his 'Jew of Malta', a tragi-

comedy, and his tragedy of 'Dido', in which he was joined
with Nash.

20. WILLIAM WINSTANLEY

1687

William Winstanley (1628-90) was, according to Anthony à
Wood, at one time a barber, but though he forsook the
razor he kept the scissors, 'for he borrowed without stint,
and without acknowledgement'. He was an inveterate compiler of biographical and historical matters.
   From 'The Lives of the most Famous English Poets, or
the Honour of Parnassus' (1687), 134.

Christopher Marlow was ... not only contemporary with
William Shakespear, but also, like him, rose from a Actor,
to be a maker of Comedies and Tragedies, yet was he much
inferior to *Shakespear*, not only in the number of his
Plays, but also in the elegancy of his Style. His pen was
chiefly employed in Tragedies [lists 'Tamburlaine' 1 and
2, 'Lust's Dominion', 'Massacre', 'Jew', 'Dido']. But
none made such a great noise as his Comedy of 'Doctor
Faustus' with his Devils, and such like tragical Sport,
which pleased much the humors of the Vulgar. He also
began a Poem of 'Hero and Leander'; wherein he seemed to
have a resemblance of that clear and unsophisticated Wit
which was natural to *Musaeus* that incomparable Poet. This
Poem being left unfinished by *Marlow*, who in some riotous
Fray came to an untimely and violent end, was thought
worthy of the finishing hand of *Chapman* ... in the performance whereof, nevertheless he fell short of the Spirit
and Invention with which it was begun.

21. GERARD LANGBAINE

1691

Gerard Langbaine (1656-92), biographer and critic, had the distinction of being numbered among Dryden's enemies. From 'An Account of the English Dramatick Poets' (1691).

Christopher MARLOE

An Author that was Cotemporary with the Incomparable *Shakespear*, and One who trod the Stage with Applause both from Queen *Elisabeth*, and King *James*. Nor was he accounted a less Excellent Poet by the Judicious *Johnson*: and *Heywood* his Fellow Actor, stiles him, the Best of Poets. In what esteem he was in his time may be gathered from part of a copy of Verses writ in that Age, call'd a 'Censure of the Poets', where he is thus Characteriz'd:

[Quotes Drayton; see No. 15, above.]

He writ besides a Poem, call'd 'Hero and Leander'; *whose mighty Lines* (says One)* Mr. *Benjamin Johnson, a Man sensible enough of his own Abilities, was often heard to say, that they were Examples fitter for Admiration, than Paralel.* This Poem being left imperfect by our Author, who (according to Mr. *Philips*) *in some riotous fray, came to an untimely and violent End; it was finished by Mr. Chapman, and printed octavo Lond. 1606.*

Note

*Bosworth's Poems, Pref.

22. ANTHONY À WOOD

1691

Anthony à Wood (1632-95), the historian of Oxford and
biographer of its scholars, was noted not only for his
learning but for the intemperance of his judgments.
Note how he has embroidered Beard and Meres (Nos 8 and 12
above). Edward Phillips had attributed 'Tamburlaine' to
Thomas Newton; hence the intrusion of Marlowe into an
Oxford book.
   From 'Athenae Oxonienses' (1691), article on Thomas
Newton (ed. 1815), II, col. 9.

But in the end, so it was, that this Marlo giving too
large a swing to his own wit, and suffering his lust to
have the full reins, fell to that outrage and extremity,
as Jodelle a French tragical poet did, (being an epicure
and an atheist,) that he denied God and his Son Christ,
and not only in word blasphemed the Trinity, but also (as
it was credibly* reported) wrote divers discourses
against it, affirming our Saviour to be a deceiver, and
Moses to be a conjurer: The holy *Bible* also to contain
only vain and idle stories, and all religion but a device
of policy. But see the end of this person, which was
noted by all, especially the precisians. For so it fell
out, that he being deeply in love with a certain woman,
had for his rival a bawdy serving-man, one rather fit to
be a pimp, than an ingenious amoretto as Marlow conceived
himself to be. Whereupon Marlo taking it to be an high
affront, rush'd in upon, to stab, him, with his dagger:
But the serving-man being very quick, so avoided the
stroke, that withal catching hold of Marlo's wrist, he
stab'd his own dagger into his own head, in such sort,
that notwithstanding all the means of surgery that could
be wrought, he shortly after died of his wound, before
the year 1593.

Note

*See in Tho. Beard's *Theatre of God's Judgments*, lib. I,
chap. 23.

23. THEOPHILUS CIBBER

1753

Theophilus Cibber (1703-58) was the son of Colley Cibber,
the actor-dramatist pilloried by Pope, and himself connected with the theatre. His 'Lives of the Poets' in five
volumes was largely, it appears, the work of one Robert
Shiels.
From 'The Lives of the Poets' (1753), I, 85-7.

CH[R]ISTOPHER MARLOE

Was bred a student in Cambridge, but there is no account
extant of his family. He soon quitted the University, and
became a player on the same stage with the incomparable
Shakespear. He was accounted, says Langbaine, a very fine
poet in his time, even by Ben Johnson himself, and Heywood
his fellow-actor stiles him the best of poets. In a copy
of verses called the Censure of the Poets, he was thus
characterized.

Next Marloe bathed in Thespian springs,
Had in him those brave sublunary things,
That your first poets had; his raptures were
All air and fire, which made his verses clear;
For that fine madness still he did retain,
Which rightly should possess a poet's brain.

His genius inclined him wholly to tragedy, and he
obliged the world with six plays, besides one he joined
for with Nash, called 'Dido Queen of Carthage'; but before
I give an account of them, I shall present his character
to the reader upon the authority of Anthony Wood, which is
too singular to be passed over. This Marloe, we are told,
presuming upon his own little wit, thought proper to practise the most epicurean indulgence, and openly profess'd
atheism; he denied God, Our Saviour; he blasphemed the
adorable Trinity, and, as it was reported, wrote several
discourses against it, affirming Our Saviour to be a
deceiver, the sacred scriptures to contain nothing but
idle stories, and all religion to be a device of policy
and priestcraft; but Marloe came to a very untimely end,
as some remarked, in consequence of his execrable blasphemies. It happened that he fell deeply in love with a

low girl, and had for his rival a fellow in livery, who
looked more like a pimp than a lover. Marloe, fired with
jealousy, and having some reason to believe that his mistress granted the fellow favours, he rushed upon him to
stab him with his dagger; but the footman being quick,
avoided the stroke, and catching hold of Marloe's wrist
stabbed him with his own weapon, and notwithstanding all
the assistance of surgery, he soon after died of the
wound, in the year 1593. Some time before his death, he
had begun and made a considerable progress in an excellent
poem called 'Hero and Leander', which was afterwards
finished by George Chapman, who fell short, as it is said,
of the spirit and invention of Marloe in the execution of
it.

What credit may be due to Mr. Wood's severe representation of this poet's character, the reader must judge for
himself. For my part, I am willing to suspend my judgment
till I meet with some other testimony of his having thus
heinously offended against his God, and against the best
and most amiable system of Religion that ever was, or ever
can be: Marloe might possibly be inclined to free-thinking,
without running the unhappy lengths that Mr. Wood tells us,
it was reported he had done. We have many instances of
characters being too lightly taken up on report, and mis-
takenly represented thro' a too easy credulity; especially
against a man who may happen to differ from us in some
speculative points, wherein each party however, may think
himself Orthodox: The good Dr. Clarke himself, has been as
illspoken of as Wood speaks of Marloe.

His other works are

1. 'Dr. Faustus', his tragical history printed in 4to.
London, 1661.

2. 'Edward the Second', a Tragedy, printed in 4to.
London - when this play was acted is not known.

3. 'Jew of Malta', a Tragedy played before the King and
Queen at Whitehall, 1633. This play was in much esteem in
those days; the Jew's part being performed by Mr. Edward
Alleyn, the greatest player of his time, and a man of real
piety and goodness; he founded and endowed Dulwich hospi-
tal in Surry; he was so great an actor, that Betterton,
the Roscius of the British nation, used to acknowledge
that he owed to him those great attainments of which he
was master.

4. 'Lust's Dominion; or the Lascivious Queen', published by Mr. Kirkman, 8vo. London, 1661. This play was
altered by Mrs. Behn, and acted under the title of the
'Moor's Revenge'.

5. 'Massacre of Paris, with the death of the Duke of
Guise', a Tragedy, played by the Right Honourable the Lord

Admiral's servants. This play is divided into acts; it begins with the fatal marriage between the King of Navarre, and Margurete de Valois, sister to King Charles IX; the occasion of the massacre, and ends with the death of Henry III of France.

6. 'Tamerlain the Great; or the Scythian Shepherd', a Tragedy in two parts, printed in an old black letter, 8vo. 1593. This is said to be the worst of his productions.

24. THOMAS WARTON

1781

Thomas Warton (1728-90) was Professor of Poetry at Oxford (1757-67), and Poet Laureate (1785-90). His 'Observations on the Faerie Queene of Spenser' (1754), and his 'History of English Poetry' (1774-81) both show, in addition to their general usefulness, a modest appreciation of the 'romantic' sensibility. For the extracts from the 'History' concerning Marlowe, I have chosen to use the 1824 edition, with its 'numerous additional notes by the late Mr. Ritson, the late Dr. Ashby, Mr. Douce, Mr. Park, and other eminent antiquaries', since it gives useful information for the state of Marlowe scholarship and criticism during the period.

From 'The History of English Poetry from the Close of the Eleventh to the Commencement of the Eighteenth Century' (1824), IV, 246, 260-6.

The 'Elegies' of Ovid, which convey the obscenities of the brothel in elegant language, but are seldom tinctured with the sentiments of a serious and melancholy love, were translated by Christopher Marlowe below mentioned, and printed at Middleburgh without date. This book was ordered to be burnt at Stationers' hall, in 1599, by command of the archbishop of Canterbury and the bishop of London....

Christopher Marlowe, or Marloe, educated in elegant letters at Cambridge, Shakespeare's cotemporary on the stage, often applauded both by queen Elisabeth and king James the First, as a judicious player, esteemed for his poetry by Jonson and Drayton, and one of the most

distinguished tragic poets of his age, translated
Coluthus's 'Rape of Helen' into English rhyme, in the
year 1587. I have never seen it; and I owe this information to the manuscript papers of a diligent collector of
these fugacious anecdotes. (i) But there is entered to
Jones, in 1595, 'A booke entituled "Raptus Helenae,"
Helens Rape, by the Athenian duke Theseus.' (k)
Coluthus's poem was probably brought into vogue, and
suggested to Marlowe's notice, by being paraphrased in
Latin verse the preceding year by Thomas Watson, the
writer of sonnets just mentioned. (l) Before the year
1598, appeared Marlowe's translation of the 'Loves of
Hero and Leander,' the elegant prolusion of an unknown
sophist of Alexandria, but commonly ascribed to the
antient Musaeus. It was left unfinished by Marlowe's
death*; but what was called a second part, which is
nothing more than a continuation from the Italian,
appeared by one Henry Petowe, in 1598. (m) Another
edition was published, with the first book of Lucan,
translated also by Marlowe, and in blank verse, in
1600. (n) At length George Chapman, the translator of
Homer, completed, but with a striking inequality†,
Marlowe's unfinished version, and printed it at London
in quarto, 1606. (o) Tanner takes this piece to be one
of Marlowe's plays. It probably suggested to Shakespeare
the allusion to Hero and Leander, in the 'Midsummer
Night's Dream,' under the player's blunder of Limander and
Helen, where the interlude of Thisbe is presented. (p)
It has many nervous and polished verses. His tragedies
manifest traces of a just dramatic conception, but they
abound with tedious and uninteresting scenes, or with such
extravagancies as proceeded from a want of judgment, and
those barbarous ideas of the times, over which it was the
peculiar gift of Shakespeare's genius alone to triumph and
to predominate. (q) His 'Tragedy of Dido queen of Carthage' was completed and published by his friend Thomas
Nashe, in 1594. (r)
    Although Jonson mentions Marlowe's MIGHTY MUSE, yet the
highest testimony Marlowe has received, is from his cotemporary Drayton; who from his own feelings was well qualified to decide on the merits of a poet. It is in
Drayton's Elegy, To my dearly loved friend Henry Reynolds
of Poets and Poesie.

    Next Marlowe, bathed in the Thespian springes,
    Had in him those braue translunary (s) thinges,
    That the first poets had: his raptvres were
    All air, and fire, which made his verses clear:
    For that fine madness still he did retaine
    Which rightly should possesse a poet's braine. (t)

In the 'Return from Parnassus', a sort of critical
play, acted at Cambridge in 1606, Marlowe's *buskined* MUSE
is celebrated. (u) His cotemporary Decker, Jonson's
antagonist, having allotted to Chaucer and *graue* Spenser,
the highest seat in the Elisian *grove of Bayes*, has thus
arranged Marlowe. 'In another companie sat learned
Atchlow and, (tho he had ben a player molded out of their
pennes,††yet because he had been their louer and register
to the Muse) inimitable Bentley§: these were likewise
carowsing out of the holy well, &c. Whilst Marlowe,
Greene, and Peele, had gott under the shadow of a large
vyne, laughing to see Nashe, that was but newly come to
their colledge, still haunted with the same satyricall
spirit that followed him here vpon earth.' (w)
Marlowe's wit and spriteliness of conversation had
often the unhappy effect of tempting him to sport with
sacred subjects; more perhaps from the preposterous ambition of courting the casual applause of profligate and
unprincipled companions, than from any systematic disbelief of religion. His scepticism, whatever it might be,
was construed by the prejudiced and peevish puritans into
absolute atheism: and they took pains to represent the
unfortunate catastrophe of his untimely death, as an
immediate judgment from heaven upon his execrable impiety.
(x) He was in love, and had for his rival, to use the
significant words of Wood, 'a bawdy servingman, one rather
fitted to be a pimp, than an ingenious *amoretto*, as
Marlowe conceived himself to be.' (y) The consequence
was, that an affray ensued; in which the antagonist having
by superior agility gained an opportunity of strongly
grasping Marlow's wrist, plunged his dagger with his own
hand into his own head. Of this wound he died rather
before the year 1593. (z) One of Marlowe's tragedies is
'The tragical history of the life and death of doctor John
Faustus'. (a) A proof of the credulous ignorance which
still prevailed, and a specimen of the subjects which then
were thought not improper for tragedy. A tale which at
the close of the sixteenth century had the possession of
the public theatres of our metropolis, now only frightens
children at a puppet-show in a country-town. But that the
learned John Faust continued to maintain the character of
a conjuror in the sixteenth century even by authority,
appears from a 'Ballad of the life and death of doctor
Faustus the *great congerer*,' which in 1588 was licenced to
be printed by the learned Aylmer bishop of London. (b)
As Marlowe, being now considered as a translator, and
otherwise being generally ranked only as a dramatic poet,
will not occur again, I take this opportunity of remarking
here, that the delicate sonnet called the Passionate

Shepherd to his Love, falsely attributed to Shakespeare,
and which occurs in the third act of 'The Merry Wives
of Windsor,' followed by the nymph's Reply, was written
by Marlowe. (c) Isaac Walton in his 'Compleat Angler,' a
book perhaps composed about the year 1640, although not
published till 1653, has inserted this sonnet, with the
reply, under the character of 'that smooth song which was
made by Kit Marlowe, not at least fifty years ago: and –
an Answer to it which was made by sir Walter Raleigh, in
his younger days: old fashioned poetry, but choicely
good.' In 'England's Helicon,' a miscellany of the year
1600, it is printed with Christopher Marlowe's name, and
followed by the Reply, subscribed IGNOTO, Raleigh's constant signature. (d) A page or two afterwards, it is
imitated by Raleigh. That Marlowe was admirably qualified
for what Mr. Mason, with a happy and judicious propriety,
calls PURE POETRY, will appear from the following passage
of his forgotten tragedy of 'Edward the Second,' written
in the year 1590, and first printed in 1598. The highest
entertainments, then in fashion, are contrived for the
gratification of the infatuated Edward, by his profligate
minion Piers Gaveston*¶.

[Quotes I, i, 51-64, 66-71.]

Notes

i MSS. Coxeter.
k April 12. REGISTR. STATION. B. fol. 131. b.
l Printed at Lond. 1586. 4to.
* [Nashe in his 'Lenten Stuffe' 1599, asks whether any
   body in Yarmouth hath heard of Leander and Hero, of
   whom divine Musaeus sung, and a diviner Muse than him
   Kit Marlow? p. 42. It is the suggestion of Mr. Malone,
   that if Marlow had lived to finish his 'Hero and
   Leander,' he might perhaps have contested the palm with
   Shakspeare in his 'Venus and Adonis,' and 'Rape of
   Lucrece.' Shaksp. x. p. 72. edit. 1791. Marlow's
   translation of Ovid's 'Elegies' is noticed at p. 246.
   supr. – PARK.]
m For Purfoot, 4to. See Petowe's Preface, which has a
   high panegyric on Marlowe. He says he begun where
   Marlowe left off. In 1593, Sept. 28, there is an entry
   to John Wolfe of 'A book entitled "Hero and Leander,"
   beinge an amorous poem devised by Christopher Marlowe.'
   REGISTR. STATION. B. fol. 300. b. The translation, as
   the entire work of Marlowe, is mentioned twice in
   Nashe's 'Lenten Stuff,' printed in 1599. It occurs

again in the registers of the Stationers, in 1597,
1598, and 1600. REGISTR. C. fol. 31. a. 34. a. I
learn from Mr. Malone, that Marlowe finished only the
two first Sestiads, and about one hundred lines of the
third. Chapman did the remainder. Petowe published
the 'Shipping of Runawaies,' for Burbie, in 1603.
There is an old ballad on Jephtha judge of Israel,
by William Petowe. In the year 1567, there is an
entry to Alexander Lacy, of 'A ballett intituled the
Songe of Jesphas dowghter at his death.' REGISTR.
STATION. A. fol. 162. a. Perhaps this is the old song
of which Hamlet in joke throws out some scraps to
Polonius, and which has been recovered by Mr. Steevens.
'Hamlet,' Act ii. Sc. 7. [See also Jeffa judge of
Israel, in REGISTR. D. fol. 93. Dec. 14, 1624.] This
is one of the pieces which Hamlet calls *pious chansons*,
and which taking their rise from the Reformation,
abounded in the reign of Elisabeth. Hence, by the way,
we see the propriety of reading *pious chansons*, and not
pons chansons, or ballads sung on *bridges*, with Pope.
Rowe arbitrarily substituted *rubric*, not that the
titles of old ballads were ever printed in red. *Rubric*
came at length simply to signify *title*, because, in
the old manuscripts, it was the custom to write the
titles or heads of chapters in red ink. In the Stat-
utes of Winchesters and New college, every statute is
therefore called a RUBRICA.

n   But this version of Lucan is entered, as above, Sept.
28, 1593, to John Wolfe, Ibid. fol. 300. b. Nor does
it always appear at the end of 'Museus' in 1600. There
is an edition that year by P. Short.

†   [Chettle in his 'Englands Mourning Garment,' does not
admit of this inequality, when he describes Chapman as

          Coryn, full of worth and wit,
      That finish'd dead Musaeus' gracious song,
      With grace as great, and words and verse as fit.

To the joint version of Marlow and Chapman, Cokain thus
alludes in his 'Remedy for Love:'

      MUSAEUS Englished by *two poets* shun;
      It may undo you though it be well done.

Dr. Anderson, however, is of opinion, that the work is
worthy of republication. British Poets. - PARK.]

o   There is another edition in 1616, and 1629. 4to. The
edition of 1616, with Chapman's name, and dedicated to
Inigo Jones, not two inches long and scarcely one

broad, is the most diminutive product of English typo-
graphy. But it appears a different work from the edition of 1606. The 'Ballad of Hero and Leander' is
entered to J. White, Jul. 2, 1614. REGISTR. STATION.
C. fol. 252. a. Burton, an excellent Grecian, having
occasion to quote MUSAEUS, cites Marlowe's version,
'Melancholy,' pag. 372. seq. fol. edit. 1624.

p Act v. Sc. ult.

q Nashe in his Elegy prefixed to Marlowe's 'Dido,'
mentions five of his plays. Mr. Malone is of opinion,
from a similarity of style, that the Tragedy of
'Locrine,' published in 1595, attributed to Shakespeare, was written by Marlowe. SUPPL. SHAKESP. ii.
190. He conjectures also Marlowe to be the author of
the old 'King John.' Ibid. i. 163. And of 'Titus
Andronicus,' and of the lines spoken by the players in
the interlude in 'Hamlet.' Ibid. i. 371.

r In quarto. At London, by the widow Orwin, for Thomas
Woodcocke. Played by the children of the chapel. It
begins,

     'Come gentle Ganimed!'

It has been frequently confounded with John Right-
wise's play on the same subject performed at saint
Paul's school before Cardinal Wolsey, and afterwards
before queen Elisabeth at Cambridge, in 1564.
   [I doubt whether any play that had been acted before
Cardinal Wolsey, could be performed again before queen
Elizabeth, as on such occasions I believe they never
exhibited stale or second-hand goods, but fresh for
the nonce. - ASHBY.]
   I have before mentioned the Latin tragedy of Dido
and Eneas, performed at Oxford, in 1583, before the
prince Alasco. [See supr. iii. 210.] See what Hamlet
says to the first Player on this favorite story. In
1564, was entered a 'ballet of a lover blamynge his
fortune by Dido and Eneas for thayre vntruthe.'
REGISTR. STATION. A. fol. 116. a. In the 'Tempest,'
Gonzalo mentions the 'widow Dido.' ACT iii. Sc. i.
On old ballads we read the Tune of queen Dido. Perhaps
from some ballad on the subject, Shakespeare took his
idea of Dido standing with a willow in her hand on the
sea-shore, and beckoning Eneas back to Carthage.
'Merch. Ven.' ACT v. Sc. i. Shakespeare has also
strangely falsified Dido's story, in the S. P. of
'K. Henry the Sixth,' ACT iii. Sc. ii. I have before
mentioned the interlude of Dido and Eneas at Chester.

s Langbaine, who cites these lines without seeming to

know their author, by a pleasant mistake has printed this word *sublunary*. 'Dram. Poets,' p. 324.

t Lond. edit. 1753. iv. p. 1256. That Marlowe was a favorite with Jonson, appears from the Preface to one Bosworth's poems; who says, that Jonson used to call the *mighty lines* of Marlowe's 'Musaeus' fitter for admiration than parallel. Thomas Heywood, who published Marlowe's 'Jew of Malta,' in 1633, wrote the Prologue, spoken at the Cockpit, in which Marlowe is highly commended both as a player and a poet. It was in this play that Allen, the founder of Dulwich college, acted the JEW with so much applause.

u Hawkins's 'Old Pl.' iii. p. 215. Lond. 1607. 4to. But it is entered in 1605, Oct. 16, to J. Wright, where it is said to have been acted at saint John's. REGISTR. STATION. C. fol. 130. b. See other cotemporary testimonies of this author, in 'Old Plays.' (in 12 vol.) Lond. 1780. 12mo. vol. ii. 308.

‡ [Another edition of this tract, with out date, introduces at this place 'learned Watson, industrious Kyd, and ingenious Atchlow.' Watson has been mentioned as a sonneteer, and Kyd was a writer of tragedy. - PARK.]

§ [Nash thus speaks of Bentley, in his 'Prince Pennilesse,' after noticing Ned Allen and the principal actors. - 'If I write any thing in Latine (as I hope one day I shall), not a man of any desert here amongst us, but I will have up: - Tarlton, Knell, *Bentley*, shall be made known to Fraunce, Spayne, and Italie,' &c. Heywood, in his Apologie, celebrates 'Knell, *Bentley*, *Mills*, Wilson, and Lanam, as players who by the report of many judicial auditors, performed many parts so absolute, that it were a sin to drowne their works in Lethe.' John Bentley is introduced by Ritson in 'Bibl. Poetica,' as the author of a few short poems in an ancient MS. belonging to Samuel Lysons, Esq. Robert Mills, a schoolmaster of Stamford, has various verses in one of Rawlinson's MSS. in the Bodleian library, entitled Miscellanea Poetica. temp. Eliz. - PARK.]

w 'A Knight's Conjuring,' Signat. L. 1607. 4to. To this company Henry Chettle is admitted, [See supr. p. 116.] and is saluted in bumpers of Helicon on his arrival.

['In comes Chettle, sweating and blowing, by reason of his fatnes: to welcome whom, because he was of olde acquaintance, all rose up and fell presentlie on their knees, to drink a health to all lovers of Helicon.' - PARK.]

x See Beard's 'Theatre of God's Judgments,' lib. i. ch. xxiii. And 'Account of the blasphemous and damnable

opinions of Christ. Marley and 3 others, who came to a
sudden and fearfull end of this life.' MSS. HARL.
6853.80. fol. 320.
    [For the sake of exposing Mr. Warton's urbane though
injudicious apology for the atheism of Marlow, this
paper was printed in Ritson's Observations, and it too
glaringly exhibits the diabolical tenets and debauched
morals of unhappy Christoph[er] Marlow. - PARK.]
y 'Ath. Oxon.' i. 338. See Meres, 'Wits Tr.' fol. 287.
z Marston seems to allude to this catastrophe, 'Certaine
Satyres.' Lond. for Edmond Matts, 1598, 12mo. SAT. ii.

    Tis loose-leg'd Lais, that same common drab,
    For whom good Tubro tooke the mortall stab.

By the way, Marlowe in his 'Edward the Second,' seems
to have ridiculed the puritans under the character of
the scholar Spencer, who 'says a long grace at a tables
end, wears a little band, buttons like pins heads, and

            - 'is curate-like in his attire,
    Though inwardly licentious enough,'
        &c.

    [It is at least probable, that Marlow dressed his
scholar from what he saw wore in or before the year
1593. Small conical buttons &c. were then the prevailing fashion. See the pictures of Lord Southampton, Sir
Philip Sidney and Sir Walter Raleigh, who was 'curate-
like' in his attire. - ASHBY.]
a Entered, I think for the first time, to T. Bushell,
Jan. 7, 1600. REGISTR. STATION. C. fol. 67. b. Or
rather 1610, Sept 13, to J. Wright. Ibid. fol. 199. b.
b REGISTR. STATION. B. fol. 241. b.
c See Steevens's 'Shakesp.' vol. i, p. 297. edit. 1778.
d Signat. P. 4. edit. 1614. [The publisher of 'England's
Helicon' never conceals the names of his writers
where he knows them; where he does not, he subscribes
the word IGNOTO (Anonymous). - RITSON.]
    [The Nymphs Reply to the passionate Shepherd, is in
'England's Helicon.' Isaac Walton informs us, that
this reply was made by Sir Walter Raleigh in his younger days. Mr. Warton observes, that this Reply is subscribed IGNOTO, Raleigh's constant signature. Another
very able critic (Ritson) contends that this signature
was affixed by the publisher to express by it his
ignorance of the author's name. Mr. Warton, however,
had perhaps good reasons for his opinion though he
neglected to adduce them; and it is to be observed,

that in Mr. Steevens's copy of the first edition of
England's Helicon, the original signature was W. R.
the second subscription of IGNOTO (which has been
followed in the subsequent editions) being rather
awkwardly pasted over it. Caley's Life of Raleigh.
- PARK.]
¶ [It seems somewhat remarkable that Marlow, in describing the pleasures which Gaveston contrived to debauch
the infatuated Edward, should exactly employ those
which were exhibited before the sage Elizabeth. But
to her they were only occasional and temporary relaxa-
tions. - ASHBY.]

25. JOSEPH RITSON

1782

Joseph Ritson (1752-1803) was a combative and eccentric
antiquary and a morose vegetarian, editor of important
collections of popular poetry, and author of many works
consulted with profit by students of the literary tradition, for example, 'Bibliographia Poetica' (1802). His
censure of Warton's 'History' was based on his opinion
that it was 'a tolerable specimen of the numerous errors,
falsities, and plagiarisms, of which he had been guilty
in the course of his History'. For the benefit of those
influenced by Warton's tolerant account of Marlowe's
opinions, he reproduced, after the preface below, the
'Note' of Richard Baines (No. 4).
  From 'Observations on the Three First Volumes of the
History of English Poetry in a Familiar Letter to the
Author' (1782), 39 ff.

A great deal has been sayed about Marlow, his opinions and
exit, from age to age; from Beard to Warton: the oldest
writers ('prejudiced and peevish Puritans') directly
arraigned him of atheism and blasphemy; and those of more
modern times (pious and orthodox churchmen) generously
labour to rescue his character; either by boldly denying,
or artfully extenuating the crimes alleged against him:
but not an iota of evidence has been produced on either
side. I have a great respect for Marlow as an ingenious

poet, but I have a much higher regard for truth and justice; and will therefore take the liberty to produce the
strongest (if not the whole) proof that now remains of his
diabolical tenets, and debauched morals; and if you, Mr.
Warton, still choose to think him innocent of the charge,
I shall be very glad to see him thoroughly white-washed in
your next edition. The paper is transcribed from an old
MS. in the Harleian library, cited in one of your notes,
and was never before printed.

[Baines's 'Note' follows, 40-2.]

III
1782-1896

26. THOMAS DERMODY

1800

Thomas Dermody (1775-1802) was born in Ennis, County
Clare, went to Dublin to become a poet, and died of dissi-
pation. His collected poems were published in 1807.
From 'The Pursuit of Patronage', in 'Poems: Moral and
Descriptive' (1800), 53.

Who, led by sweet Simplicity aside
From pageants that we gaze at to deride,
Has not, while wilder'd in the bow'ry grove,
Oft sigh'd: 'Come, live with me, and be my love'?
Yet, oh! be love transformed to deadly hate,
As freezes memory at Marlow's fate:
Disastrous bard! by too much passion warm'd,
His fervid breast a menial beauty charm'd;
Nor, vers'd in arts deceitful woman knows,
Saw he the prospect of his future woes.
Vain the soft plaint, that sordid breast to fire
With warmth refin'd or elegant desire;
Vain his melodious magic, to impart
Affections foreign to th' unfeeling heart;
In guardless ecstacy's delicious glow,
He sinks beneath a vassal murd'rer's blow.
O'er his dread fate my kindred spirit stands
Smit with commutual wound, and Pity wrings her hands.
Ah! had some genial ray of bounty shone
On talents that but lack'd its aid alone,

Had some soft pennon of protection spread
Its eider plumage o'er that hapless head,
What emanations of the beauteous mind
Had deck'd thy works, the marvel of mankind:
Snatch'd from low-thoughted Care thy stooping soul,
And plac'd thee radiant on Fame's deathless roll;
Where still anneal'd, thy own unequall'd strain
Shall crown'd by sensibility remain!

27. CHARLES LAMB

1808

Charles Lamb (1775-1834), schoolfellow and friend of
Coleridge, clerk in India House for more than thirty
years, is best remembered for the 'Essays of Elia' (1823).
The 'Specimens' was influential in establishing a romantic
sentiment about Marlowe. Lamb loved old books.
    From 'Specimens of English Dramatic Poets who lived
about the Time of Shakespeare' (ed. 1835), I, 19-45.

[Lamb reproduces an extract from 'Lust's Dominion'; the
descriptions of the hero in 1 'Tamburlaine', II, i,
7-30, and IV, i, 50-64; proceeds with 2 'Tamburlaine',
IV, iii, 1 ff. ('Holla, ye pamper'd jades', etc.);
Gaveston's invitation to delights in 'Edward II', I, i,
71; the deposition scene (V, i) of that play, and the
murder (V, v, 44 ff.); the opening soliloquy of Barabas in
'The Jew of Malta', I, i, 1-47; and the final scenes of
'Doctor Faustus'.]

The lunes of Tamburlaine are perfect 'midsummer madness.'
Nebuchadnazar's are mere modest pretensions compared with
the thundering vaunts of this Scythian Shepherd. He comes
in (in the Second Part) drawn by conquered kings, and
reproaches these *pampered jades of Asia* that they can *draw
but twenty miles a day*. Till I saw this passage with my
own eyes, I never believed that it was anything more than
a pleasant burlesque of Mine Ancient's. But I assure my
readers that it is soberly set down in a Play which their
Ancestors took to be serious. I have subjoined the genuine speech for their amusement. *Enter Tamburlaine, drawn*

in his chariot by Trebizon and Soria, with bits in their
mouths, reins in his left hand, in his right hand a whip,
with which he scourgeth them....
This tragedy is in a very different style from 'mighty
Tamburlaine.' The reluctant pangs of abdicating Royalty
in Edward furnished hints which Shakspeare scarce improved
in his Richard the Second; and the death-scene of
Marlowe's king moves pity and terror beyond any scene,
ancient or modern, with which I am acquainted...
Marlowe's Jew does not approach so near to Shakspeare's
as his Edward II. does to Richard II. Shylock, in the
midst of his savage purpose, is a man. His motives, feelings, resentments, have something human in them. 'If you
wrong us, shall we not revenge?' Barabas is a mere monster, brought in with a large painted nose, to please the
rabble. He kills in sport, poisons whole nunneries,
invents infernal machines. He is just such an exhibition
as a century or two earlier might have been played before
the Londoners, *by the Royal command*, when a general pil-
lage and massacre of the Hebrews had been previously
resolved on in the cabinet. It is curious to see a superstition wearing out. The idea of a Jew (which our pious
ancestors contemplated with such horror) has nothing in it
now revolting. We have tamed the claws of the beast, and
pared its nails, and now we take it to our arms, fondle
it, write plays to flatter it: it is visited by princes,
affects a taste, patronises the arts, and is the only
liberal and gentleman-like thing in Christendom...
The growing horrors of Faustus are awfully marked by
the hours and half hours as they expire and bring him
nearer and nearer to the exactment of his dire compact.
It is indeed an agony and bloody sweat.
Marlowe is said to have been tainted with atheistical
positions, to have denied God and the Trinity. To such
a genius the history of Faustus must have been delectable
food: to wander in fields where curiosity is forbidden to
go, to approach the dark gulf near enough to look in, to
be busied in speculations which are the rottenest part of
the core of the fruit that fell from the tree of knowledge. Barabas the Jew, and Faustus the conjurer, are
offsprings of a mind which at least delighted to dally
with interdicted subjects. They both talk a language
which a believer would have been tender of putting into
the mouth of a character though but in fiction. But the
holiest minds have sometimes not thought it blameable to
counterfeit impiety in the person of another, to bring
Vice in upon the stage speaking her own dialect, and,
themselves being armed with an Unction of self-confident
impunity, have not scrupled to handle and touch that

familiarly, which would be death to others. Milton, in
the person of Satan has started speculations hardier than
any which the feeble armoury of the atheist ever furnished:
and the precise strait-laced Richardson has strengthened
Vice, from the mouth of Lovelace, with entangling sophis-
tries and abstruse pleas against her adversary Virtue
which Sedley, Villiers, and Rochester, wanted depth of
Libertinism sufficient to have invented.

28. REVIVAL OF 'THE JEW OF MALTA' BY EDMUND KEAN

1818

A thorough discussion of this revival, on 24 April 1818,
at Drury Lane, by Edmund Kean (1789-1833), the reigning
tragic actor of that age, may be found in James L. Smith,
'The Jew of Malta' in the Theatre, 'Christopher Marlowe'
(Mermaid Critical Commentaries), ed. Brian Morris (1968),
7-11. Kean and his collaborator, Samson Penley, tore the
play apart and re-shaped it as a vehicle for Kean's playing 'the noble alien monstrously wronged and magnificently
revenged'. I reproduce here extracts from two contemporary reviews, and a retrospective comment from a life of
Kean.

(a) From an unsigned review in 'Blackwood's Magazine'
(May 1818), iii, 209-10.

'The Jew of Malta' is, on many accounts, a very curious
and interesting work. It is undoubtedly the foundation
of Shakespeare's Jew. But it possesses claims to no
common admiration for itself; for, besides the high poetical talent it exhibits, it may be considered as the first
regular and consistent English drama; the first unassisted
and successful attempt to embody that dramatic unity which
had been till then totally neglected or overlooked. The
dramatic poems which preceded the 'Jew of Malta' could be
considered as dramas only in so far as they exhibited
events, instead of relating them. The poet, instead of
telling a story himself, introduced various persons to
speak their own thoughts and feelings, as they might be
supposed to arise from certain events and circumstances;

but his characters, for the most part, expressed themselves in a style and language moulded and tinctured by
his particular habits of thinking and feeling.

Marlow was the first poet before Shakespeare who
possessed any thing like real *dramatic* genius, or who
seemed to have any distinct notion of what a drama should
be, as distinguished from every other kind of poetical
composition. It is with some hesitation that we dissent
from the opinion of an able writer in this Magazine, in
thinking, that the 'Jew of Malta' is Marlow's best play.
Not that we *like* it better than the 'Faustus' or 'Edward
II.', but it is better *as a play*. There is more variety
of character, and more of moral purpose, in the 'Edward
II.', and the Faustus exhibits loftier and more impassioned poetry; but neither of those plays possess, in so
great a degree as the one before us, that rare, and when
judiciously applied, most important quality, which we have
called dramatic unity, - that tending of all its parts to
engender and sustain the same kind of feeling throughout.
In the 'Jew of Malta', the characters are all, without
exception, wicked, in the common acceptance of the term.
Barabas, the Governor, Ithamore, the Friars, Abigail, to
compass their own short-sighted views, all set moral restraint at defiance, and they are all unhappy, - and their
unhappiness is always brought about by their own guilt.
We cannot agree with many persons in thinking, that this
play is without a moral purpose; or that Barabas is a mere
monster, and not a man. We cannot allow, that even Ithamore is *gratuitously* wicked. There is no such thing in
nature - least of all in human nature, and Marlow knew
this. It is true that Ithamore appears to be so at first
sight. He finds it a pleasant pastime to go about and
kill men and women who have never injured him. But it
must not be forgotten that he is *a slave*; and a slave
should no more be expected *to* keep a compact with the
kind from which he is cut off, than a demon or a wild
beast. Who shall limit the effects of slavery on the
human mind? Let those answer for the crimes of Ithamore
who broke the link that united him to his species. For a
more full account of this play in its original state, we
refer the reader to Vol. II. p. 260, of this Magazine.

The alterations in the 'Jew of Malta', as it has now
been performed, are chiefly confined to omissions, with
the exception of a long and tedious scene between Lodowick
and Mathias at the commencement, in which each tells the
other and the audience the story of his love for Abigail,
the Jew's daughter, which said love nobody cares any thing
about. What could be the inducement to change the fine
and characteristic commencement of the original, in which

we are at once introduced to Barabas in his counting-
house, among his gold? Lodowick and Mathias are very
uninteresting and intrusive people at best; and it is
quite time enough to be troubled with them when the author
wants them in order to heighten his principal character.
But it is a remarkable fact, that managers of theatres
seem to know less of the true purposes and bearings of
the dramatic art than any other given set of people whatever. After saying this generally, it is but fair to add,
that we noticed two slight alterations in this play, which
seemed to evince something that looked almost like genius.
In the third act, after having purchased the slave Ithamore, in order to ascertain whether he will suit his purposes, Barabas desired to know his 'birth, condition, and
profession.' Ithamore answers, that his profession is any
thing his new master pleases. 'Hast thou no trade?' says
Barabas, 'then listen to my words;' and then, after coun-
selling him to discard all natural affections, proceeds,
in a horrible and most unnatural speech, to sum up all his
own past crimes, by describing how *he* has been accustomed
to employ his time.

> As for myself, I walk abroad a-nights,
> And kill sick people groaning under walls:
> Sometimes I go about and poison wells, &c.

Instead of omitting this speech altogether in the acted
play, Barabas is made (aside) to feign that he has done
all this, in order to try Ithamore's disposition. This
is a very happy thought; and the answer of Ithamore is not
less so. Instead of echoing back in a boasting confession
of the same kind of guilt, as he does in the original,
Ithamore, with a low and savage cunning worthy of the
character, hints, generally, that he knows and has prac-
tised better tricks, to plague mankind, than even those
his master has just spoken of, but that *none shall know
them!*' We consider both these as very lucky hits, though
not likely to tell, or even be noticed in the representation. We willingly offer the credit of them, wherever it
is due.
The other chief alterations from the original, are the
omission of every thing relating to the poisoning of the
nuns, and some change, not much for the better, in the
manner of Barabas's death.
We think the play, upon the whole, greatly injured by
the alterations, and see no reason for any of them,
except those we have particularised above, and they are
only adapted to the closet. The performance flags very
much during the second and third acts, and is not likely

to become a favourite with the public.
The whole weight of the play lies upon Mr Kean. No one
has a single line that can be made any thing of in the way
of acting. The character of Barabas is, as far as it
goes, well enough adapted to display some of Mr Kean's
peculiar powers, but not those of the highest or rarest
kind. In some parts, however, - and those the very best,
- he made more of the character than the author has done.
There was something very fine and sepulchral in his manner
of delivering that admirable speech at the beginning of
the second act, where he goes before daylight to seek for
Abigail, who is to bring him the concealed remnant of his
treasures.

Thus, like the sad presaging raven, that tolls
The sick man's passport in her hollow beak,
And in the shadow of the silent night
Doth shake contagion from her sable wings,
Vexed and tormented runs poor Barabas
With fatal curses towards these Christians, &c.

The next speech is still finer than this; and Mr Kean's
manner of delivering was beautifully solemn and impressive.

Now I remember those old womens' words,
Who, in my wealth, would tell me winter's tales,
And speak of spirits and ghosts that glide by night
About the place where treasure hath been hid;
And now methinks that I am one of those:
For whilst I live, here lives my soul's sole hope,
And when I die, here shall my spirit walk.

Also, when Barabas recovers the gold he has concealed,
nothing could surpass the absolute delirium of drunken
joy with which he gives the speech, - or rather the string
of exclamations in the same scene, beginning 'Oh, my girl!
my gold!' &c.
Upon the whole, Mr Kean's Barabas was as fine as the
character would admit of its being made; but it bore no
more comparison to that of Shylock, than the play of the
'Jew of Malta' does to the 'Merchant of Venice'.
We would willingly omit to notice the song that Mr Kean
was made to sing, when disguised as the minstrel. This
contemptible degradation could never be of his own choos-
ing. He surely knows himself better! If he likes to
amuse himself, or his private friends, in this way, in the
name of all that's pleasant, let him! But his public fame
should not be trifled with for 'an old song,' much less
for a new one.

(b) From an unsigned review in the 'European Magazine, and
London Review' (May 1818), lxxiii, 429-30.

April 24. Marlowe's tragedy of 'The Jew of Malta' was
revived this evening. This we conceive to be a fairer
description of the performance than appeared in the printed bills, where it was called 'a play *founded on*
Marlowe's tragedy.' In fact, the variations from the original plot, if any, are too inconsiderable to be noticed,
and even the text is permitted to stand without much
interference. There may, perhaps, be an odd sentence here
and there, belonging to the modern author, but they are
neither numerous nor conspicuous enough to establish a
partnership in that production, with respect to which he
can claim little more than the credit of having recommend-
ed it. The tragedy itself is pretty generally known; but
we doubt however, whether, with all its merits, it has
struck many of its readers in the present day, as a drama
much adapted to our stage. *Barabas* the chief character,
is powerfully conceived. The events in which he is concerned are various, the motives by which he is actuated
are terrific, but whether from the recollection of Shakespeare's *Shylock*, or from a distaste to the simplicity of
our antient writers, or, as we would rather hope, from a
disinclination to recognize within the limits of probability the multitude of atrocities ascribed to the Jew,
he does not make that impression upon the whole which was
to be expected from so great a name. We are now alluding
merely to the Play, for if ever there was an instance when
the acting was likely to overbear all obstacles in the
production itself, it was that of Mr. Kean as *Barabas*.
Unfortunately for the general impression of the Tragedy,
the first act was that in which he had most scope for display. Perhaps there is no act taken altogether, in any of
the numerous parts he has already performed, which exhibit
a more favourable and continued specimen of his wonderful
powers. But the succeeding ones are by no means equal to
the promise of the first, and the catastrophe is so forced
and artificial, that we doubt whether there is another
performer on the stage who could have saved it from a
laugh. Not only did he succeed in doing so, but in commu-
nicating to it a high degree of tragic solemnity. It
would require more time than we can devote to it at present, to enumerate the different instances in which he
manifested the perfection of his art, but to mention only
a few, we would select his deportment before the Senate,
where commanded to surrender half his wealth, his directions to his daughter where his treasure lay concealed,
his soliloquy, descriptive of the prosperity of his tribe,

his joy on receiving the money bags, and that spirit of
insatiable revenge which he kept constantly before the
audience, from the rising until the falling of the curtain. He sung a song in the disguise of a harper, which
produced a very powerful effect, and was rapturously
encored. Our readers will readily suppose that this vocal
undertaking was more remarkable for its taste than its
compass; and if the piece should become popular, it will
owe that popularity to Mr. Kean. His is the only character worth mentioning, and the applause, which was vehement
in the first act, became more moderate as the play
advanced, until at the end it broke out with all its
former vehemence. We had nearly forgotten to mention
Ithamore, performed by Mr. Harley, whose character forms
an exception to the general censure we passed upon the
subordinate personages. Though not of the tragic cast
it is an original and impressive portrait, and was
extremely well sustained. The piece was announced for
repetition with loud and unmixed applause.

April 30. Mr. Kean performed the part of *Barabas*, in 'The
Jew of Malta', with his usual spirit this evening, but
having resisted a very general *encore* at the conclusion of
the Harper's song, the audience testified their disappro-
bation by opposing the further progress of the piece.
Mr. Kent came forward in this juncture, and stated on the
part of Mr. Kean, that he felt himself so much indisposed
as to be scarcely able to go through the remainder of the
character. This explanation restored the good humour
which was for a moment suspended, and the piece proceeded
to its conclusion with much applause.

(c) From F. W. Hawkins, 'The Life of Edmund Kean' (1869),
I, 39-43.

The production of this tragedy, considering that it had
experienced a total and inconsiderate neglect of two centuries, was certainly the most hazardous experiment in the
whole series of Kean's revivals, inasmuch as the poetical
power, fervid passion, and wild grandeur characteristic of
Marlowe's works but ill compensate the playgoer for the
imperfect construction of his plots, the disorder and
improbability of his incidents, and the alternate reality
and insignificance with which his characters are impressed.
The 'Jew of Malta' exhibits more of his defects than any
of the other six plays from his pen that have descended to
posterity; it is powerless to enchain that absorbed and
riveted interest with which we contemplate his 'Faust'
(the prototype of Goethe's) on the brink of everlasting

ruin; or move us to that pity and terror which redeem his
'Edward II', from the disgust otherwise provoked by his
irresolution and effeminacy. The character of Barabbas is
obviously drawn to second and stimulate the popular hatred
against the Jews of the Elizabethan period, and, in fur-
therance of this intention, Marlowe has compounded him of
the most malignant passions which can agitate the human
breast, without one shade of natural feeling or worthy
impulse to relieve the inherent gloom associated with the
character. How we miss in Barabbas those minor considera-
tions, that beautiful element of humanity which pervades
the action, those ever-glancing lights and shadows which
make the Shylock of Shakspeare 'more than half a Christian!' The 'Jew of Malta' can no longer retain a hold of
the stage when the combined influences of philosophy and
civilization teach us to remember that -

On every sect pernicious passions fall,
And vice and virtue reign alike in all.

The play is almost exclusively occupied with the development and fulfilment of schemes organized by Barabbas in
revenge for the deprivation of his wealth by the Governor
of Malta for the payment of the Turkish tribute. Alleyn,
its original representative, succeeded, we are told, in
throwing around it a sort of dignity, but after his death
it quickly faded from the memory, and the play was
scarcely ever heard of until Kean recalled it into a
transient vitality. In its revival much of the rancour
against the Jews which sully Marlowe's pages was expur-
gated; all expressions incompatible with a better sense
of morality and refinement than that of the Elizabethan
period was removed; and the quaint and obsolete phraseo-
logy with which the original abounds was corrected and
modernized. There was no intention to insult the general
body of the Jews by producing the play during the feast of
the Passover, as was supposed at the time, for it was
expressly stated in the prologue that it was foreign to
the intention of the revivers to attach any stigma or
opprobrium to the Hebrew name. Kean's Barabbas was a very
fine and impressive performance. He illumined and rendered tolerable a dark and gloomy portrait, and it only
needs to record this fact to convey the highest eulogy on
his acting. He seized upon every passage that could diffuse an air of truth and probability around the character
with instinctive discrimination. If ever there was an
instance when the acting of a principal performer overbore
all obstacles in the production itself, it was that of
Kean in Barabbas. His deportment before the senate when

commanded to surrender his wealth; his bitter execration
on its confiscation; his directions to his daughter
where his treasure lay concealed; the soliloquy descriptive of the persecution of his tribe; and the scene where
the discovery of the gold and jewels enabled him to resume
his former splendour and means of mischief, were treated
in a manner possible only to the highest order of histrionic superiority. Nothing could have been finer than the
absolute delirium of drunken joy with which he burst out,
'Oh, my girl, - my gold!' The heaviness of the fourth act
was finely relieved by a song warbled by the tragedian in
the disguise of a harper. It was executed à *merveille*,(1)
and produced a powerful effect.

Note

1 Superbly.

29. WILLIAM HAZLITT

1820

William Hazlitt (1778-1830) was a vivid and formidable
figure in the literary life of his time, associate and
interpreter of his Romantic contemporaries. He was a
liberal in politics, life and criticism, and his comments
on Marlowe constitute part of his tribute to a literary
heritage which he found undervalued.
    From Lectures chiefly on the Dramatic Literature of the
Age of Elizabeth, in 'Complete Works', ed. P. P. Howe,
VI (1931). 175-6, 202-3, 207, 209-10, 211.

Perhaps the genius of Great Britain (if I may so speak
without offence or flattery), never shone out fuller or
brighter, or looked more like itself, than at this period.
Our writers and great men had something in them that
savoured of the soil from which they grew: they were not
French, they were not Dutch, or German, or Greek, or
Latin; they were truly English. They did not look out of
themselves to see what they should be; they sought for
truth and nature, and found it in themselves. There was

no tinsel, and but little art; they were not the spoiled
children of affectation and refinement, but a bold, vigorous, independent race of thinkers, with prodigious
strength and energy, with none but natural grace, and
heartfelt unobtrusive delicacy. They were not at all
sophisticated. The mind of their country was great in
them, and it prevailed. With their learning and unexampled acquirement, they did not forget that they were men:
with all their endeavours after excellence, they did not
lay aside the strong original bent and character of their
minds. What they performed was chiefly nature's handy-
work; and time has claimed it for his own. – To these,
however, might be added others not less learned, nor with
a scarce less happy vein, but less fortunate in the event,
who, though as renowned in their day, have sunk into 'mere
oblivion;' and of whom the only record (but that the noblest) is to be found in their works. Their works and
their names, 'poor, poor dumb names,' are all that remains
of such men as Webster, Deckar, Marston, Marlow, Chapman,
Heywood, Middleton, and Rowley! 'How lov'd, how honour'd
once, avails them not:' though they were the friends and
fellow-labourers of Shakespear, sharing his fame and fortunes with him, the rivals of Jonson, and the masters of
Beaumont and Fletcher's well-sung woes! They went out one
by one unnoticed, like evening lights; or were swallowed
up in the headlong torrent of puritanic zeal which succeeded, and swept away every thing in its unsparing
course, throwing up the wrecks of taste and genius at
random, and at long fitful intervals, amidst the painted
gew-gaws and foreign frippery of the reign of Charles II,
and from which we are only now recovering the scattered
fragments and broken images to erect a temple to true
Fame! How long, before it will be completed?...
    Marlowe is a name that stands high, and almost first in
this list of dramatic worthies. He was a little before
Shakespear's time,* and has a marked character both from
him and the rest. There is a lust of power in his writings, a hunger and thirst after unrighteousness, a glow of
the imagination, unhallowed by any thing but its own energies. His thoughts burn within him like a furnace with
bickering flames; or throwing out black smoke and mists,
that hide the dawn of genius, or like a poisonous mineral,
corrode the heart. His 'Life and Death of Doctor Faustus,'
though an imperfect and unequal performance, is his greatest work. Faustus himself is a rude sketch, but it is a
gigantic one. This character may be considered as a per-
sonification of the pride of will and eagerness of curiosity, sublimed beyond the reach of fear and remorse. He
is hurried away, and, as it were, devoured by a tormenting

desire to enlarge his knowledge to the utmost bounds of
nature and art, and to extend his power with his knowledge. He would realise all the fictions of a lawless
imagination, would solve the most subtle speculations of
abstract reason; and for this purpose, sets at defiance
all mortal consequences, and leagues himself with demonia-
cal power, with 'fate and metaphysical aid.' The idea of
witchcraft and necromancy, once the dread of the vulgar
and the darling of the visionary recluse, seems to have
had its origin in the restless tendency of the human mind,
to conceive of and aspire to more than it can atchieve by
natural means, and in the obscure apprehension that the
gratification of this extravagant and unauthorised desire,
can only be attained by the sacrifice of all our ordinary
hopes, and better prospects to the infernal agents that
lend themselves to its accomplishment. Such is the foundation of the present story. Faustus, in his impatience to
fulfil at once and for a moment, for a few short years, all
the desires and conceptions of his soul, is willing to give
in exchange his soul and body to the great enemy of mankind. Whatever he fancies, becomes by this means present
to his sense: whatever he commands, is done. He calls back
time past, and anticipates the future: the visions of
antiquity pass before him, Babylon in all its glory, Paris
and Oenone: all the projects of philosophers, or creations
of the poet pay tribute at his feet: all the delights of
fortune, of ambition, of pleasure, and of learning are
centered in his person; and from a short-lived dream of
supreme felicity and drunken power, he sinks into an abyss
of darkness and perdition. This is the alternative to
which he submits; the bond which he signs with his blood!
As the outline of the character is grand and daring, the
execution is abrupt and fearful. The thoughts are vast
and irregular; and the style halts and staggers under them,
'with uneasy steps'; - 'such footing found the sole of
unblest feet.' There is a little fustian and incongruity
of metaphor now and then, which is not very injurious to
the subject.... The intermediate comic parts, in which
Faustus is not directly concerned, are mean and grovelling
to the last degree. One of the Clowns says to another:
'Snails! what hast got there? A book? Why thou can'st not
tell ne'er a word on 't.' Indeed, the ignorance and barbarism of the time, as here described, might almost justify
Faustus's overstrained admiration of learning, and turn the
heads of those who possessed it, from novelty and unaccus-
tomed excitement, as the Indians are made drunk with wine!
Goethe, the German poet, has written a drama on this tradition of his country, which is considered a master-piece.
I cannot find, in Marlowe's play, any proofs of the atheism

or impiety attributed to him, unless the beliefs in witchcraft and the Devil can be regarded as such; and at the
time he wrote, not to have believed in both, would have
been construed into the rankest atheism and irreligion.
There is a delight, as Mr. Lamb says, 'in dallying with
interdicted subjects'; but that does not, by any means,
imply either a practical or speculative disbelief of
them....
      'Edward II.' is, according to the modern standard of
composition, Marlowe's best play. It is written with few
offences against the common rules, and in a succession of
smooth and flowing lines. The poet however succeeds less
in the voluptuous and effeminate descriptions which he
here attempts, than in the more dreadful and violent
bursts of passion. 'Edward II.' is drawn with historic
truth, but without much dramatic effect. The management
of the plot is feeble and desultory; little interest is
excited in the various turns of fate; the characters are
too worthless, have too little energy, and their punishment is, in general, too well deserved, to excite our com-
miseration; so that this play will bear, on the whole, but
a distant comparison with Shakespear's 'Richard II.' in
conduct, power, or effect. But the death of Edward II, in
Marlow's tragedy, is certainly superior to that of Shakespear's King; and in heart-breaking distress, and the sense
of human weakness, claiming pity from utter helplessness
and conscious misery, is not surpassed by any writer whatever.
      I do not think 'The Rich Jew of Malta' so characteris-
tic a specimen of this writer's powers. It has not the
same fierce glow of passion or expression. It is extreme
in act, and outrageous in plot and catastrophe; but it has
not the same vigorous filling up. The author seems to
have relied on the horror inspired by the subject, and the
national disgust excited against the principal character,
to rouse the feelings of the audience: for the rest, it is
a tissue of gratuitous, unprovoked, and incredible atrocities, which are committed, one upon the back of the other,
by the parties concerned, without motive, passion, or
object. There are, notwithstanding, some striking passages in it, as Barabbas's description of the bravo, Philia
Borzo; the relation of his own unaccountable villanies to
Ithamore; his rejoicing over his recovered jewels 'as the
morning lark sings over her young;' and the backwardness
he declares in himself to forgive the Christian injuries
that are offered him, which may have given the idea of one
of Shylock's speeches, where he ironically disclaims any
enmity to the merchants on the same account. It is perhaps hardly fair to compare the 'Jew of Malta' with the

'Merchant of Venice'; for it is evident, that Shakespear's
genius shews to as much advantage in knowledge of character, in variety and stage-effect, as it does in point of
general humanity....

Note

* He died about 1594.

30. J. P. COLLIER

1820

John Payne Collier (1789-1883) was a research scholar of
great industry and unusual gifts, contributor to the
publications of the Camden Society, the Percy Society, and
the Shakespeare Society, editor of an annotated Shakespeare in eight volumes (1842-4). Unhappily, his addiction
to forgery makes anything that passed through his hands
(and he had access to an immense number of documents)
subject to suspicion. The brief extracts below, from
early contributions to the 'Edinburgh Review', are conventional and free of 'discoveries'.
   From the 'Edinburgh Review' (June 1820), vi, 521;
(August 1820), vii, 151-2.

[Collier quotes 1 'Tamb.', IV, ii, 1-40, and proceeds:]

It is not to be denied that this address of 'Tamburlaine'
is extravagant, perhaps bombastic; but besides the
author's purpose to surprise by striking novelty, we ought
to take into account the country in which his scene
principally lies - Persia - the seat of grandeur and
luxury; and in order to keep up mere probability, according to existing notions, Marlow was obliged to make his
language correspond with the nature of the clime, and the
dignity of the characters represented, as far as the properties of the theatre would allow in the utmost gorgeousness of oriental splendour: what was wanting in the scenery and dresses, he was, in a manner, bound to make up for
in the glitter and glare of description. As for any

rhodomontades put into the mouth of Tamburlaine, (for they
are confined almost exclusively to him,) they are not half
so exaggerated and wind-swollen as the sentiments Dryden
has in many places given to his favourite Almanzor in 'The
Conquest of Grenada.' Nathan Lee's 'Alexander the Great'
has also gone beyond it in several well known instances;
and if Marlow has represented his hero as drawn in his car
by captive princes, he but complied with the popular
notion of the character of Tamburlaine and the truth of
history, as far as either was known to audiences at
theatres. I will venture to assert, that there is nothing
from the beginning to the end of the two parts of 'Tamburlaine' to compare with the absurd, not to say ridiculous speeches of Cethegus in Ben Jonson's 'Catiline.' How
often has Lucan been lashed for the inflated and disgust-
ing picture he has given of the slaughters of Marius and
Sylla; but Ben Jonson has not only put the whole of it
into the mouth of Cethegus, but he has out-heroded Herod
in the accumulation of bloated epithets and offensive
impossibilities. I could easily verify what is stated by
quotations, but they would lead us out of the way, and are
perhaps unnecessary. Recollecting, with Drayton, that
Marlow's 'raptures were all air and fire,' and that he was
gifted with that 'fine madness,' with which poets' brains
ought to be possessed, we may read the subsequent description of Zenocrate, the mistress of Tamburlaine, with much
admiration.

[Quotes i 'Tamb.', V, ii, 72-110.]

The other dramatic productions in which Marlow was
alone concerned are five in number, and as we have before
alluded to the gradual change he occasioned from rhyme to
blank verse, from low comedy to stately tragedy, and
subsequently from inflated bombast to a more refined and
chastened style, it is comparatively easy to trace the
course and progress of his muse. His plays were all
printed at very different dates, between 1590 to 1657; but
the order in which they were written may be arrived at
without much difficulty or uncertainty. His first effort
was, doubtless, that the examination of which we have just
completed, and his last, his 'Edward II.' which, as a
historical play, has more to recommend it than the 'True
Tragedy of Richard Duke of York,' with many of the materials of which Shakespeare constructed his 'Henry VI.' Part
3. All Marlow's other pieces are in various gradations of
improvement, with the exception, perhaps, of 'The Massacre

of Paris,' which was obviously a work of great haste, and
got up for the purpose of gratifying the vulgar feeling
at that date against popery: indeed, it has hardly any
thing to recommend it, and I forbear to quote from it,
because though its excessive rarity may render it curious,*
it would throw but a faint light on this undertaking. I
may say, however, that the plot, as far as it deserves the
name, is most irregularly conducted, and is little better
than mere bustle and confusion, and incongruity from
beginning to end. Scarcely a single poetical passage is
to be found in it; and though the name of Marlow be upon
the title-page, I feel satisfied that it is merely the
imposition of the bookseller, availing himself of the
popularity of so esteemed a poet.

On the other hand, 'The Tragical Historie of Dr Faustus,' 'The Rich Jew of Malta,' 'Lusts Dominion,' and the
English historical play of 'Edward II.' all possess, in a
greater or less degree, strong claims to our admiration.
The first of these has had justice done to it in Mr Lamb's
'Specimens,' where several characteristic extracts are
inserted. It is well known that the greatest living poet
of Germany has constructed a tragedy upon the same story.
There is one circumstance in Marlow's play of 'Faustus'
deserving remark, and that is the repetition of the incident in his 'Tamburlaine,' where the hero mounts his
throne on the back of the prostrate Bajazet: in 'Faustus,'
the Pope is made to employ the same kind of footstool in
ascending his chair, using the back of the 'Saxon Bruno,'
who had put in claims to the See of Rome. Of 'The Rich
Jew of Malta' I shall say nothing, because it has recently
been introduced upon the public stage, where Kean represented Barabas. 'Lusts Dominion, or the Lascivious
Queen,' contains some beautiful poetry and harmonious
versification, though here and there we find traces of
that bombastic style Marlow at first employed to gratify
his audiences: Thus, in one place, Eleazar, the Moor,
tells his king,

> My liege, the tongue of true obedience
> Must not gainesay his soueraign's impose:
> By heauen, I will not kiss the cheek of sleep
> Till I have fetched those traitors to the court.

This puffed-up stuff may well be contrasted with such
delightful passages as the following, in which the Queen
is endeavouring to assuage the angry Moor:

> Looke smoothly on me! -
> Chime out your softest strains of harmony,

And on delicious musick's silken wings
Send ravishing delight to my loue's ears,
That he may be inamour'd of your tunes.

The 'Edward II,' of the same author in no respect differs from some of the historical plays attributed to
Shakespeare, excepting in its superiority, both in conduct
and poetry. It has been already said, that the 'Richard
II.' of the latter has been drawn upon the model of
Marlow's unhappy monarch, whose vacillating character is
quite as finely contrasted with that of the rash and blus-
tering Mortimer, as the disposition and conduct of Richard
is with the hot aspiring Bolingbroke. I had purposed to
go into some detail on the peculiar merits of this play,
but to do so with any success would demand an article of
itself, and it is the less necessary as the historical
tragedy is inserted in Dodsley's Collection. Your readers
will also, perhaps, be of opinion that I have already
dwelt long enough upon Marlow.

Note

* A copy of it was not many months since sold by Mr Evans
   of Pall-Mall for about ten guineas.

31. JAMES BROUGHTON

1830

James Broughton (fl. 1830) discovered Marlowe's burial
registered in St Nicholas, Deptford, dismissed the tradition that he was an actor, and examined the 'evidence'
about his character and opinions with critical detachment.
His notes in the British Museum copy of the 1826 edition
of the 'Works' should also be noted.
    From Life and Writings of Christopher Marlowe, in the
'Gentleman's Magazine' (January-June 1830), c, 3-6, 121-6,
222-4, 313-15, 593-7, *passim*:

[1.]

Having now expressed my opinion pretty fully upon the
question of Marlowe's imputed blasphemies, I have little
more to offer upon this point, except to entreat that the
reader, whatever he may think of my humble attempt to vin-
dicate the poet's fame, will not form his conclusions
without deliberately reperusing and comparing the eviden-
ces upon which the charge has been grounded; dispassionately weighing the probability of the several narratives;
and, above all, taking into full consideration the circumstance that he who first broached the tale which others
have heedlessly adopted, was a fierce and vindictive Puritan. Let him call to mind the rancorous malignity displayed by the members of that intolerant sect towards
those who distinguished themselves by encouraging the arts
which impart grace and elegance to society; and, above
all, towards those who upheld the enormities of the Drama.
Let him recollect of what extravagancies this same spirit,
sometimes dormant, but never extinct, has impelled man to
the commission in our times, when the conflagration of one
theatre has been styled from the pulpit a national bless-
ing, and the sudden downfall of another described (in a
strain of impious buffoonery) as the triumphant issue of a
contest between the Deity and the Evil Principle for the
possession of its site*; when a writer, who probably would
feel offended at being termed a fanatical fool, has ventured to assert, in print, that 'thousands of unhappy
spirits, and thousands yet to increase the number, will
look back with unutterable anguish on the nights and days
in which the plays of Shakspeare ministered to their
guilty delights†!' Let him ask himself whether a writer
capable of seriously, and perhaps conscientiously, promul-
gating such a sentiment as this, would hesitate to go a
step further, and blacken by any means in his power the
moral character of the author whose writings he so earnest-
ly decries? Or whether he would not deem the invention of
any libel, having a tendency to deter men from the perusal
of them, a mere pious fraud - a piece of commendable dupli-
city? That Beard, with whom originated the charges against
Marlowe, reasoned and acted somewhat after this fashion, is
my firm conviction; but the reader, who has now before him
all the accessible materials whereon to form an opinion,
will dispassionately weigh the probabilities....
    The date at which Marlowe began to write for the stage
I imagine to have been about 1588, when was performed the
tragedy of 'Tamburlaine the Great,' to which, however, his
title has recently been questioned. Nothing at least has
transpired to shew that he commenced the trade of author-

ship at an earlier period; nor does any proof whatever
exist of his having been an actor, though his biographers,
drawing their inferences from the probability of the
thing, have universally pronounced that it actually was
the case; and Warton even declares, that 'he was often
applauded by Queen Elizabeth and King James the First, as
a judicious player.' With respect to Elizabeth, this
assertion, for which no authority is quoted, is probably
akin to the blunder which long confounded his tragedy of
'Dido' with the Latin piece of that name, acted before her
at Cambridge; and as to James, it may be sufficient to
remark that he never was in England till 1603, ten years
after Marlowe's death;.so that his applause, if expressed
at all, must have been bestowed somewhat at hazard;
unless, indeed, Christopher undertook a journey to Edinburgh purposely to convince the Scottish monarch of his
histrionic abilities. 'Tis true that Guthrie, in his
'History of Scotland,' says that James, to prove how
thoroughly he was emancipated from the tutelage of his
clergy, desired Queen Elizabeth, in the year 1599, to send
him a company of English comedians; which she did, and he
gave them a license to act in his capital and in his
court; but as Marlowe had then been six years in his
grave, it is clear that he was not one of the party.

    This erroneous supposition, that Marlowe was an actor,
arose, I believe, from an equivocal expression made use of
by Greene in his 'Groat's-worth of Wit,' where he styles
him a 'famous gracer of *tragedians*;' but at this period
the words tragedian and comedian, which now seldom signify
anything but *actor*, were commonly put for *dramatist*; and,
in fact, a century after, they were still used in that
sense.

2. 'DOCTOR FAUSTUS,' 1604.

This tragedy was originally represented about 1590, and
long continued to be a popular performance, retaining
possession of the stage till towards the close of the 17th
century. Phillips (Theatr. Poetar.) says that it 'made
more noise than any of Marlowe's plays.' There are five
old editions, all of which have in the title page a rude
wood-cut, depicting Faustus raising a devil. The most
recent of them, dated 1663, is of no authority, being
carelessly printed, and interpolated with passages from
'The Jew of Malta;' but variations from the original text
had apparently been made before, since in the accounts
kept by Philip Henslowe, proprietor of the Rose Theatre,
the following item occurs:

Lent unto the Company, the 22 of november, 1602, to
pay unto Wm. Birde and Samuel Rowley, for their
adycions in Doctor Fostes, the some of iiii lb.

The latest alteration of the piece was made by Mount-
fort the player, and acted at the Theatre in Dorset Gar-
dens; a contemptible pròduction, in which Harlequin and
Scaramouch are the principal performers; and at the conclusion, after Faustus has been torn asunder by the
devils, his limbs reunite, and he joins the other personages of the drama in a jig.

The beauties of this play have been eloquently expatia-
ted upon by numerous writers, and though defective as a
whole, it certainly merits all the praise it has received.
Some exquisitely poetical passages might be selected from
it, especially the apostrophe of Faustus to the shade of
Helen, with his last impassioned soliloquy of agony and
despair, which is surpassed by nothing in the whole circle
of the English Drama, and cannot fail to excite in the
reader a thrill of horror, mingled with pity for the mis-
erable sufferer. The appearance of the devils in this
scene, to bear away their victim, seems to have shocked
many persons, as bordering upon profanity; and among the
relaters of marvels, there was long current a story, that
upon a certain occasion Satan actually made one of the
party, with consequences very fearful to those who had
assumed his shape. Alleyn, the founder of Dulwich College, was the original representative of Faustus, and if
I mistake not, the compilers of the 'Biographical Dictionary' assert, upon some authority or other, that he was
first urged to that pious undertaking by those serious
reflections which the occurrence alluded to very naturally
excited. This strange tale is thus mentioned in Prynne's
'Histrio-Mastix,' 1633, fol. 556....

3. 'EDWARD THE SECOND,' 1598.

Viewed as a whole, this is by far the best of Marlowe's
plays. The character of Edward is admirably drawn; his
infatuated attachment to his worthless minions, his
imbecility, his indecision, his bursts of passion, his
arrogance in prosperity and abject prostration in adver-
sity, are severally depicted with an adherence to nature
and a boldness of colouring which impart the deepest
interest to the various scenes, and place Marlowe in the
first class of dramatic writers. The picture was evidently the prototype of Shakspeare's 'Richard the Second,'
with which it may challenge comparison, and scarcely be

deemed inferior. *Mortimer, jun.* as evidently gave the hint for *Hotspur.*
The play was entered on the Stationers' Books, in July, 1593, and printed 1598. There are two other old editions, dated 1612 and 1622.

4. 'THE JEW OF MALTA,' 1633.

This tragedy, which, after a slumber of almost two centuries, was revived at Drury Lane in 1818, possesses many beauties, but the interest depends too exclusively upon the character of the Jew; the plot is excessively wild and improbable, nor can the charms of the language compensate for the extravagance of the incidents, in contriving which the author seems to have thought it the perfection of skill to accumulate horror upon horror. The play was coolly received on its reproduction in 1818, and soon laid aside.

The character of *Barabbas,* an original and vigorous conception, no doubt suggested to Shakspeare that of *Shylock,* and both were designed to fall in with and humour the popular prejudices against Jews, which in Elizabeth's days raged in an extravagant manner. Alleyn, who was greatly celebrated for his performance of *Barabbas,* was doubtless the original representative. To render the appearance of the Israelite more hideous, he was equipped with a huge false nose, which, as appears from various passages in old plays, was the customary decoration of userers upon the stage. To this, *Ithamore,* his servant, alludes, when he says (act 2), 'O brave master! I worship thy nose for this;' and again (act 3), 'I have the bravest, gravest, secret, subtle, *bottle-nosed* knave for my master, that ever gentleman had.' A play in a similar taste apparently preceded that of Marlowe, since Gosson, in his 'School of Abuse,' 1579, remarks, 'The Jew shown at the Bull represents the greediness of worldly choosers, and the bloody mindes of vsvrers.'

I here take my leave of Marlowe and his productions. That my feeble arguments will suffice wholly to wipe from his memory the stigma with which for upwards of two centuries it has been branded, I cannot so far flatter myself as to suppose. Many, after examining the question, will doubtless remain unconvinced; while others, without considering it at all, will continue to take for granted the current tale of his enormities, and stedfastly to believe that

> his steep aim
> Was, Titan-like, on daring doubt to pile
> Thoughts which should call down thunder
>   and the flame
> Of Heaven again assailed, if Heaven the while,
> On man and man's research could deign do more than
>   smile.

My end, however, will be accomplished, should but some
few be induced to pause ere they condemn him; and, at all
events, the facts and dates accumulated in these papers,
which have not been collected without some large expence
of time and trouble, cannot fail to be of service to any
one who may hereafter be engaged in a kindred enquiry.
  Yours, &c.   JAMES BROUGHTON.

Notes

* See 'The Ground of the Theatre,' by the *Rev*. G. Smith.
  1828.
† 'Eclectic Review,' Vol. iii. Pt. i. p. 76.

32. LEIGH HUNT

1844

Leigh Hunt (1784-1859), essayist, journalist, minor poet,
was editor of the 'Examiner' (1808-21), and served a term
in prison for reflections on the Prince Regent in that
journal. A gracious and ephemeral writer, he was a cata-
lyst for the Romantic poets, and Dickens's caricature in
Harold Skimpole ('Bleak House') hardly does him justice.
  From 'Imagination and Fancy' (1844), 136-41.

If ever there was a born poet, Marlowe was one. He perceived things in their spiritual as well as material relations, and impressed them with a corresponding felicity.
Rather, he struck them as with something sweet and glowing
that rushes by; - perfumes from a censer, - glances of
love and beauty. And he could accumulate images into as
deliberate and lofty a grandeur. Chapman said of him,

that he stood

> Up to the chin in the Pierian flood.

Drayton describes him as if inspired by the recollection:-

> Next Marlowe, bathed in the Thespian springs,
> Had in him *those brave translunary things,*
> *That the first poets had; his raptures were*
> *All air and fire,* which made his verses clear:
> *For that fine madness still he did retain,*
> *Which rightly should possess a poet's brain.*

But this happy genius appears to have had as unhappy a
will, which obscured his judgment. It made him condescend
to write fustian for the town, in order to rule over it;
subjected him to the charge of impiety, probably for nothing but too scornfully treating irreverent notions of the
Deity; and brought him, in the prime of his life, to a
violent end in a tavern. His plays abound in wilful and
self-worshipping speeches, and every one of them turns
upon some kind of ascendency at the expense of other
people. He was the head of a set of young men from the
university, the Peeles, Greens, and others, all more or
less possessed of a true poetical vein, who, bringing
scholarship to the theatre, were intoxicated with the new
graces they threw on the old bombast, carried to their
height the vices as well as wit of the town, and were
destined to see, with indignation and astonishment, their
work taken out of their hands, and done better, by the
uneducated interloper from Stratford-upon-Avon.
    Marlowe enjoys the singular and (so far) unaccountable
honour of being the only English writer to whom Shakspeare
seems to have alluded with approbation. In 'As You Like
It,' Phoebe says,

> Dead Shepherd! now I know thy saw of might, -
> 'Who ever lov'd that lov'd not at first sight?'

The 'saw' is in Marlowe's 'Hero and Leander,' a poem not
comparable with his plays.
    The ranting part of Marlowe's reputation has been
chiefly owing to the tragedy of 'Tamburlaine,' a passage
in which is laughed at in 'Henry the Fourth,' and has
become famous. Tamburlaine cries out to the captive monarchs whom he has yoked to his car, -

> Holla, ye pampered jades of Asia,
> What! can ye draw but twenty miles a day,

And have so proud a chariot at your heels,
And such a coachman as great Tamburlaine?

Then follows a picture drawn with real poetry:-

The horse that *guide the golden eye of Heaven,*
And blow the morning from their nostrils (read
nosterils)
Making their fiery gait above the clouds,
Are not so honour'd in their governor,
As you, ye slaves, in mighty Tamburlaine.

Marlowe, like Spenser, is to be looked upon as a poet
who had no native precursors. As Spenser is to be criti-
cised with an eye to his poetic ancestors, who had nothing
like the Faerie Queene, so is Marlowe with reference to
the authors of Gorbodue. He got nothing from them; he
prepared the way for the versification, the dignity, and
the pathos of his successors, who have nothing finer of
the kind to show than the death of Edward the Second -
not Shakspeare himself: - and his imagination, like
Spenser's, haunted those purely poetic regions of ancient
fabling and modern rapture, of beautiful forms and passionate expressions, which they were the first to render the
common property of inspiration, and whence their language
drew 'empyreal air.' Marlowe and Spenser are the first of
our poets who perceived the beauty of words; not as apart
from their significance, nor upon occasion only, as Chaucer did (more marvellous in that than themselves, or than
the originals from whom he drew), but as a habit of the
poetic mood, and as receiving and reflecting beauty
through the feeling of the ideas.

33. ALEXANDER DYCE

1850

Alexander Dyce (1798-1869) early abandoned the active
exercise of holy orders for literary pursuits, chiefly
editions of early poems and plays. His edition of Shakespeare (1857), like his Marlowe and others, continues to be
useful. His knowledge of Elizabethan literature was
remarkable, and he was meticulous in his use of the
authorities at his command.

From Some Account of Marlowe and His Writings, in 'The
Works of Christopher Marlowe' (1850), I, xv, xix-xx, xxi-
xxiii, xxiv-xxv, xlv-xlviii.

With very little discrimination of character, with much
extravagance of incident, with no pathos where pathos was
to be expected, and with a profusion of inflated language,
'Tamburlaine' is nevertheless a very impressive drama, and
undoubtedly superior to all the English tragedies which
preceded it; - superior to them in the effectiveness with
which the events are brought out, in the poetic feeling
which animates the whole, and in the nerve and variety of
the versification. Marlowe was yet to shew that he could
impart truthfulness to his scenes; but not a few passages
might be gleaned from 'Tamburlaine,' as grand in thought,
as splendid in imagery, and as happy in expression, as any
which his later works contain....
    The well-known fact, that our early dramatists usually
borrowed their fables from novels or 'histories,' to which
they often servilely adhered, has been thought no deroga-
tion from their merits. Yet the latest biographer of
Marlowe dismisses 'Faustus' as 'unworthy of his reputation,' chiefly because it 'closely follows a popular rom-
ance of the same name.' Certain it is that Marlowe has
'closely followed' the prose 'History of Doctor Faustus';
but it is equally certain that he was not indebted to that
'History' for the poetry and the passion which he has infused into his play, for those thoughts of surpassing
beauty and grandeur with which it abounds, and for that
fearful display of mental agony at the close, compared to
which all attempts of the kind by preceding English dramatists are 'poor indeed.' In the opinion of Hazlitt,
'"Faustus," though an imperfect and unequal performance,
is Marlowe's greatest work.' Mr. Hallam remarks, 'There
is an awful melancholy about Marlowe's Mephistophiles,
perhaps more impressive than the malignant mirth of that
fiend in the renowned work of Goethe. But the fair form
of Margaret is wanting.' In the comic scenes of 'Faustus'
(which are nearly all derived from the prose 'History' we
have buffoonery of the worst description; and it is difficult not to believe that Marlowe is answerable for at
least a portion of them, when we recollect that he had
inserted similar scenes in the original copy of his 'Tamburlaine.'
    In what year Marlowe produced 'The Jew of Malta' we are
unable to determine. The words in the Prologue, 'now the
Guise is dead,' are evidence that it was composed after

23rd Dec. 1588; and Mr. Collier thinks that it was probably
written about 1589 or 1590. Barabas was originally performed by Alleyn; and the aspect of the Jew was rendered
as grotesque and hideous as possible by means of a false
nose. In Rowley's 'Search for Money,' 1609, a person is
described as having 'his visage (or vizard) like the arti-
ficiall Jewe of Maltae's nose;' and a speech in the play
itself, 'Oh, brave, master! I worship your nose for
this,' is a proof that Marlowe intended his hero to be
distinguished for the magnitude of that feature. It would
seem, indeed, that on our early stage Jews were always
furnished with an extra quantity of nose: it was thought
that a race so universally hated could hardly be made to
appear too ugly....
    The character of Barabas, upon which the interest of
the tragedy entirely depends, is delineated with no ordinary power, and possesses a strong individuality.
Unfortunately, however, it is a good deal overcharged;
but I suspect, that in this instance at least, Marlowe
violated the truth of nature, not so much from his love of
exaggeration, as in consequence of having borrowed all
the atrocities of the play from some now-unknown novel,
whose author was willing to flatter the prejudices of his
readers by attributing almost impossible wickedness to a
son of Israel. 'The first two acts of "The Jew of
Malta,"' observes Mr. Hallam, 'are more vigorously conceived, both as to character and circumstance, than any
other Elizabethan play, except those of Shakespeare:' but
the latter part is in every respect so inferior, that we
rise from a perusal of the whole with a feeling akin to
disappointment. If the dialogue has little poetry, it
has often great force of expression. - That Shakespeare
was well acquainted with this tragedy cannot be doubted;
but that he caught from it more than a few trifling hints
for 'The Merchant of Venice' will be allowed by no one who
has carefully compared the character of Barabas with that
of Shylock. - An alteration of 'The Jew of Malta' was produced at Drury-lane Theatre in 1818, when Kean was in the
zenith of his fame, and, owing to his exertions in Barabas, it was very favourably received.
    Warton incidentally mentions that Marlowe's 'Edward the
Second' was 'written in the year 1590;' and, for all we
know, he may have made the assertion on sufficient
grounds, though he has neglected to specify them. Mr.
Collier, who regards it (and, no doubt, rightly) as one
of our author's latest pieces, has not attempted to fix
its date. It was entered in the Stationers' Books 6th
July 1593, and first printed in 1598.
    From that heaviness, which prevails more or less in all

'chronicle histories' anterior to those of Shakespeare,
this tragedy is not wholly free; its crowded incidents do
not always follow each other without confusion; and it has
few of those 'raptures,' for which Marlowe is eulogized by
one of his contemporaries. But, taken as a whole, it is
the most perfect of his plays; there is no overdoing of
character, no turgidity of language. On the two scenes
which give the chief interest to this drama Lamb remarks:
'the reluctant pangs of abdicating royalty in Edward furnished hints which Shakespeare scarce improved in his
Richard the Second; and the death-scene of Marlowe's king
moves pity and terror beyond any scene ancient or modern
with which I am acquainted.' The excellence of both
scenes is indisputable; but a more fastidious critic than
Lamb might perhaps justly object to such an exhibition of
physical suffering as the latter scene affords....
     'The Massacre at Paris' was printed without date (per-
haps about 1595 or 1596), either from a copy taken down,
during representation, by some unskilful and ignorant
short-hand-writer, or from a very imperfect transcript
which had belonged to one of the theatres.
     It would be rash to decide on the merits of a play
which we possess only with a text both mutilated and
abounding in corruptions; I strongly suspect, however,
that 'The Massacre at Paris,' even in its pristine state,
was the very worst of Marlowe's dramas.
     We must now turn from his works to the personal history
of Marlowe. - It is not to be doubted that by this time he
had become acquainted with most of those who, like himself, were dramatists by profession; and there can be
little doubt too that beyond their circle (which, of
course, included the actors) he had formed few intimacies.
Though the demand for theatrical novelties was then
incessant, plays were scarcely recognized as literature,
and the dramatists were regarded as men who held a rather
low rank in society: the authors of pieces which had
delighted thousands were generally looked down upon by the
grave substantial citizens, and seldom presumed to approach the mansions of the aristocracy but as clients in
humble attendance on the bounty of their patrons.
Unfortunately, the discredit which attached to dramatic
writing as an occupation was greatly increased by the
habits of those who pursued it: a few excepted, they were
improvident, unprincipled, and dissolute, - now rioting in
taverns and 'ordinaries' on the profits of a successful
play, and now lurking in the haunts of poverty till the
completion of another drama had enabled them to resume
their revels. - At a somewhat later period, indeed, a
decided improvement appears to have taken place in the

morals of our dramatic writers: and it is by no means
improbable that the high respectability of character which
was maintained by Shakespeare and Jonson may have operated
very beneficially, in the way of example, on the playwrights around them. - But among those of superior station
there was at least one person with whom Marlowe lived on
terms of intimacy: the publisher of his posthumous fragment, 'Hero and Leander,' was induced to dedicate it 'to
the worshipful Sir Thomas Walsingham, knight,' because he
had 'bestowed upon the author many kind favours, entertaining the parts of reckoning and worth which he found
in him with good countenance and *liberal affection*.' Nor
is this the only proof extant that Sir Thomas Walsingham
cultivated a familiarity with the dramatists of his day;
for to him, as to his 'long-loved and honourable *friend*,'
Chapman has inscribed by a sonnet the comedy of 'Al
Fooles,' 1605....
    This version of the 'Amores,' taken altogether, does so
little credit either to Marlowe's skill as a translator or
to his scholarship, that one is almost tempted to believe
it was never intended by him to meet the eye of the world,
but was made, merely as a literary exercise, at an early
period of life, when classical studies chiefly engaged
his attention. We look in vain for the graces of Ovid.
In many passages we should be utterly puzzled to attach a
definite meaning to the words, if we had not the original
at hand; and in many others the Latin is erroneously
rendered, the mistranslations being sometimes extremely
ludicrous. I doubt if more can be said in praise of this
version than that it is occasionally spirited and flowing.
Of the XVth Elegy of the First Book there are two translations, - the second, which is by B. J. (i.e. Ben Jonson)
being, however, only an alteration of the first....
    A paraphrase on the very elegant production of the
Pseudo-Musaeus had been projected and was already partly
composed by Marlowe, when death put an end to his labours;
and as much of 'Hero and Leander' as could be discovered
after his decease, having been entered in the Stationers'
Books 28th September, 1593, was given to the press in
1598. - While the poem of the Greek grammarian is com-
prised in 341 verses, the fragment in question extends to
above 800.
    In this paraphrase Marlowe has somewhat impeded the
progress and weakened the interest of the story by introducing extraneous matter and by indulging in whimsical and
frivolous details; he occasionally disregards costume; he
is too fond of conceits, and too prodigal of 'wise saws'
and moral axioms. But he has amply redeemed these faults
by the exquisite perception of the beautiful which he

displays throughout a large portion of the fragment, by
descriptions picturesque and vivid in the extreme, by
lines which glow with all the intensity of passion, by
marvellous felicities of language, and by skilful modulation of the verse. - The quotation from this poem in 'As
You Like It' may be considered as a proof that it was
admired by Shakespeare; and the words which are there
applied to the author, - 'dead shepherd,' - sound not
unlike an expression of pity for his sad and untimely end.
Jonson, too, in 'Every Man in his Humour' has cited 'Hero
and Leander'; and he is reported to have spoken of it
often in terms of the highest praise.

34. G. H. LEWES

1864

George Henry Lewes (1817-78) was a versatile and accomplished man of letters, and layman's philosopher. This
post-Goethean treatment of 'Doctor Faustus' and its age
is most suggestive for the general Victorian view.
  From 'The Life and Works of Goethe' (1864), 475-8.

'Doctor Faustus' has many magnificent passages, such as
Marlowe of the 'mighty line' could not fail to write; but
on the whole it is wearisome, vulgar, and ill-conceived.
The lowest buffoonery, destitute of wit, fills a large
portion of the scenes; and the serious parts want dramatic
evolution. There is no character well drawn. The melancholy figure of Mephistophilis has a certain grandeur,
but he is not the Tempter, according to the common conception, creeping to his purpose with the cunning of the
serpent; nor is he the cold, ironical 'spirit that
denies'; he is more like the Satan of Byron, with a touch
of piety and much repentance. The language he addresses
to Faustus is such as would rather frighten than seduce
him.
  The reader who opens 'Faustus' under the impression
that he is about to see a philosophical subject treated
philosophically, will have mistaken both the character of
Marlowe's genius and of Marlowe's epoch. 'Faustus' is no
more philosophical in intention than the 'Jew of Malta',

or 'Tamburlaine the Great'. It is simply the theatrical
treatment of a popular legend, - a legend admirably
characteristic of the spirit of those ages in which men,
believing in the agency of the devil, would willingly have
bartered their future existence for the satisfaction of
present desires. Here undoubtedly is a philosophical
problem, which even in the present day is constantly
presenting itself to the speculative mind. Yes, even in
the present day, since human nature does not change, -
forms only change, the spirit remains; nothing perishes, -
it only manifests itself differently. Men, it is true, no
longer believe in the devil's agency; at least, they no
longer believe in the power of calling up the devil and
transacting business with him; otherwise there would be
hundreds of such stories as that of 'Faust'. But the
spirit which created that story and rendered it credible
to all Europe remains unchanged. The sacrifice of the
future to the present is the spirit of that legend. The
blindness to consequences caused by the imperiousness of
desire; the recklessness with which inevitable and
terrible results are braved in perfect consciousness of
their being inevitable, provided that a temporary pleasure
can be obtained, is the spirit which dictated Faust's
barter of his soul, which daily dictates the barter of
men's souls. We do not make compacts, but we throw away
our lives; we have no Tempter face to face with us offering illimitable power in exchange for our futurity: but
we have our own Desires, imperious, insidious, and for
them we barter our existence, - for one moment's pleasure
risking years of anguish.
     The story of Faustus suggests many modes of philosoph-
ical treatment, but Marlowe has not availed himself of
any: he has taken the popular view of the legend, and
given his hero the vulgarest motives. This is not meant
as a criticism, but as a statement. I am not sure that
Marlowe was wrong in so treating his subject; I am only
sure that he treated it so. Faustus is disappointed with
logic, because it teaches him nothing but debate, - with
physic, because he cannot with it bring dead men back to
life, - with law, because it concerns only the 'external
trash', - and with divinity, because it teaches that the
reward of sin is death, and that we are all sinners.
Seeing advantage in none of these studies he takes to
necromancy, and there finds content; and how?

[Quotes I, i. 94-98.]

There may in this seem something trivial to modern appre-
hensions, yet Marlowe's audience sympathized with it,

having the feelings of an age when witches were burned, when men were commonly supposed to hold communication with infernal spirits, when the price of damnation was present enjoyment.

The compact signed, Faustus makes use of his power by scampering over the world, performing practical jokes and vulgar incantations, - knocking down the Pope, making horns sprout on the heads of noblemen, cheating a jockey by selling him a horse of straw, and other equally vulgar tricks, which were just the things the audience would have done had they possessed the power. Tired of his buffooneries he calls up the vision of Helen; his rapture at the sight is a fine specimen of how Marlowe can write on a fitting occasion.

His last hour now arrives: he is smitten with remorse, like many of his modern imitators, when it is too late; sated with his power, he now shudders at the price. After some tragical raving, and powerful depicted despair, he is carried off by devils. The close is in keeping with the commencement: Faustus is damned because he made the compact. Each part of the bargain is fulfilled; it is a tale of sorcery, and Faustus meets the fate of a sorcerer.

The vulgar conception of this play is partly the fault of Marlowe, and partly of his age. It might have been treated quite in conformity with the general belief; it might have been a tale of sorcery, and yet magnificently impressive. What would not Shakespeare have made of it? Nevertheless, we must in justice to Marlowe look also to the state of opinion in his time; and we shall then admit that another and higher mode of treatment would perhaps have been less acceptable to the audience. Had it been metaphysical, they would not have understood it; had the motives of Faustus been more elevated, the audience would not have believed in them. To have saved him at last, would have been to violate the legend, and to outrage their moral sense. For, why should the black arts be unpunished? why should not the sorcerer be damned? The legend was understood in its literal sense, in perfect accordance with the credulity of the audience. The symbolical significance of the legend is entirely a modern creation.

35. EDWARD DOWDEN

1870

Edward Dowden (1843-1913) was Professor of English Literature at Trinity College, Dublin (1867-1913). His most
influential work was his 'Shakspere, His Mind and Art'
(1875). His references to a Marlowe 'cult' and his attack
on German criticism are especially interesting.
From 'Transcripts and Studies' (1888), 431-53, first
published in the 'Fortnightly Review', January 1870.

The study of Shakspere and his contemporaries is the study
of one family consisting of many members, all of whom have
the same life-blood in their veins, all of whom are recognisable by accent and bearing, and acquired habits, and
various unconscious self-revealments as kinsmen, while
each possesses a character of his own, and traits of mind
and manners and expression which distinguish him from the
rest. The interest of the study lies chiefly in the
gradual apprehension, now on this side, now on that, of
the common nature of this great family of writers, until
we are in complete intellectual possession of it, and in
tracing out the characteristics peculiar to each of its
individuals. There is, perhaps, no other body of literature towards which we are attracted by so much of unity,
and at the same time by so much of variety. If the school
of Rubens had been composed of greater men than it was, we
should have had an illustrious parallel in the history of
painting to the group of Shakspere and his contemporaries
in the history of poetry.
    The 'school of Rubens' we say; we could hardly speak
with accuracy of the 'school of Shakspere.' Yet there can
be little doubt that he was in a considerable degree the
master of the inferior and younger artists who surrounded
him. It is the independence of Ben Jonson's work and its
thorough individuality, rather than comparative greatness
or beauty of poetical achievement, which have given him a
kind of acknowledged right to the second place amongst
the Elizabethan dramatists, a title to vice-president's
chair in the session of the poets. His aims were different from those of the others, and at a time when plays and
playwrights were little esteemed, he had almost a nineteenth-century sense of the dignity of art, and of his own
art in particular:-

And he told then plainly he deserved the bays,
For his were called Works, where others were but Plays.

But Webster, and Massinger, and Beaumont and Fletcher,
and Shirley (who were content, like Shakspere, to write
'plays,' and did not aspire to 'works') are really followers of the greatest of all dramatic writers, and very different handiwork they would probably have turned out had
they wrought in their craft without the teaching of his
practice and example. Shakspere's immediate predecessors
were men of no mean powers; but they are separated by a
great gulf from his contemporaries and immediate successors. That tragedy is proportioned to something else than
the number of slaughtered bodies piled upon the stage at
the end of act five, that comedy has store of mirth more
vital, deeper, happier, more human than springs from

Jigging veins of rhyming mother wits,
And such conceits as clownage keeps in pay -

these were discoveries in art made by Shakspere; and is it
too much to suppose that but for him these discoveries
might have come later by a dozen years or more? The works
of the pre-Shaksperians are of small interest for the most
part, except as illustrating a necessary stage of growth
in the history of the drama. They do not win upon us with
the charm, the singleness of aim, the divine innocency,
the sacred inexperience, the unction of art, which we are
sensible of in the works of Raphael's predecessors.
Italian painting may be personified under the figure of a
royal maiden who, after a period of chaste seclusion and
tender virginity, came forth into the world, and was a
queen and mother of men. The English drama was, first, a
schoolboy, taught rude piety by the priests, and rude
jokes by his fellows; then a young man, lusty, passionate,
mettlesome, riotous, aspiring, friendly, full of extravagant notions and huffing words, given to irregular ways
and disastrous chances and desperate recoveries, but, like
Shakspere's wild prince, containing the promise of that
grave, deep-thoughted, and magnificent manhood which was
afterwards realised.
     It is, however, amongst the pre-Shaksperians that we
find the man who, of all the Elizabethan dramatists,
stands next to Shakspere in poetical stature, the one man
who, if he had lived longer and accomplished the work
which lay clear before him, might have stood even *beside*
Shakspere, as supreme in a different province of dramatic
art. Shakspere would have been master of the realists or
naturalists; Marlowe, master of the idealists. The

starting-point of Shakspere, and of those who resemble
him, is always something concrete, something real in the
moral world - a character and an action; to no more
elementary components than human characters and actions
can the products of their art be reduced in the alembic of
critical analysis; further than these they are irredu-
cible. The starting-point of Marlowe, and of those who
resemble Marlowe, is something abstract - a passion or an
idea; to a passion or an idea each work of theirs can be
brought back. Revenge is not the subject of the 'Merchant
of Venice;' Antonio and Shylock, Portia and Nerissa,
Lorenzo and Jessica, Bassanio and Gratiano - these, and a
passage in the lives of these, are the true subjects.
Even of 'Romeo and Juliet' the subject is not love, but
two young and loving hearts surrounded by a group of most
living figures, and overshadowed by a tyrannous fate.
Those critics, and they are unfortunately numerous since
German criticism became a power in this country, who
attempt to discover an intention, idea, or, as they say,
motiv presiding throughout each of Shakspere's plays, have
got upon an entirely mistaken track, and they inevitably
come out after labyrinthine wanderings at the other end of
nowhere. Shakspere's trade was not that of preparing nuts
with concealed mottoes and sentiments in them for German
commentators to crack. Goethe, who wrought in Shakspere's
manner (though sometimes with a self-consciousness which
went hankering after ideas and intentions), Goethe saw
clearly the futility of all attempts to release from their
obscurity the secrets of his own works, as if the mystery
of what he had created were other than the mystery of
life.... But Marlowe worked, as Milton also worked, from
the starting-point of an idea or passion, and the critic
who might dissect all the creatures of Shakspere's art
without ever having the honour to discover a soul, may
really, by dexterous anatomy, come upon the souls of Marlowe's or of Milton's creatures - intelligent monads
seated observant in the pineal gland.
   Shakspere and Marlowe, the two foremost men of the
Elizabethan artistic movement, remind us in not a few par-
ticulars of the two foremost men of the artistic movement
in Germany eighty or ninety years ago, Goethe and Schiller.
Shakspere and Goethe are incomparably the larger and
richer natures, their art is incomparably the greater and
more fruitful; yet they were themselves much greater than
their art. Shakspere rendered more by a measureless sum
of a man's whole nature into poetry than Marlowe did; yet
his own life ran on below the rendering of it into poetry,
and was never wholly absorbed and lost therein. We can
believe that under different circumstances Shakspere might

never have written a line, might have carried all that lay
within him unuttered to his grave. While still in the
full manhood of his powers, he chose to put off his gar-
ments of enchantment, break his magic staff, and dismiss
his airy spirits; or, in plain words, bring to a close his
career as poet, and live out the rest of his life as
country gentleman in his native town. It is a suggestive
fact, too, that the scattered references to Shakspere
which we find in the writings of his contemporaries, show
us the poet concealed and sometimes forgotten in the man,
and make it clear that he moved among his fellows with no
assuming of the bard or prophet, no aspect as of one inspired, no air of authority as of one divinely commis-
sioned; that, on the contrary, he appeared as a pleasant
comrade, genial, gentle, full of civility in the large
meaning of that word, upright in dealing, ready and bright
in wit, quick and sportive in conversation. Goethe, also,
though he valued his own works highly, valued them from a
superior position as one above them, and independent of
them. But Marlowe, like Schiller, seems to have lived in
and for his art. His poetry was no episode in his life,
but his very life itself. With an university education,
and a prospect, which for a man of his powers can hardly
have been an unpromising one, of success in one of the
learned professions (not necessarily the Church), he must
abandon his hardly-earned advantages, return to the
poverty from which he had sprung, and add to poverty the
disgrace of an actor's and playwright's life. His contemporaries usually speak of him as a man would be spoken
of who was possessed by his art, rather than as one who,
like Shakspere, held it in possession.

> That fine madness still he did retain,
> Which rightly should possess a poet's brain.

So wrote Drayton; and according to Chapman's fine hyper-
bole he

> Stood
> Up to the chin in the Pierian flood.

This is not the way in which Shakspere is spoken of.
Nor is it an uncharacteristic circumstance that probably
while he lay for a short time tortured with the wound of
his own dagger, and death was hastening, one of Marlowe's
chief anxieties, if the tradition be trustworthy, was
about the fate of his 'Hero and Leander,' and that he
commended it for completion to the man of all others best
fitted for the task - the great translator of Homer, whose

words have just been quoted.

But if Marlowe be the Schiller - the subjective poet,
the idealist, as Shakspere is the Goethe, objective and
naturalistic, of Elizabethan art - he is a Schiller of a
decidedly Satanic school. With an important critical
movement behind him, around him a regulated state of society, and many influences calling into activity the better
part of his nature, the true Schiller's head and heart and
sensibilities as an artist passed through their 'Sturm und
Drang' fever, and came forth illuminated, purified, and
elevated. On the other hand, the world amidst which he
moved was too much one of merely cultured refinement; no
rude but large and ardent popular heart beat in his hearing; rather, in the court and *salons* and theatre of
Weimar, official waistcoats rose and fell with admirable
but not very inspiring regularity over self-possessed and
decorous bosoms. The talk was of poems, pictures, busts,
medals, and the last little new law of the Duke. It is
not surprising that Schiller's art should have a touch of
coldness in it. Marlowe had behind him, not a critical
movement like the German, but the glare of Smithfield
fires and the ghostly procession of noble figures dealt
with by the headsman on Tower Hill, terrible religious and
political battles, and the downfall of a faith. For his
own part, taking art as the object of his devotion, he
thrust all religions somewhat fiercely aside, and professed an angry Atheism. The Catholic hierarchy and creed
he seems to have hated with an energy profoundly different from the feeling of Shakspere, distinguished as that
was by a discriminating justice. The reckless Bohemian
London life which Marlowe shared with his companions,
Greene, Peele, Nash, and other wild livers, had nothing
in it to sober his judgment, to chasten and purify his
imagination and taste, nothing or very little to elevate
his feelings. But it was quick and passionate. The
'Sturm und Drang' through which our English dramatists
passed was of far sterner stress than that of Germany.
But Marlowe did pass through it. He perished unhappily
before he had acquired mastery in his second style. He
lived long enough to escape from the period, so to speak,
of his 'Robbers,' not long enough to attain to the serene
ideality of a 'Wilhelm Tell.' But Marlowe possessed one
immense advantage over Schiller - he stood not in the
midst of a petty ducal court, but in the centre of a great
nation, and at a time when that nation was all air and
fire, its baser elements disappearing in the consciousness
of a new-found power, a time when the nation was no aggre-
gation of atoms cohering by accident, and each clamorous
for its own particular rights, but a living body, with

something like a unity of ideas, and with feelings self-
organised around splendid objects of common interest,
pride, and admiration. The strength and weakness of what
Marlowe accomplished in literature correspond with the
influences from the real world to which he was subject.
He is great, ardent, aspiring; but he is also without
balance, immoderate, unequal, extravagant. There is an
artistic grace which is the counterpart of the theological
grace of charity. It pervades everything that Shakspere
has written; there is little of it in Marlowe's writings.
There is in them 'a hunger and thirst after unrighteousness, a glow of the imagination unhallowed by anything but
its own energies. His thoughts burn within him like a
furnace with bickering flames, or throwing out black smoke
and mists that hide the dawn of genius, or like a poisonous mineral corrode the heart.'* If a Schiller, then,
surely a Schiller of a Satanic school.

Marlowe's works consist of six or seven plays and some
translations, one of which - a paraphrase of the 'Hero and
Leander' of the pseudo-Musaeus - is remarkable as evidenc-
ing, more than any other of his writings, the Renaissance
feeling for sensuous beauty which Marlowe possessed in a
degree hardly, if at all, less than that displayed by
Shakspere in his youthful 'Venus and Adonis.' Of the
dramas, one was produced in conjunction with Nash, and we
cannot safely assign to its authors their respective
shares in the work. One - 'The Massacre at Paris' - seems
to have been thrown off to meet some temporary occasion;
and certainly, however this may have been, it may without
remorse be set down as of little worth. A third was written, we can hardly doubt, when the poet was in the transition period from his early to what would have been, if he
had lived, his mature style. Though in some respects the
best, it is in truth the least characteristic of all his
more important writings. There are critics who can more
readily forgive any literary deficiencies or incapacities
than sins of actual commission, who can bear with every
evidence of dulness of poetical vision, languor of the
thinking power, uncertainty of the shaping hands, but who
have no toleration for splendid crimes, the sins of the
sanguine temperament, extravagant fancies, thoughts that
climb too high, turbulency of manner, and great swelling
words of vanity. These have pronounced 'Edward the
Second' Marlowe's best play. And it is, doubtless, free
from the violence and extravagance of the dramas that preceded it, from the vaulting ambition of poetical style,
which 'o'erleaps itself, and falls o' the other;' but,
except in a few scenes, and notably the closing ones, it
wants also the clear raptures, the high reaches of wit,

the 'brave translunary things,' the single lines - each
one enough to ransom a poet from captivity - which especially characterise Marlowe. The historical matter he is
unable to handle as successfully as a subject of an imaginative or partly mythical kind; it does not yield and take
shape in his hands as readily, and accordingly 'Edward the
Second,' though containing a few splendid passages, is
rather a series of scenes from the chronicles of England
than a drama.

Three plays remain, and on these the fame of Marlowe
may safely rest - 'Tamburlaine the Great,' 'The Tragical
History of Dr Faustus,' and 'The Jew of Malta.' Each of
these is admirably characteristic, and could have proceeded from no other brain than that of its creator. The
three together form a great achievement in literature for
a man probably not more than twenty-seven years of age
when the latest was written; and they still stand apart
from the neighbouring crowd of dramatic compositions, and
close to one another - a little group distinguished by
peculiar marks of closest kinship, a peculiar physiognomy,
complexion, demeanour, and accent. Each of the three is
the rendering into artistic form of the workings of a
single passion, while at the same time each of these
several passions is only a different form of life assumed
by one supreme passion, central in all the great characters of Marlowe, magisterial, claiming the whole man, and
in its operation fatal.

The subject of 'Tamburlaine' - probably Marlowe's
earliest work, certainly the first which made an impression on the public - if we would express it in the sim-
plest way, is the mere lust of dominion, the passion of
'a mightly hunter before the Lord' for sovereign sway,
the love of power in its crudest shape. This, and this
alone, living and acting in the person of the Scythian
shepherd, gives unity to the multitude of scenes which
grow up before us and fall away, like the fiery-hearted
blossoms of some inexhaustible tropical plant, blown with
sudden and strong vitality, fading and dropping away at
night, and replaced next morning by others as sanguine
and heavy with perfume. There is no construction in
'Tamburlaine.' Instead of two plays there might as well
have been twenty, if Marlowe could have found it in his
heart to husband his large supply of kings, emperors,
soldans, pashas, governors, and viceroys who perish before
the Scourge of God, or had he been able to discover
empires, provinces, and principalities with which to endow
a new race of rulers. The play ends from sheer exhaustion
of resources. As Alexander was reduced to weep for
another world to conquer, so Tamburlaine might have wept

because there were no more emperors to fill his cages, no
more monarchs to increase his royal stud. He does not
weep, but what is much better, dies. The play resembles
in its movement no other so much as the 'Sultan Amurath'
of De Quincey's elder brother. 'What by the bowstring,
and what by the scimitar, the sultan had so thinned the
population with which he commenced business that scarcely
any of the characters remained alive at the end of Act the
first.' Five crops had to be taken off the ground in the
tragedy, amounting, in short, to five tragedies involved
in one. The difference is, that Marlowe could not be
satisfied with less than ten crops and a corresponding
number of tragedies.

Yet 'Tamburlaine' is the work of a master-hand, untrained. If from some painting ill-composed, full of
crude and violent colour, containing abundant proofs of
weakness and inexperience, and having half its canvas
crowded with extravagant grotesques which the artist took
for sublime - if from such a painting one wonderful face
looked out at us, the soul in its eyes and on its lips,
a single desire possessing it, eager and simple as a
flame, should we question the genius of the painter? And
somewhat in this manner the single passion which has the
hero of the piece for its temporary body and instrument
looks out at us from the play of 'Tamburlaine.' The lust
and the pride of conquest, the ambition to be a god upon
earth, the confident sense that in one's own will resides
the prime force of nature, disdain of each single thing,
how splendid soever, which the world can offer by way of
gift or bribe, because less than the possession of all
seems worthless - these are feelings which, though evidence from history that they are real is not wanting, are
yet even imagined in a vivid way by very few persons. The
demands which most of us make on life are moderate; our
little lives run on with few great ambitions, and this
gross kind of ambition is peculiarly out of relation to
our habits of desire. But Marlowe, the son of the Canterbury shoemaker, realised in imagination this ambition as
if it were his very own, and gave it most living expression....

Faustus is the Paracelsus of Marlowe. Over the soul of
the Würtemberg doctor the passion for knowledge dominates,
and all influences of good and evil, the voices of damned
and of blessed angels reach him faint and ineffectual as
dreams, or distant music, or the suggestions of long-
forgotten odours, save as they promise something to glut
the fierce hunger and thirst of his intellect. All subjects, however, in the stream of Marlowe's genius are
hurried in a single direction. Pride of will drew to

itself all other forces of his nature, and made them
secondary and subordinate; and accordingly we are not surprised when we find that, in Marlowe's hands, the passion
for knowledge which possesses Faustus becomes little more
than a body, as it were, giving a special form of life to
the same consuming lust of power which he had treated in
the earlier drama of 'Tamburlaine.' To Faustus, in the
suggestion of the Tempter, the words 'knowing good and
evil' grow dim in the unhallowed splendour of the promise
'Ye shall be as gods.' All secrets of Nature and of Fate
he desires to penetrate, but not in order that he may
contemplate their mysteries in philosophic calmness, not
that he may possess his soul in the serene light of ascer-
tained primal truths; rather it is for the lordship over
men and things which knowledge places in his hands that he
chiefly desires it. Logic, law, physic, divinity, have
yielded their whole stores into his keeping, but they have
left his intellect unsatisfied, craving for acquisition of
a less formal, a more natural and living kind, and they
have afforded him no adequate field, and but feeble
instruments for the display of the forces of his will.
It is magic which with every discovery to the intellect
unites a corresponding gift of power:-

Tis magic, magic that hath ravished me.

What is knowledge worth if it does not enable him to
obtain mastery over gross matter, over the lives and fortunes of men, over the elements of air and earth, of fire
and water, and over the strong elemental spirits? To be
surrounded with proofs and witnesses of the transcendent
might of his own will, - this is the ultimate desire of
Faustus, as in other circumstances and seeking other
manifestations, it was of Tamburlaine. But the scholar
does not ever disappear in the magician. In the first
heated vision of the various objects towards which the
new agency at his command might be turned, projects rise
before him of circling Germany with brass, of driving the
Prince of Parma from the land, and reigning 'sole king of
all the provinces;' yet even in that hour there mingle
with more vulgar ambitions the ambitions of the thinker and
the student; he would have his subject spirits resolve him
of all ambiguities, and read to him strange philosophies.
The pleasure, which afterwards he seeks, less for its own
sake than to banish the hated thought of the approaching
future, is the quintessence of pleasure. He is not made
for coarse delights. He desires no beauty but that of
'the fairest maid in Germany,' or the beauty of Helen of
Troy:-

Was this the face that launch'd a thousand ships.
And burnt the topless towers of Ilium?
Sweet Helen, make me immortal with a kiss.

He chooses no song but Homer's song, no music but that of
Amphion's harp:-

Long ere this I should have slain myself
Had not sweet pleasure conquer'd deep despair.
Have not I made blind Homer sing to me
Of Alexander's love and Oenon's death?
And hath not he that built the walls of Thebes,
With ravishing sound of his melodious harp,
Made music with my Mephistophilis?

And in the scene of parting with the two scholars,
immediately preceding the uncompanioned agony of the
doomed man's latest hour - a scene distinguished by a
lofty pathos which we find nowhere else in Marlowe - there
is throughout an atmosphere of learning, of refinement, of
scholarly urbanity, which makes us feel how thoroughly
Marlowe had preserved his original conception of the
character of Faustus, even while he degraded him to the
low conjuror of certain passages, introduced by a writer
singularly devoid of humour, to make sport for the
groundlings of the theatre.
A grosser air is breathed throughout 'The Jew of
Malta.' The whole play is murky with smoke of the pit.
Evil desires, evil thoughts, evil living, fill its five
acts to the full. Nine-tenths of the picture are as
darkly shadowed as some shadowy painting of Rembrandt;
but, as might also be in one of Rembrandt's paintings, in
the centre there is a head relieved against the gloom, lit
by what strange light we do not know, unless it be the
reflection from piles of gold and gems - a head fascinating and detestable, of majestic proportions, full of
intellect, full of malice and deceit, with wrinkled brow,
beak-like nose, cruel lips, and eyes that, though half-
hooded by leathery lids, triumph visibly in the success of
something devilish. Barabas is the dedicated child of sin
from his mother's womb. As he grew in stature he must
have grown in crooked wisdom and in wickedness. His heart
is a nest where there is room for the patrons of the seven
deadly sins to lodge, but one chief devil is its permanent
occupier - Mammon. The lust of money is the passion of
the Jew, which is constantly awake and active. His bags
are the children of his heart, more loved than his Abigail, and the dearer because they were begotten through
deceit or by violence. Yet Barabas is a superb figure.

His energy of will is so great; his resources and inven-
tions are so inexhaustible; he is so illustrious a representative of material power and of intellectual. Even his
love of money has something in it of sublime, it is so
huge a desire. He is no miser treasuring each contemptible coin. Precisely as Tamburlaine looked down with
scorn at all ordinary kingships and lordships of the
earth, as Faustus held for worthless the whole sum of
stored-up human learning in comparison with the infinite
knowledge to which he aspired, so Barabas treats with
genuine disdain the opulence of common men....
     It has not seemed necessary here to dwell upon all that
is worthless, and worse than worthless, in Marlowe's
plays - on the midsummer madness of 'Tamburlaine,' the
contemptible buffoonery of 'Dr Faustus,' and the overloaded sensational atrocities of 'The Jew of Malta.' Such
criticism every one but an Ancient Pistol does for himself. We all recognise the fustian of Marlowe's style,
and the ill effects of the demands made upon him by
sixteenth-century play-goers for such harlequinade as
they could appreciate. A more important thing to recognise is that up to the last Marlowe's great powers were
ripening, while his judgment was becoming sane, and his
taste purer. He was escaping, as has been already said,
from his 'Sturm und Drang' when he was lost to the world.
'Tamburlaine' was written at the age of twenty-two,
'Faustus' two or three years later. At such an age
accomplishment is rare; we usually look for no more than
promise. If Shakspere had died at the age when Marlowe
died we should have known little of the capacity which
lay within him of creating a Macbeth, a Lear, an Othello,
a Cleopatra. Marlowe has left us three great ideal figures of Titanic strength and size. That we should say is
much. In one particular a most important advance from
'Tamburlaine' to 'Dr Faustus' and the later plays is dis-
cernible - in versification. His contemporaries appear
to have been much impressed by the greatness of his verse
- Marlowe's 'mighty line;' and it was in the tirades of
'Tamburlaine' that blank verse was first heard upon a
public stage in England. But in this play the blank verse
is like a gorgeous robe of brocade, stiff with golden
embroidery; afterwards in his hands it becomes pliable,
and falls around the thought or feeling which it covers
in nobly significant lines.

Note

* Hazlitt.

36. H. A. TAINE

1872

Hippolyte Adolphe Taine (1828-93) sought, in literary his-
tory, to determine how 'la race, le milieu et le moment'
interplay in creative activity. The first edition of the
'Histoire' was published in 1863-4.
From 'A History of English Literature', trans. H. Van
Laun (Edinburgh, 1872), I, 234, 237-9, 243-4.

Thus was this theatre produced; a theatre unique in history, like the admirable and fleeting epoch from which it
sprang, the work and the picture of this young world, as
natural, as unshackled, and as tragic as itself. When an
original and national drama springs up, the poets who
establish it, carry in themselves the sentiments which it
represents. They display better than other men the public
spirit, because the public spirit is stronger in them than
in other men. The passions which surround them, break
forth in their heart with a harsher or a juster cry, and
hence their voices become the voices of all.... Equally
in England the poets are in harmony with their works.
Almost all are Bohemians, born of the people, yet educated, and for the most part having studied at Oxford or
Cambridge, but poor, so that their education contrasts
with their condition. Ben Jonson is the step-son of a
bricklayer, and himself a bricklayer; Marlowe is the son
of a shoemaker; Shakspeare of a woollen merchant; Massinger of a servant. They live as they can, get into debt,
write for their bread, go on the stage. Peele, Lodge,
Marlowe, Jonson, Shakspeare, Heywood, are actors; most of
the details which we have of their lives are taken from
the journal of Henslowe, an old pawnbroker, later a money-
lender and manager of a theatre, who gives them work,
advances money to them, receives their manuscripts or
their wardrobes as security. For a play he gives seven or
eight pounds; after the year 1600 prices rise, and reach
as high as twenty or twenty-five pounds. It is clear
that, even after this increase, the trade of author
scarcely brings in bread. In order to earn money, it was
necessary, like Shakspeare, to become a manager, to try
to have a share in the property of a theatre; but the case
is rare, and the life which they lead, a life of comedians
and actors, improvident, full of excess, lost amid

debauchery and acts of violence, amidst women of evil
fame, in contact with young profligates, in provocations
and misery, imagination and licence, generally leads them
to exhaustion, poverty, and death. Men received enjoyment
from them, and neglected and despised them....
Marlowe was an ill-regulated, dissolute, outrageously
vehement and audacious spirit, but grand and sombre, with
the genuine poetic frenzy; pagan moreover, and rebellious
in manners and creed. In this universal return to the
senses, and in this impulse of natural forces which
brought on the Renaissance, the corporeal instincts and
the ideas which give them their warrant, break forth
impetuously. Marlowe, like Greene, like Kett, is a sceptic, denies God and Christ, blasphemes the Trinity,
declares Moses 'a juggler,' Christ more worthy of death
than Barabbas, says that 'yf he wer to write a new religion, he wolde undertake both a more excellent and more
admirable methode,' and 'almost in every company he com-
meth, perswadeth men to Athiesme.' Such were the rages,
the rashnesses, the excesses which liberty of thought gave
rise to in these new minds, who for the first time, after
so many centuries, dared to walk unfettered. From his
father's shop, crowded with children, from the stirrups
and awls, he found himself at Cambridge, probably through
the patronage of a great man, and on his return to London,
in want, amid the licence of the green-room, the low
houses and taverns, his head was in a ferment, and his
passions were heated. He turned actor; but having broken
his leg in a scene of debauchery, he remained lame, and
could no longer appear on the boards. He openly avowed
his infidelity, and a prosecution was begun, which, if
time had not failed, would probably have brought him to
the stake. He made love to a drab, and trying to stab his
rival, his hand was turned, so that his own blade entered
his eye and his brain, and he died, still cursing and
blaspheming. He was only thirty years old. Think what
poetry could emanate from a life so passionate, and
occupied in such a manner! First, exaggerated declamation, heaps of murder, atrocities, a pompous and furious
display of tragedy soaked in blood, and passions raised to
a pitch of madness. All the foundations of the English
stage, 'Ferrex and Porrex,' 'Cambyses,' 'Hieronymo,' even
the 'Pericles' of Shakspeare, reach the same height of
extravagance, force, and horror. It is the first out-
break of youth. Recall Schiller's 'Robbers,' and how
modern democracy has recognised for the first time its
picture in the metaphors and cries of Charles Moor. So
here the characters struggle and jostle, stamp on the
earth, gnash their teeth, shake their fists against

heaven. The trumpets sound, the drums beat, coats of mail
file past, armies clash together, men stab each other, or
themselves; speeches are full of gigantic threats or lyrical figures; kings die, straining a bass voice; 'now doth
ghastly death with greedy talons gripe my bleeding heart,
and like a harpy tires on my life.' The hero in 'Tamburlaine the Great' is seated on a chariot drawn by chained
kings, burns towns, drowns women and children, puts men to
the sword, and finally, seized with an invisible sickness,
raves in monstrous outcries against the gods, whose hands
afflict his soul, and whom he would fain dethrone. There
already is the picture of senseless pride, of blind and
murderous rage, which passing through many devastations,
at last arms against heaven itself. The overflowing of
savage and immoderate instinct produces this mighty sound-
ing verse, this prodigality of carnage, this display of
overloaded splendours and colours, this railing of demon-
iac passions, this audacity of grand impiety. If in the
dramas which succeed it, 'The Massacre at Paris,' 'The
Jew of Malta,' the bombast decreases, the violence remains.
     There is the living, struggling, natural, personal man,
not the philosophic type which Goethe has created, but a
primitive and genuine man, hot-headed, fiery, the slave of
his passions, the sport of his dreams, wholly engrossed in
the present, moulded by his lusts, contradictions, and
follies, who amidst noise and starts, cries of pleasure
and anguish, rolls, knowing it and willing it, down the
slope and crags of his precipice. The whole English drama
is here, as a plant in its seed, and Marlowe is to Shakspeare what Perugino was to Raphael.

37. H. N. HUDSON

1872

H. N. Hudson (1814-86), a Vermont man, was a scholarly
popularizer, and editor of the 'New Hudson Shakespeare'
(1880-1). There is nothing new in what he has to say
about Marlowe, but it is representative of the critical
assumptions of the period.
     From Shakespeare: His Life, Art, and Characters'
(Boston, Mass., 1872), 109-19.

The scene of these two plays ['Tamburlaine'], which are substantially one, takes in the whole period of time from the hero's first conquest till his death; so that the action ranges at large over divers kingdoms and empires. Except the hero, there is little really deserving the name of characterization, this being a point of art which Marlowe had not yet reached, and which he never attained but in a moderate degree, taking Shakespeare as the standard. But the hero is drawn with grand and striking proportions, and perhaps seems the larger, that the bones of his individuality stand out in undue prominence; the author lacking that balance of powers which is requisite, to produce the symmetry and roundness met with in the higher forms of Nature. And he knew not, apparently, how to express the hero's greatness *in word*, but by making him bethump the stage with tempestuous verbiage; which, to be sure, is not the style of greatness at all, but only of one trying to be great, and *trying* to be so, because he is not so. For to talk big is the instinct of ambitious littleness. But Tamburlaine is also represented *in act* as a most magnanimous prodigy: amidst his haughtiest strides of conquest, we have strains of gentleness mingling with his iron sternness; and he everywhere appears lifted high with generous passions and impulses: if he regards not others, he is equally ready to sacrifice himself, his ease, pleasure, and even life, in his prodigious lust of glory.

As to the rest, this drama consists rather of a long series of speeches than any genuine dialogue. And the persons all speak from one brain, the hero talking just like the others, only more so; as if the author had no way to discriminate character but by different degrees of the same thing: in which respect the work has often reminded me of divers more civilized stage preparations, such as Addison's 'Cato,' Young's 'Revenge,' et *id genus omne*.(1) For the proper constituent of dramatic dialogue is, that the persons strike fire out of each other by their sharp collisions of thought, so that their words relish at once of the individual speaking and the individual spoken to. Moreover the several parts of this work are not moulded together in any thing like vital unity; the materials seem bundled up arbitrarily, and for stage effect, instead of being assorted on any principle of organic coherence; everything thus going by the author's will, not by any law of reason or art. But this is a high region, from which there was in that age but one man big enough to be seen: so it's no use speaking of the rest. Therewithal the work affects us, throughout, as a dead-level of superlatives; everywhere we have nearly the same boisterous wind of tragical storm-and-stress: so that the effect is much like that of a picture all foreground, with no perspective, no proportionateness of light and shade, to give us distinct impressions.

'The Jew of Malta' shows very considerable advance towards a chaste and sober diction, but not much either in development of character or composition of parts. Barabas the Jew is a horrible monster of wickedness and cunning, yet not without strong lines of individuality. The author evidently sought to compass the effect of tragedy by accumulation of murders and other hellish deeds; which shows that he had no steady ideas as to wherein the true secret of tragic terror lies: he here strives to reach it by overfilling the senses; whereas its proper method stands in the joint working of the moral and imaginative powers, which are rather stifled than kindled by causing the senses to 'sup full of horrors.' The piece, however, abounds in quick and caustic wit; in some parts there is a good share of dialogue as distinguished from speech-making; and the versification is far more varied and compact than in 'Tamburlaine.' Still the work, as a whole, shows little that can properly be called dramatic power as distinguished from the general powers of rhetoric and wit.

'The Tragical History of Doctor Faustus,' probably written before 1590, exhibits Marlowe in a higher vein of workmanship. I think it must be acknoweldged that he here wields the right elements and processes of tragic effect with no ordinary subtlety and power. Faustus, the hero, is a mighty necromancer, who has studied himself into direct communion with preternatural beings, and beside whom Friar Bacon sinks into a tame forger of bugbears. A Good Angel and a Bad Angel figure in the piece, each trying to win Faustus to his several way. Lucifer is ambitious to possess 'his glorious soul,' and the hero craves Lucifer's aid, that he may work wonders on the Earth. At his summons, Mephistophilis, who acts as Lucifer's prime minister, visits him to negotiate an arrangement. I must quote a brief passage from their interview:

[Quotes I, iii, 65-99.]

This passage, especially the hero's cool indifference in questioning about things which the fiend shudders to consider, has often struck me as not altogether unworthy to be thought of in connection with Milton....

'The Jew of Malta' has divers passages in a far higher and richer style of versification than any part of 'Tamburlaine.' The author's diction has grown more pliant and facile to his thought; consequently it is highly varied in pause and movement; showing that in his hand the noble

instrument of dramatic blank-verse was fast growing into
tune for a far mightier hand to discourse its harmonies
upon. I must add that considerable portions both of this
play and the preceding are meant to be comical. But the
result only proves that Marlowe was incapable of comedy.
No sooner does he attempt the comic vein than his whole
style collapses into mere balderdash. In fact, though
plentifully gifted with wit, there was not a particle of
real humour in him; none of that subtle and perfusive
essence out of which the true comic is spun; for these
choice powers can hardly live but in the society of certain moral elements that seem to have been left out of
his composition.

'Edward the Second,' probably the latest, certainly
much the best, of Marlowe's dramas, was printed in 1598.
Here, for the first time, we meet with a genuine specimen
of the English Historical Drama. The scene covers a
period of twenty years; the incidents pass with great
rapidity, and, though sometimes crushed into indistinct-
ness, are for the most part well used both for historic
truth and dramatic effect; and the dialogue, generally,
is nervous, animated, and clear. In the great article
of character, too, this play has very considerable merit.
The King's insane dotage of his favourites, the upstart
vanity and insolence of Gaveston, the artful practice and
doubtful virtue of Queen Isabella, the factious turbulence
of the nobles, irascible, arrogant, regardless of others'
liberty, jealous of their own, sudden of quarrel, eager
in revenge, are all depicted with a goodly mixture of
energy and temperance. Therewithal the versification
moves, throughout, with a freedom and variety, such as may
almost stand a comparison with Shakespeare in what may be
called his earlier period; as when, for instance, 'King
Richard the Second' was written. It is probable, however,
that by this time, if not before, Marlowe had begun to
feel the power of that music which was to charm him, and
all others of the time, out of audience and regard. For
we have very good evidence, that before Marlowe's death
Shakespeare had far surpassed all of that age who had
ever been competent to teach him in any point of dramatic
workmanship.

Marlowe is of consequence, *mainly*, as one of the first
and greatest improvers of dramatic poetry in so far as
relates to diction and metrical style; which is my reason
for emphasizing his work so much in that regard....

Others have thought that Marlowe, if he had lived,
would have made some good approach to Shakespeare in
tragic power. A few years more would no doubt have lifted
him to very noble things, that is, provided his powers

could have been kept from the eatings and cripplings of debauchery; still, any approach to that great Divinity of the Drama was out of the question for him. For, judging from his life and works, the moral part of genius was constitutionally defective in him; and, with this so defective, the intellectual part cannot be truly itself; and his work must needs be comparatively weak in those points of our being which it touches, because it does not touch them all: for the whole must be moved at once, else there can be no great moving of any part. No, no! there was not, there could not have been in Marlowe, great as he was, a tithe of Shakespeare, for tragedy, nor any thing else. To go no further, he was, as we have seen, destitute of humour; the powers of comedy evidently had no place in him; and these powers are indispensable to the production of high tragedy: a position affirmed as long ago as the days of Plato; sound in the reason of the thing; and, above all, made good in the instance of Shakespeare; who was *Shakespeare*, mainly because he had *all* the powers of the human mind in harmonious order and action, and *used* them all, explicitly or implicitly, in every play he wrote.

Note

1 And all of that kind.

38. WILLIAM MINTO

1874

William Minto (1845-93) held the chair of Logic and English in the University of Aberdeen from 1880 to 1893. The comment here reproduced may be taken as the typical response to Marlowe at that time.
    From 'Characteristics of English Poets' (1874; Boston, 1897), 233, 236-7.

Marlowe's alleged writings against the Trinity have never been seen; in all probability, like some alleged infidel works of the Middle Ages, they never existed: but there

seems no reason to doubt that he was, as his accusers
stated, a man that neither feared God nor regarded man.
Beauty, which he worshipped with passionate devotion, was
the only sunshine of his life, and it shone with a burning
fierceness proportioned to the violence of his tempestuous
moods. The vision of Hero and Leander is a rapt surrender
of the whole soul to impassioned meditation on luxurious
beauty. In his life as in his plays, such intervals of
delight were probably rare. Tamburlaine is a most impassioned adorer of divine Zenocrate; Faustus hangs in ecsta-
tic worship on the lips of Helen; but these are only brief
transports in lives where energy and ambition are devour-
ingly predominant. Marlowe's genius was little adapted to
sonneteering and pastoral poetry: he stigmatized the
fashionable love-lyrics as 'egregious foppery,' and deri-
ded them with rough ridicule. He wrote no sonnets; only
one pastoral song has been ascribed to him, and it is
direct and fresh, a movement of impatient captivating
sweetness, an impulsive tone of invitation that will take
no denial. Marlowe was a clear and powerful genius, and
we often seem to catch in his poetry an undertone of
almost angry contempt for commonplace.

The most generally impressive of Marlowe's works is his
fragment on the tale of Hero and Leander, and if we founded solely upon this, we should form most erroneous notions
of his genius. We should suppose his worship of beauty,
which was but a rare and transient passion, to have been
the presiding force of his imagination. It is in his
plays that we find the world of storm and strife wherein
he delighted to expatiate, and a most titanic world it is,
immeasurably transcending nature in breadth and height of
thought, feeling, and destructive energy; a region where
everything is on a gigantic scale, peopled with creatures
that are monstrous in the largeness of their composition
and the fierceness of their passions....

'Tamburlaine' was Marlowe's first play, but the impetu-
ous swell of his conceptions cannot be said to have been
much moderated as he went on. His 'raptures all air and
fire' were not, I believe, the extravagance of youth;
still less could they have been, as Mr Collier seems to
think, the result of inexperience in blank verse, and
mistaken effort to make up by bombastic terms for the
absence of rhyme; they were part of the constitution of
this individual man. It is impossible to say what he
might have done had his life been longer: he might have
exhausted this high astounding vein, and proved himself
capable of opening up another. But as long as he lived he
found fuel for his lofty raptures. He could not repeat
another conqueror of the world, but his heroes are all

expanded to the utmost possible limit of their circumstances. The Jew of Malta is an incarnation of the devil
himself: he is no less universal in his war against all
mankind that are within reach of his power: he fights
single-handed with monstrous instruments of death against
a whole city, and does not scruple to poison even his own
daughter. Faustus is not a malevolent being, but his
ambition is even greater than Tamburlaine's; he soars
beyond the petty possibilities of humanity, leagues himself with superhuman powers, and rides through space in
a fiery chariot exploring the secrets of the universe.
Even in his historical play of Edward II., where he is
bound by the shackles of recent history more or less known
to his audience, the conflict of explosive passions is
superhuman in its energies; the king's court is a hell of
extravagant affection and fiendish spite, wanton tyranny
and mutinous unapproachable fierceness - a den of wild
beasts.

39. A. W. WARD

1875

Sir Adolphus William Ward (1837-1924) was Professor of
History and English Literature and Language, Owens
College, Manchester, 1866-97. He was author of 'A History
of English Dramatic Literature to the Death of Queen Anne'
(1875), and for a time drama critic for the 'Manchester
Guardian'.
    From 'A History of English Dramatic Literature to the
Death of Queen Anne' (1875), I, 196-8, 201-3.

The dramatic merits as well as the poetic beauties of
'Edward II' are extremely great. The construction is upon
the whole very clear, infinitely superior e.g. to that of
Peele's 'Edward I.' The two divisions into which the
reign of Edward II naturally falls, viz. the period of the
ascendancy of Gaveston and that of the ascendancy of the
Spensers, are skilfully interwoven; and after the catastrophe of the fourth act (the victory of the King's adver-
saries and his capture) the interest in what can no
longer be regarded as uncertain, viz. the ultimate fate of

the King, is most powerfully sustained. The characters
too are mostly well drawn; there is no ignobility about
the King, whose passionate love for his favourites is
itself traced to a generous motive; he is not without
courage and spirit in the face of danger; but his weakness is his doom. Misfortune utterly breaks him; and
never have the 'drowsiness of woe' (to use Charles Lamb's
expression), and, after a last struggle between pride and
necessity, the lingering expectation of a certain doom,
been painted with more tragic power. The scene in act iv,
where the King seeks refuge among the monks of Neath
Abbey, is of singular pathos; but it is perhaps even more
remarkable how in the last scene of all the unutterable
horror of the situation is depicted without our sense of
the loathsome being aroused; and how pity and terror are
mingled in a degree to which Shakspere himself only on
occasion attains. For the combined power and delicacy of
treatment, the murder of Edward II may be compared to the
murder of Desdemona in 'Othello'; for the fearful suspense
in which the spectator is kept, I know no parallel except
the 'Agamemnon' of Aeschylus, but even here the effort is
inferior, for in the English tragedy the spectator shares
the suspense, and shares the certainty of its inevitable
termination, with the sufferer on the stage himself. On
the other characters I will not dwell; but they are not
mere figures from the Chronicle. It may be worth while to
note the skill with which the character of young Edward
(afterward King Edward III) is drawn, and how our good-
will is preserved for him, even though his name is put
forward by his father's enemies. Gaveston's insolence is
admirably reproduced; he is a Frenchman, and has a touch
of lightheartedness to the last, when he expresses his indifference as to the precise *manner* of his death:

> I thank you all, my lords: then I perceive
> That heading's one, and hanging is the other,
> And death is all.

The imperious haughtiness of Young Mortimer is equally
well depicted; in the character of the Queen alone I miss
any indication of the transition from her faithful but
despairing attachment to the King to a guilty love for
Mortimer. The dignity of the tragedy is not marred by any
comic scenes, - which is well, for humour is not Marlowe's
strong point; but there is some wit in the sketch of
Baldock as an unscrupulous upstart, who fawns upon the
great, and gains influence by means of his ability to
find for everything reasons, or, as his interlocutor terms
them, *Quandoquidems*.(1)

The play is written of course in blank verse, of a
flowing as well as vigorous description; but rhymes are
not unfrequent. The author's love of classical quotations
finds vent on several occasions; and the number of classical allusions is extraordinary; besides Leander and Gany-
mede, who from different reasons were naturally in Marlowe's mind, Circe, the Cyclops, Proteus, Danaë, Helen,
Atlas, Pluto, Charon, and Tisiphone, as well as Catiline
and other historical parallels, are mentioned....

Having dwelt at the utmost length which I could permit
myself upon the several plays attributable without doubt
to Marlowe, I must be brief in my concluding remarks on
his position as a dramatist. His services to our dramatic
literature are two-fold. As the author who first introduced blank verse to the popular stage he rendered to our
drama a service which it would be difficult to over-
estimate. No innovation could have done more to preserve
it from the danger of artificiality of form, which so
readily leads to artificiality of matter, to which the
drama is at all times peculiarly exposed. It is obvious
that on the stage no form of rhymed verse can, except in
isolated lyrical passages, prevail except the rhymed *couplet*; and it is the couplet in particular which leads to an
antithetical arrangement of thoughts, which is of its
essence a constant application of rhetorical practice.
Thus rhymed couplets, while their use in special cases
(such as the close of a speech or even any other peculiarly emphatic passage) will always commend itself, cannot
without great danger both to the continuity and the nat-
uralness of dramatic movement be employed as the ordinary
form of dramatic verse. It is not too much to say that
their use in the French drama has contributed to mould the
character of a whole development, which continues to this
day, of French dramatic literature, while their abandon-
ment by the English popular stage had an equally decisive
effect upon our own. In substituting blank verse, Marlowe
at first thought it necessary to compensate by rhetorical
efforts of another kind for the loss of immediate effect
entailed by the change; but already in his later plays it
is perceptible how unnecessary he had come to feel the
substitution of rant for antithesis; and as the metre
easily adapted itself to his hand, he recognised in practice its supreme merit of flexibility; so that whereas his
earlier blank verse is monotonous, his later is varied in
rhythm and cadence. The English drama never returned to
rhyme, except in a phase of its history which is to be
regarded as a conscious aberration from its national
course; and it soon relinquished an endeavour forced upon
it by the influence of foreign examples, finally renounced

on this head by the most eminent of their English followers. Altogether, it may well be doubted whether any
literary innovation has ever been so rapidly and so perma-
nently successful as this, in which the critically important step is associated with the name of Marlowe.

His second service to the progress of our dramatic
literature, though not perhaps admitting of so precise a
statement, is even more important than the other. The
genius of Marlowe, as it displays itself in the few works
which have come down to us from the brief career which he
ran as a dramatic author, is far from satisfying all the
demands of his art. In construction, though by no means
unskilful and at times eminently successful, he is careless; and it is only rarely that he applies himself to the
development of character. It is not just to say of the
author of 'Edward II' that he never represents any dramatic conflicts except those between human impatience of all
control and of all limits, and the control and the limits
which the conditions of human life impose; it is not just
to deny that he can move the springs of pity as well as
of terror, and depict other passions besides those of
ambition and defiant self-exultation. But during his
brief poetic career he had not learnt the art of mingling,
except very incidentally, the operation of other human
motives of action with those upon which his ardent spirit
more especially dwelt; and of the divine gift of humour,
which lies so close to that of pathos, he at the most
exhibits occasional signs. The element in which as a
poet he lived was passion; and it was he and no other who
first inspired with true poetic passion the form of literature to which his chief efforts were consecrated. After
Marlowe had written, it was impossible for our dramatists
to return to the cold horrors or tame declamation of the
earlier tragic drama; the 'Spanish Tragedy' and 'Gorboduc'
had alike been left behind. 'His raptures were all ayre
and fire;' and it is this gift of passion which, together
with his services to the outward form of the English drama,
makes Marlowe worthy to be called not a predecessor, but
the earliest in the immortal company, of our great dramatists.

Note

1 Quandoquidem: 'seeing that', or 'Since indeed', a
  pedantic opening.

40. FAUST ON THE STAGE

1879

An interesting comment on the persistence of belief in
the principalities and powers of the air and on Marlowe
vs Goethe. The article is titled Faust on the Stage.
From 'All the Year Round' (28 June, 1879), xliii, 40-1.

'The Tragical History of Doctor Faustus' is then the
earliest literary work extant purporting to treat of the
Wittenberg savant and conjuror - terms almost synonymous
in the age in which he lived. To the average mind of the
fifteenth century, astronomy and astrology, chemistry and
alchemy, signified exactly the same thing; in fact, our
prosaic and matter-of-fact ancestors cared very much more
for the arts of divination, the transmutation of metals,
and the secret of perpetual youth, than for any abstract
idea of science. What may be called the poetry of science, the love of knowledge for its own sake, is a recent
invention, like the love of picturesque scenery, and the
arts of spelling accurately, and speaking decently and
modestly. Some of these last are not very widely distributed even now, any more than a knowledge of the difference between science and quackery. In queer lower strata
lurk 'survivals' of the thoughts and customs of centuries
long gone by, changed a little as to outward form and
expression, but in essentials just as of old. There are
thousands of people now in England who know no more difference between astronomy and astrology than their ancestors of four hundred years ago. White witches are yet to
be found in Devonshire, and gipsies everywhere that a
silver spoon is to be picked up. More than this, the present Astronomer Royal, like Flamsteed, who lived a century
and a half before him, is besieged with requests to find
lost linen and spoons, to 'take the stars off' a favourite
son who has a strange knack of losing his watch when he
goes to market, to 'fix the planets' for a pet daughter,
or to find the whereabouts of stolen property. A yearly
average arrives at the Observatory at Greenwich of letters
containing droll requests of this kind, proving that
vulgar human nature is profoundly penetrated with the
wisdom of Buckle's apothegm that 'the chief use of knowledge of the past is to predict the future.' In a rough
kind of way these good people agree with the philosopher,

albeit they import the revelations of the planets into
their calculations. In Marlowe's time nobody doubted his
own star for an instance. During the lifetime of the
English poet, the greatest living woman saving Elizabeth
herself, Catherine de Medicis, spent a part of every day
with Ruggieri, her necromancer, in the tower since built
into the wall of the Paris corn-market, or in his loftier
observatory at Blois. It was in the latter that the
Italian juggler cast the horoscope of Henry of Navarre,
and found that he would reign in France; a prediction
which absolutely drew away the queen from the Huguenots,
the natural allies of the monarchy against the overweening
Guises, backed by Spain and the Pope. It was, therefore,
not astonishing that the world should have a lively sense
of the personal presence of Lucifer, at the time Kit Marlowe tippled sack at Deptford. Honest Kit himself never
doubted the personality of angel or devil. He presents us
with the personality of Tamburlaine the Great, after the
fashion caricatured by Shakespeare, and gives us Doctor
Faustus in all good faith, without sceptical reservation,
cold realism, or metaphysical abstraction. To Marlowe
Faustus is an entity - a genuine living man, as unlike
Goethe's Faust as may be; a real personage, making a real
compact with a real devil, and paying the penalty with
body and soul. In reading Marlowe's remarkable work it is
impossible to imagine that the author doubted the possibility of the events he puts before the spectator. This
simple faith gives a genuineness to the Tragical History
of Doctor Faustus, that one is far from finding in the
great work of Goethe. Marlowe's work is the outcome of an
undoubting mind - not the statement of a great problem yet
unsolved. After the old simple fashion, Marlowe points
his moral before he begins to adorn his tale, and tells
us, through the medium of the chorus, how Faustus is

> graced with Doctor's name,
> Excelling all, and sweetly can dispute
> In the heavenly matters of theology:
> Till swoln with cunning, and a self-conceit,
> His waxen wings did mount above his reach,

and so 'surfeits on the cursed necromancy.' Marlowe
wrote, as Goethe could not write, in the firm belief of
the possibility of what he wrote. Goethe's earth and air
spirits are abstractions; Marlowe's are concrete actuali-
ties, and throughout the Englishman's wonderful play there
is no hint, any more than there is in a mediaeval mystery,
that the events in it are either impossible or even improbable. There is another curious point of difference;

not with the last thought of Goethe in the second part of
Faust, but in the first or dramatic part - a difference
clearly ascribable to the fervent religious faith of the
sixteenth century. Throughout Marlowe's play there is the
constant interposition of good counsel and warning to repentance. Faustus signs the contract, but it is throughout suggested that it might have been annulled had he
turned back in time; the Christian doctrine of repentance
is never forgotten, and Faustus is constantly opened a
loophole of escape.
    Weary of success as a learned doctor, he asks:

    Are not thy bills hung up as monuments,
    Whereby whole cities have escaped the plague,
    And thousand desperate maladies been cured?

Human knowledge being compassed, he aspires to the supernatural, and accordingly calls in two doctors learned in
the art magical, 'the German Valdes,' whose name hath a
most un-Teutonic sound, and Cornelius. These worthies
instruct him how to use the works of Bacon and Albertus
Magnus, in conjunction with the Hebrew Psalter and New
Testament, so as to raise spirits more potent than those
whom Owen Glendower (teste Hotspur) called in vain. His
interview with Mephistopheles is marked by several pecu-
liarities, notably one not overlooked by Milton:

    FAUST. Where are you damned?
    MEPH.   In hell.
    FAUST. How comes it then that thou art come out of
hell?
    MEPH.   Why, this is hell, nor am I out of it;
    Think'st thou that I, that saw the face of God
    And tasted the eternal joys of Heaven,
    Am not tormented with ten thousand hells
    In being deprived of everlasting bliss?

    This Mephistopheles is not the mocking fiend of Goethe,
but rather the awful Lucifer of Milton. He is determined
to secure the soul of Faustus, and during his twenty-four
years of service realises every kind of impossibility for
his temporary master. Some persistence on the part of the
fiend is required, for Marlowe's Faustus is a shabby
client, ever trying to escape performance of his bond.
This is not astonishing when the spirit of the age is
taken into consideration. The mystic and comprehensive
answer to Where is hell?

Hell hath no limits, nor is circumscribed
In one self place: but where we are is hell,
And where hell is there must we ever be,

must not be understood too literally. Nothing would have
been farther from Marlowe's purpose than to shake popular
belief in an actual fixed place of eternal punishment.
Firstly, such doctrine would have been utterly opposed to
the theology of his day; secondly, it would have made an
end of his tragedy. The reality of the infernal regions
is as necessary to Marlowe as to Dante. Neither doubted
their existence, while, on the other hand, Goethe held
what are called 'advanced views' on such subjects, and,
whether he chose openly to avow his disbelief in eternal
punishment or not, treats his angels and spirits in Faust
as mere poetical machinery, just as Julius Caesar, according to Sallust, treated the old Pagan gods in that memorable speech in the senate house, touching the conspiracy
of Catiline. There is no real good or evil spirit in
Goethe's wonderful work, and the malicious Mephistopheles
is rather recollected as a saver of good things than as a
malignant fiend. Now Marlowe, on the contrary, is very
real. Not only is Faustus duly handed over to the foul
fiend at the conclusion of the tragedy, but a perpetual
conflict is maintained between his good and bad angels.
He is warned over and over again, and it is implied that
even such contract as he has signed with Lucifer may be
voided by prompt renunciation and repentance. He is
shown, within the compass of eight days, the face of
heaven, of earth, and of hell. The seven deadly sins
appear before him, and describe their attributes; he is
given every chance of repentance in vain. Yet he is not
shown to be oppressed by the Greek destiny. On the contrary, his power to decide is assumed by the frequency of
the appeals made to him. He is vanquished by one weakness - sensuality.

41. A. C. BRADLEY

1880

Andrew Cecil Bradley (1851-1935) is best known for his
'Shakespearean Tragedy' (1904); twentieth-century critics
take off from it, either by way of repudiation or

accommodation. His comments on Marlowe, in which he
shares the assumptions of his contemporaries, are still
important.
From Christopher Marlowe, in 'The English Poets,
Selections', ed. T. H. Ward (1880), I, 411-17.

Marlowe has one claim on our affection which everyone is
ready to acknowledge; he died young. We think of him
along with Chatterton and Burns, with Byron, Shelley, and
Keats. And this is a fact of some importance for the
estimate of his life and genius. His poetical career
lasted only for six or seven years, and he did not outlive
his 'hot days, when the mad blood's stirring.' An old
ballad tells us that he acted at the Curtain theatre in
Shoreditch and 'brake his leg in one rude scene, When in
his early age.' If there is any truth in the last statement, we may suppose that Marlowe gave up acting and confined himself to authorship. He seems to have depended
for his livelihood on his connection with the stage; and
probably, like many of his fellows and friends, he lived
in a free and even reckless way. A more unusual characteristic of Marlowe's was his 'atheism.' No reliance can
be placed on the details recorded on this subject; but it
was apparently only his death that prevented judicial
proceedings being taken against him on account of his
opinions. The note on which these proceedings would have
been founded was the work of one Bame, who thought that
'all men in christianitei ought to endeavour that the
mouth of so dangerous a member may be stopped,' and was
hanged at Tyburn about eighteen months afterwards. But
other testimony points in the same direction; and a
celebrated passage in Greene's 'Groatsworth of Wit' would
lead us to suppose that Marlowe was given to blatant pro-
fanities. Whatever his offences may have been - and there
is nothing to make us think he was a bad-hearted man - he
had no time to make men forget them. He was not thirty
when he met his death.
    The plan of the present volumes excludes selections
from Marlowe's plays; but as his purely poetical works
give but a one-sided idea of his genius, and as his importance in the history of literature depends mainly on his
dramatic writings, some general reference must be made to
them. Even if they had no enduring merits of their own,
their effect upon Shakespeare - an effect which, to say
nothing of 'Henry VI,' is most clearly visible in 'Richard
II' - and their influence on the drama would preserve them
from neglect. The nature of this influence may be seen by

a glance at Marlowe's first play. On the one hand it stands at the opposite pole to the classic form of the drama as it is found in Seneca, a form which had been adopted in 'Gorboduc,' and which some of the more learned writers attempted to nationalise. There is no Chorus in 'Tamburlaine' or in any of Marlowe's plays except 'Dr. Faustus'; and the action takes place on the stage instead of being merely reported. On the other hand, in this, the first play in blank verse which was publicly acted, he called the audience

From jigging veins of rhyming mother-wits,
And such conceits as clownage keeps in pay,

and fixed the metre of his drama for ever as the metre of English tragedy. And, though neither here nor in 'Dr. Faustus' could he yet afford to cast off all the conceits of clownage, he was in effect beginning to substitute works of art for the formless popular representations of the day. Doubtless it was only a beginning. The two parts of 'Tamburlaine' are not great tragedies. They are full of mere horror and glare. Of the essence of drama, a sustained and developed action, there is as yet very little; and what action there is proceeds almost entirely from the rising passion of a single character. Nor in the conception of this character has Marlowe quite freed himself from the defect of the popular plays, in which, naturally enough, personified virtues and vices often took the place of men. Still, if there is a touch of this defect in 'Tamburlaine,' as in the 'Jew of Malta,' it is no more than a touch. The ruling passion is conceived with an intensity, and portrayed with a sweep of imagination unknown before; a requisite for the drama hardly less important than the faculty of construction is attained, and the way is opened for those creations which are lifted above the common and yet are living flesh and blood. It is the same with the language. For the buffoonery he partly displaced Marlowe substitutes a swelling diction, 'high astounding terms,' and some outrageous bombast, such as that which Shakespeare reproduced and put into the mouth of Pistol. But, laugh as we will, in this first of Marlowe's plays there is that incommunicable gift which means almost everything, *style*; a manner perfectly individual, and yet, at its best, free from eccentricity. The 'mighty line' of which Jonson spoke, and a pleasure, equal to Milton's, in resounding proper names, meet us in the very first scene; and in not a few passages passion, instead of vociferating, finds its natural expression, and we hear the fully-formed style, which in Marlowe's best writing is, to use his own words,

Like his desire, lift upward and divine.

'Lift upward' Marlowe's style was at first, and so it
remained. It degenerates into violence, but never into
softness. If it falters, the cause is not doubt or
languor, but haste and want of care. It has the energy
of youth; and a living poet has described this among its
other qualities when he speaks of Marlowe as singing

With mouth of gold, and morning in his eyes.

As a dramatic instrument it developed with his growth and
acquired variety. The stately monotone of 'Tamburlaine,'
in which the pause falls almost regularly at the end of
the lines, gives place in 'Edward II' to rhythms less
suited to pure poetry, but far more rapid and flexible.
In 'Dr. Faustus' the great address to Helen is as different in metrical effect as it is in spirit from the last
scene, where the words seem, like Faustus heart, to 'pant
and quiver.'...
     The expression 'lift upward' applies also, in a sense,
to most of the chief characters in the plays. Whatever
else they may lack, they know nothing of half-heartedness
or irresolution. A volcanic self-assertion, a complete
absorption in some one desire, is their characteristic.
That in creating such characters Marlowe was working in
dark places, and that he developes them with all his
energy, is certain. But that in so doing he shows (to
refer to a current notion of him) a 'hunger and thirst
after unrighteousness,' a desire, that is, which never has
produced or could produce true poetry, is an idea which
Hazlitt could not have really intended to convey. Marlowe's works are tragedies. Their greatness lies not
merely in the conception of an unhallowed lust, however
gigantic, but in an insight into its tragic significance
and tragic results; and there is as little food for a
hunger after unrighteousness (if there be such a thing)
in the appalling final scene of 'Dr. Faustus,' or, indeed,
in the melancholy of Mephistopheles, so grandly touched by
Marlowe, as in the catastrophe of 'Richard III' or of
Goethe's 'Faust.' It is true, again, that in the later
acts of the 'Jew of Malta' Barabas has become a mere monster; but for that very reason the character ceases to
show Marlowe's peculiar genius, and Shakespeare himself
has not portrayed the sensual lust after gold, and the
touch of imagination which redeems it from insignificance,
with such splendour as the opening speech of Marlowe's

play. Whatever faults however the earlier plays have, it
is clear, if 'Edward II' be one of his latest works, that
Marlowe was rapidly outgrowing them. For in that play,
to say nothing of the two great scenes to which Lamb gave
such high praise, the interest is no longer confined to a
single character, and there is the most decided advance
both in construction and in the dialogue.

Of the weightier qualities of Marlowe's genius the
extracts from his purely poetical works give but little
idea; but just for that reason they testify to the variety
of his powers. Everyone knows the verses 'Come live with
me, and be my love,' with their pretty mixture of gold
buckles and a belt of straw. This was a very popular
song; Raleigh wrote an answer to it; and its flowing music
has run in many a head beside Sir Hugh Evans's. But the
shepherd would hardly be called 'passionate' outside the
Arcadia to which the lyric really belongs. Of the beautiful fragment in *ottava rima* nothing is known, except that
it was first printed with Marlowe's name in 'England's
Parnassus,' 1600. The translations of Lucan and Ovid (the
former in blank verse) were perhaps early studies. It is
curious that Marlowe should have set himself so thankless
a task as a version of Lucan which literally gives line
for line; but the choice of the author is characteristic.
The translation of Ovid's 'Amores' was burnt on account of
its indecency in 1599, and it would have been no loss to
the world if all the copies had perished. The interest of
these translations is mainly historical. They testify to
the passion for classical poetry, and in particular to
that special fondness for Ovid of which the literature of
the time affords many other proofs. The study of Virgil
and Ovid was a far less mixed good for poetry than that of
Seneca and Plautus; and it is perhaps worth noticing that
Marlowe, who felt the charm of classical amatory verse,
and whose knowledge of Virgil is shown in his 'Queen Dido,'
should have been the man who, more than any other, secured
the theatre from the dominion of inferior classical dramas.

How fully he caught the inspiration, not indeed of the
best classical poetry, but of that world of beauty which
ancient literature seemed to disclose to the men of the
Renascence, we can see in many parts of his writings, in
Faust's address to Helen, in Gaveston's description of
the sports at Court, in the opening of 'Queen Dido'; but
the fullest proof of it is the fragment of 'Hero and Leander.' Beaumont wrote a 'Salmacis and Hermaphroditus,'
Shakespeare a 'Venus and Adonis,' but both found their
true vehicle in the drama. Marlowe's poem not only stands
far above one of these tales, and perhaps above both, but
it stands on a level with his plays; and it is hard to say

what excellence he might not have reached in the field of
narrative verse. The defect of his fragment, the intrusion of ingenious reflections and of those conceits with
one of which our selection unhappily terminates, was the
fault of his time; its merit is Marlowe's own. It was
suggested indeed by the short poem of the Pseudo-Musaeus,
an Alexandrian grammarian who probably wrote about the end
of the fifth century after Christ, and appears to have
been translated into English shortly before 1580; but it
is in essence original. Written in the so-called heroic
verse, it bears no resemblance to any other poem in that
metre composed before, nor, perhaps, is there any written
since which decidedly recalls it, unless it be 'Endymion.'
'Pagan' it is in a sense, with the Paganism of the Renascence: the more pagan the better, considering the subject.
Nothing of the deeper thought of the time, no 'looking
before and after,' no worship of a Gloriana or hostility
to an Acrasia, interferes with its frank acceptance of
sensuous beauty and joy. In this, in spite of much resemblance, it differs from 'Endymion,' the spirit of which is
not fruition but unsatisfied longing, and in which the
vision of a vague and lovelier ideal is always turning the
enjoyment of the moment into gloom. On the other hand, a
further likeness to Keats may perhaps be traced in the
pictorial quality of Marlowe's descriptions. His power
does not lie in catching in the aspect of objects or
scenes those deeper suggestions which appeal to an imagination stored with human experience as well as sensitive
to colour and form; for this power does not necessarily
result in what we call pictorial writing; but his soul
seems to be in his eyes, and he renders the beauty which
appeals directly to sense as vividly as he apprehends it.
Nor is this the case with the description of objects
alone. The same complete absorption of imagination in
sense appears in Marlowe's account of the visit to Hero's
tower. This passage is in a high degree voluptuous, but
it is not prurient. For prurience is the sign of an unsatisfied imagination, which, being unable to present its
object adequately, appeals to extraneous and unpoetic
feelings. But Marlowe's imagination is completely satisfied; and therefore, though he has not a high theme (for
it is a mere sensuous joy that is described, and there is
next to no real emotion in the matter), he is able to make
fine poetry of it. Of the metrical qualities of the poem
there can be but one opinion. Shakespeare himself, who
quoted a line of it,* never reached in his own narrative
verse a music so spontaneous and rich, a music to which
Marlowe might have applied his own words -

That calls my soul from forth his living seat
To move unto the measures of delight.

Marlowe had many of the makings of a great poet: a
capacity for Titanic conceptions which might with time
have become Olympian; an imaginative vision which was
already intense and must have deepened and widened; the
gift of style and of making words sing; and a time to
live in such as no other generation of English poets has
known. It is easy to reckon his failings. His range of
perception into life and character was contracted: of
comic power he shows hardly a trace, and it is incredible
that he should have written the Jack Cade scene of 'Henry
VI'; no humour or tenderness relieves his pathos; there is
not any female character in his plays whom we remember
with much interest; and it is not clear that he could have
produced songs of the first order. But it is only Shakespeare who can do everything; and Shakespeare did not die
at twenty-nine. That Marlowe must have stood nearer to
him than any other dramatic poet of that time, or perhaps
of any later time, is probably the verdict of nearly all
students of the drama. His immediate successors knew well
what was lost in him; and from the days of Peele, Jonson,
Drayton, and Chapman, to our own, the poets have done more
than common honour to his memory.

Note

* Dead shepherd, now I find thy saw of might;
    'Who ever loved that loved not at first sight?'
                          'As You Like It,' iii. 5.

42. J. A. SYMONDS

1884

John Addington Symonds (1840-93) was a cultivated European; his 'History of the Renaissance in Italy' is still
both attractive and useful. He wrote a general introduction to English drama for the first volume of Havelock
Ellis's Mermaid Series (see No. 49, below). His view of
Marlowe is a vivid expression of the received critical
opinion at that time.

From 'Shakspere's Predecessors in the English Drama'
(1884), 585-8, 606-14.

Marlowe has been styled, and not unjustly styled, the
father of English dramatic poetry. When we reflect on the
conditions of the stage before he produced 'Tamburlaine,'
and consider the state in which he left it after the
appearance of 'Edward II.,' we shall be able to estimate
his true right to this title. Art, like Nature, does not
move by sudden leaps and bounds. It required a slow
elaboration of divers elements, the formation of a public
able to take interest in dramatic exhibitions, the deter-
mination of the national taste toward the romantic rather
than the classic type of art, and all the other circumstances which have been dwelt upon in the preceding
studies, to render Marlowe's advent as decisive as it
proved. Before he began to write, various dramatic
species had been essayed with more or less success.
Comedies modelled in form upon the types of Plautus and
Terence; tragedies conceived in the spirit of Seneca;
chronicles rudely arranged in scenes for representation;
dramatised novels and tales of private life; Court comedies of compliment and allegory; had succeeded to the
religious Miracles and ethical Moralities. There was
plenty of productive energy, plenty of enthusiasm and
activity. Theatres continued to spring up, and acting
came to rank among the recognised professions. But this
activity was still chaotic. None could say where or
whether the germ of a great national art existed. To us,
students of the past, it is indeed clear enough in what
direction lay the real life of the drama; but this was not
apparent to contemporaries. Scholars despised the shows
of mingled bloodshed and buffoonery in which the populace
delighted. The people had no taste for dry and formal
disquisitions in the style of 'Gorboduc.' The blank verse
of Sackville and Hughes rang hollow; the prose of Lyly was
affected; the rhyming couplets of the popular theatre
interfered with dialogue and free development of character. The public itself was divided in its tastes and
instincts; the mob inclining to mere drolleries and merri-
ments upon the stage, the better vulgar to formalities and
studied imitations. A powerful body of sober citizens, by
no means wholly composed of Puritans and ascetics, regarded all forms of dramatic art with undisguised hostility.
Meanwhile, no really great poet had arisen to stamp the
tendencies of either Court or town with the authentic seal
of genius. There seemed a danger lest the fortunes of the

stage in England should be lost between the prejudices of
a literary class, the puerile and lifeless pastimes of the
multitude, and the disfavour of conservative moralists.
From this peril Marlowe saved the English drama. Amid the
chaos of conflicting elements he discerned the true and
living germ of art, and set its growth beyond all risks of
accident by his achievement.
When, therefore, we style Marlowe the father and founder of English dramatic poetry, we mean that he perceived
the capacities for noble art inherent in the Romantic
Drama, and proved its adaptation to high purpose by his
practice. Out of confusion he brought order, following
the clue of his own genius through a labyrinth of dim un-
mastered possibilities. Like all great craftsmen, he
worked by selection and exclusion on the whole mass of
material ready to his hand; and his instinct in this
double process is the proof of his originality. He
adopted the romantic drama in lieu of the classic, the
popular instead of the literary type. But he saw that
the right formal vehicle, blank verse, had been suggested
by the school which he rejected. Rhyme, the earlier metre
of the romantic drama, had to be abandoned. Blank verse,
the metre of the pedants, had to be accepted. To employ
blank verse in the romantic drama was the first step in
his revolution. But this was only the first step. Both
form and matter had alike to be transfigured. And it was
precisely in this transfiguration of the right dramatic
metre, in this transfiguration of the right dramatic
stuff, that Marlowe showed himself a creative poet. What
we call the English, or the Elizabethan, or better perhaps
the Shaksperian Drama, came into existence by this double
process. Marlowe found the public stage abandoned to aim-
less trivialities, but abounding in the rich life of the
nation, and with the sympathies of the people firmly en-
listed on the side of its romantic presentation. He
introduced a new class of heroic subjects, eminently
fitted for dramatic handling. He moulded characters, and
formed a vigorous conception of the parts they had to play.
Under his touch the dialogue moved with spirit; men and
women spoke and acted with the energy and spontaneity of
nature. He found the blank verse of the literary school
monotonous, tame, nerveless, without life or movement.
But he had the tact to understand its vast capacities, so
vastly wider than its makers had divined, so immeasurably
more elastic than the rhymes for which he substituted its
sonorous cadence. Marlowe, first of Englishmen, perceived
how noble was the instrument he handled, how well adapted
to the closest reasoning, the sharpest epigram, the loftiest flight of poetry, the subtlest music, and the most

luxuriant debauch of fancy....

About Marlowe there is nothing small or trivial. His
verse is mighty; his passion is intense; the outlines of
his plots are large; his characters are Titanic; his fancy
is extravagant in richness, insolence, and pomp. Marlowe
could rough-hew like a Cyclops, though he was far from
being able to finish with the subtlety and smoothness of
a Praxiteles. We may compare his noblest studies of
character with marbles blocked out by Michel Angelo, not
with the polished perfection of 'La Notte' in San Lorenzo.
Speaking of 'Dr. Faustus,' Goethe said with admiration:
'How greatly it is all planned!' Greatly planned, and
executed with a free, decisive touch, that never hesitates
and takes no heed of modulations. It is this vastness of
design and scale, this simplicity and certainty of purpose, which strikes us first in Marlowe. He is the sculptor-poet of Colossi, aiming at such effects alone as are
unattainable in figures of a superhuman size, and careless
of fine distinctions or delicate gradations in their execution. His characters are not so much human beings, with
the complexity of human attributes combined in living personality, as types of humanity, the animated moulds of
human lusts and passions which include, each one of them,
the possibility of many individuals. They 'are the em-
bodiments or the exponents of single qualities and simple
forces.' This tendency to dramatise ideal conceptions,
to vitalise character with one dominant and tyrannous
motive, is very strong in Marlowe. Were it not for his
own fiery sympathy with the passions thus idealised, and
for the fervour of his conceptive faculty, these colossal
personifications might have been insipid or frigid. As it
is, they are far from deserving such epithets. They are
redeemed from the coldness of symbolic art, from the tire-
someness of tragic humours, by their author's intensity of
conviction. Marlowe is in deadly earnest while creating
them, believes in their reality, and infuses the blood of
his own untamable heart into their veins. We feel them to
be day-dreams of their maker's deep desires; projected
from his subjectivity, not studied from the men around
him; and rendered credible by sheer imaginative insight
into the dark mysteries of nature. A poet with a lively
sense of humour might, perhaps, have found it impossible
to conceive and sustain passions on so exorbitant a scale
with so little relief, so entire an absence of mitigating
qualities. But it was precisely on the side of humour
that Marlowe showed his chief inferiority to Shakspere.
That saving grace of the dramatic poet he lacked altogether. And it may also be parenthetically noticed as
significant in this respect that Marlowe never drew a

woman's character. His Abigail is a mere puppet. Isabella, in his 'Edward II.,' changes suddenly from almost
abject fawning on her husband to no less abject dependence
on an ambitious paramour. His Dido owes such power as the
sketch undoubtedly possesses to the poetry of the Fourth
Aeneid.

It is no function of sound criticism to decoct a poet's
work into its final and residual essence, deducing one
motive from the complex efforts and the casual essays of a
mind placed higher *ex hypothesi* in the creative order than
the critic's own; or inventing a catch-word whereby some
incommensurable series of achievements may be ticketed.
And yet, such is the nature of Marlowe's work, that it
imperatively indicates a leading motive, irresistibly
suggests a catch-word. This leading motive which pervades
his poetry may be defined as *L'Amour de l'Impossible* - the
love or lust of unattainable things; beyond the reach of
physical force, of sensual faculty, of mastering will; but
not beyond the scope of man's inordinate desire, man's
infinite capacity for happiness, man's ever-craving thirst
for beauty, power, and knowledge. This catch-word of the
Impossible Amour is thrust by Marlowe himself, in the
pride of his youthful insolence and lawlessness of spiritual lusts, upon the most diffident and sober of his
critics. Desire for the impossible - impossible not
because it transcends human appetite or capacity, but
because it exhausts human faculties in the infinite pursuit - this is the region of Marlowe's sway as poet. To
this impossible, because unlimited, object of desire he
adds another factor, suggested by his soul's revolt
against the given order of the world. He and the Titanic
characters into whom he has infused his spirit - even as a
workman through the glass-pipe blows life-breath into a
bubble, permanent so long as the fine vitreous form
endures - he and all the creatures of his fancy thirst for
things beyond man's grasp, not merely because these things
exhaust man's faculties in the pursuit, but also because
the full fruition of them has been interdicted. Thus Marlowe's lust for the impossible, the lust he has injected
like a molten fluid into all his eminent dramatic personalities, is a desire for joys conceived by the imagination, floating within the boundaries of will and sense at
some fixed moment, but transcending these firm limitations, luring the spirit onward, exhausting the corporeal
faculties, engaging the soul itself in a strife with God.
This lust assumes the shape of thirst for power, of thirst
for beauty, of thirst for knowledge. It is chiefly thirst
for power which animates this poet and his brood. When
knowledge, as in Faustus, seems to be the bait, that

knowledge will conduce to power. But there is a carnal
element in the desire itself, a sensuality which lends a
grip to Belial on the heart-strings of the lust. This sometimes soars aloft in aspirations, exhales itself in longings after Helen, the world's queen of loveliness, evoked
from Hades; sometimes it sinks to avaricious, solitary,
gluttonous delight in gems. It resolves itself again into
the thirst for power when we find that the jewels of
Barabas are hugged and gloated over for their potency of
buying states, corrupting kingdoms; when we see that the
wraith of Helen has been dragged from Lethe to flatter a
magician's vision of omnipotence.

43. A. H. BULLEN

1885

Arthur Henry Bullen (1857-1920) was a prolific and influential editor and publisher of English Renaissance dramatic
and poetic texts. As the extracts below indicate, he was
not an original or searching critic.
    From 'The Works of Christopher Marlowe', ed. A. H.
Bullen (1885), 1, xviii-xx, xxiv-xxv, xxviii-xxix, xliv-
xlv.

It is difficult to over-estimate the importance of 'Tamburlaine' in the history of the English drama. To appreciate how immensely Marlowe outdistanced at one bound all
his predecessors, the reader must summon courage to make
himself acquainted with such productions as 'Gorboduc,'
'The Misfortunes of Arthur,' and 'Sir Clyomon and Sir
Clamydes.' He will then perceive how real is Marlowe's
claim to be regarded as the father of the English drama.
That the play is stuffed with bombast, that exaggeration
is carried sometimes to the verge of burlesque, no sensible critic will venture to deny. But the characters,
with all their stiffness, have life and movement. The
Scythian conqueror, 'threatening the world in high
astounding terms,' is an impressive figure. There is
nothing mean or trivial in the invention. The young poet
threw into his work all the energy of his passionate
nature. He did not pause to polish his lines, to correct

and curtail; but was borne swiftly onward by the wings of
his imagination. The absence of chastening restraint is
felt throughout; and, indeed, the beauty of some of the
most majestic passages is seriously marred by the introduction of a weak or ill-timed verse. Take the following
passage from the First Part:-

> Nature that framed us of four elements,
> Warring within our breasts for regiment,
> Doth teach us all to have aspiring minds:
> Our souls, whose faculties can comprehend
> The wondrous architecture of the world,
> And measure every wandering planet's course,
> Still climbing after knowledge infinite,
> And always moving as the restless spheres,
> Wills us to wear ourselves and never rest
> Until we reach the ripest fruit of all,
> That perfect bliss and sole felicity,
> The sweet fruition of an earthly crown. (ii. 7.)

The ear exults in the sonorous march of the stately
verse as each successive line paces more majestically than
the preceding; but what cruel discomfiture awaits us at
the end! It seems almost inconceivable that the poet
should have spoilt so magnificent a passage by the lame
and impotent conclusion in the last line. For the moment
we are half inclined to think that he is playing some
trick upon us; that he has deliberately led up to an
anti-climax in order to enjoy the malicious satisfaction
of laughing at our irritation. The noble and oft-quoted
passage on Beauty (1 'Tamburlaine,' v. 1) is injured con-
siderably by the diffuseness of the context. Marlowe
seems to have blotted literally nothing in this earliest
play....
Before leaving 'Tamburlaine' a word must be said about
Marlowe's introduction of blank verse. Unrhymed verse of
ten syllables had been employed both for epic and dramatic
purposes before Marlowe's time. The Earl of Surrey, in
his translation of Books ii. and iv. of Virgil's 'Aeneid,'
had been the first to transplant the metre from Italy.
Surrey was a charming sonneteer and graceful lyrist; but
it would be absurd to claim that his translations from
Virgil afford the slightest hint of the capabilities of
blank verse. It is impossible to select six consecutive
lines that satisfy the ear. Without freedom or swing the
procession of languid lines limps feebly forward. When we
come to 'Gorboduc,' the first dramatic piece in which
rhyme was discarded, the case is no better. Little
advance, or rather none at all, has been made in rendering

the verse more flexible. Misled by classical usage, all
writers before Marlowe aimed at composing blank verse on
the model of Greek iambics. Confusing accent with quantity, they regarded accentuated and unaccentuated syllables as respectively long and short. Hence the aim was
to end each line with a strongly accentuated syllable,
immediately preceded by one that was unaccentuated; in
the rest of the line unaccentuated and accentuated syllables occurred alternately. Then, to complete the monotony, at the end of each verse came a pause, which effect-
ually excluded all freedom of movement. This state of
things Marlowe abolished. At a touch of the master's hand
the heavy-gaited verses took symmetry and shape. That the
blank verse of 'Tamburlaine' left much to be desired in
the way of variety is, of course, undeniable. Its sonorous music is fitted rather for epic than dramatic purposes.
The swelling rotundity of the italicised lines in the following passage recalls the magnificent rhythm of Milton:-

> The galleys and those pilling brigandines
> That yearly sail to the Venetian Gulf,
> And hover in the Straits for Christians' wreck,
> Shall lie at anchor in the Isle Asant
> Until the Persian fleet and men-of-war,
> *Sailing along the oriental sea,*
> Have fetched about the Indian continent
> *Even from Persepolis to Mexico.*

Later, Marlowe learned to breathe sweetness and softness
into his 'mighty line,' - to make the measure that had
thundered the threats of Tamburlaine falter the sobs of a
broken heart....
     But on the strength of internal evidence we might go
further, and say that the comic scenes [in 'The Jew'] are
in no instance by Marlowe. As far as possible, it is well
to avoid theorising, but I must state my conviction that
Marlowe never attempted to write a comic scene. The Muses
had dowered him with many rare qualities - nobility and
tenderness and pity - but the gift of humour, the most
grateful of all gifts, was withheld. To excite 'tears and
laughter for all time' was given to Shakespeare alone; but
all the Elizabethan dramatists, if we except Ford and
Cyril Tourneur, combined to some extent humour with tragic
power. The Elizabethan stage rarely tolerated any tragedy
that was unrelieved by scenes of mirth. It was in vain to
plead the example of classical usage, to point out that
the Attic tragedians never jested. Fortunately the
'understanding' pittites were not learned in the classical
tongues; they applauded when they were satisfied, and they

'mewed' when the play dragged. As the populace in
Horace's time clamoured 'media inter carmina,'(1) for a
bear or a boxer, so an Elizabethan audience, when it felt
bored or scared, insisted on being enlivened by a fool or
a clown. After a little fuming and fretting the poets
accepted the conditions; they soon found that the demand
of the audience was no outrage upon nature, and that there
need be no abruptness in the passage from tears to laughter. And so was realised for the first and last time in
the world's history the dream of Socrates; the theory he
propounded to Agathon, who was too drunk and drowsy for
argument or contradiction, as the dawn broke over that
memorable symposium. But Marlowe could not don alternately the buskin and the sock. His fiery spirit walked
always on the heights; no ripple of laughter reached him
as he scaled the 'high pyramides' of tragic art. But
while the poet was pursuing his airy path the actors at
the Curtain had to look after their own interests. They
knew that though they should speak with the tongues of
angels yet the audience would turn a deaf ear unless some
comic business were provided. Accordingly they employed
some hack-writer, or perhaps a member of their own company, to furnish what was required. How execrably he
performed his task is only too plain....
     Charles Lamb remarked that 'the reluctant pangs of
abdicating royalty in Edward furnished hints which Shakespeare scarce improved in his "Richard the Second"; and
the death-scene of Marlowe's king moves pity and terror
beyond any scene, ancient or modern, with which I am
acquainted.' Mr. Swinburne thinks that there is more
discrimination of character in Marlowe's play than Shakespeare's; that the figures are more life-like, stand out
more clearly as individual personalities. It may also be
urged that there is more 'business' in Marlowe's play;
that the action is never allowed to flag. The character
of the gay, frank, fearless, shameless favourite, Piers
Gaveston, is admirably drawn. Even in the presence of
death, with the wolfish eyes of the grim nobles bent on
him from every side, he loses nothing of his old jaunti-
ness. Marlowe has thoroughly realised this character, and
portrayed it in every detail with consummate ability.
Hardly less successful is the character of Young Spenser,
the insolent compound of recklessness and craft, posing as
the saviour of society, while he stealthily pursues his
own selfish projects. In his drawing of female characters, Marlowe showed no great skill or variety. The features in some of his portraits are either so dim as to
present no likeness at all, or they are excessively un-
lovely. Isabella is a vain, selfish woman, without any

strength of character. She is hurt at finding herself
neglected by the king, but the wound is only surface-deep.
She acquiesces passively in her husband's death, and with
equal indifference would have sacrificed her paramour.
Edward, with all his weakness, is not wholly ignoble. In
all literature there are few finer touches than when after
recounting his fearful suffering and privations in the
dungeon, he gathers his breath for one last kingly utterance:-

> Tell Isabel, the queen, I looked not thus
> When for her sake I ran at tilt in France,
> And there unhorsed the Duke of Cleremont.

What heart-breaking pathos in those lines! For a moment,
as his thoughts travel back across the years, he forgets
the squalor of his dungeon and rides blithely beneath the
beaming eyes of his lady. It has been objected that the
representation of the king's physical suffering oversteps
the limit of dramatic art. Euripides was censured by
ancient critics for demeaning tragedy; but to-day the
judgment of readers is on the side of Euripides, not of
his critics. Besides, if Euripides erred, Sophocles
erred also. The physical suffering of Philoctetes excites
far more disgust than anything that we find in Euripides.
There are those who think that the blinding of Gloster, in
'Lear,' surpassed in horror any scene of physical agony
enacted on the English stage. But criticism, which fears
to raise its voice against Shakespeare, shows no mercy to
Shakespeare's contemporaries.

Note

1 In the midst of (serious) dramatic presentations.

44. UNSIGNED REVIEW OF BULLEN'S EDITION OF 'THE WORKS'

1885

From the 'Nation', xl (1885), 423-4, 444-6.

MARLOWE. - I.

The English Dramatists: The Works of Christopher
Marlowe. Edited by A. H. Bullen, M.A. Boston:
Houghton, Mifflin & Co. 1885. 3 vols.

Mr. Bullen is to give us, in handsome print and paper, and
well and wisely seen to for the readings, all our dramatists, of about Shakspere's time, who have earned of their
after-comers the work and cost of printing. These will
not be very many, and all of them will be well worth the
having. 'Kit' Marlowe, who may with truth be called the
first of these, comes first from Mr. Bullen, and is set
forth by him with gentle and tender hands. Dramatic
poetry, higher up than his, had been but a worthless ooze,
or a soiled and muddy trickle. He gave it a new beginning, unlike what had been before, and on another scale.

To come upon a starting-place, or a turning-place, in
the life of the race of men, or of our English branch of
it, is a great thing. Such a thing it is to find at
Hissarlik hauberk, or helm, or shield - 'exesa . . .
scabra rubigine' - or at Bannockburn some little, crooked,
earth-eaten bit of one of the iron calthrops that tumbled
the English Edward's horses and horsemen on Scottish soil.
So, too, it would be if we could come in upon unfinished
work - work on its way to perfectness - of any one such
mastering man as Pheidias or Zeuxis. It startles us, this
day, to see, in that painting left by one of our American
masters but half done, the later and larger figure coming
forth, as it were, of its former self. Now, is it not
much to find, in its very making, our ten-syllable blank
verse - the verse of Shakspere and Milton? This we shall
find in Marlowe's plays; and these plays we shall find not
unworthy of being read by those even who can feel and
understand the sharpness of insight, and strength, and
grace, and manifoldness that are in Shakspere and Goethe,
and the mirthfulness - rather unkindly, grim, ghastly - of
the one; and of the other, frolic, neighborly and of good-
fellowship.

Two little lines, most musical, and with a dainty picture in each word, have for generations drawn men's hearts
towards Marlowe:

By shallow rivers, to whose falls
Melodious birds sing madrigals.

They are in themselves a full and rounded poem. Shakspere, a little Marlowe's younger, borrowed these, and
more, in one of his plays, and Izaak Walton, in his

'Angler,' takes in the whole piece from which they come.
Poor Marlowe! Disreputable in life, and worse in death;
loathed by all men professing godliness; yet must we think
that his heart was not all bad, and we know that he did
for our great English tongue good work, and in our tongue
did good work too, and that both these works are great and
lasting. Until we have well read his plays, and weighed
him well, we are looking to find even more in him and them
than can be found; and this because we find so much. He
was the first English writer of true plays; and as Lucretius, first of Roman writers, made great poetry for his
own use, to give philosophy through it to his countrymen,
much in the same way, though less, did Marlowe. Besides
this work - besides his plays and the verse in which he
wrote them, and his easy ten-syllable rhyme, and that one
melodious madrigal which all readers of English have loved
from boyhood, and besides, through all, his strong and
swift imagination - if all this be not enough, there is
nothing worthy in the man, or in what he did to give him
hold upon the memory of men. Yet when we say 'Poor Marlowe!' as men used to say 'Poor Burns!' (and for all the
self-same reasons, and for others too), we say it with the
assured feeling that Marlowe, though nothing like so great
as Burns, is great enough to take and stand by what
belongs to him in fair and equal weighing, though his bad
weigh heavily. He has, at the same time, as one feels
sure, enough of manhood to need and crave, if he could
speak, some good and kindly thought from fellow-men, and
has, as poet - and even as man - good right to it.
Marlowe could never claim, like Burns, to have held
fast to, and carried safely through whatever filthiness of
drinking and debauchery, a great deal of the best manli-
ness of this human nature that we all are made in, and in
which we feel each other, and take from one another the
push of thought and feeling. He cannot claim, like
Burns, to have used whatever he had of that best manli-
ness for the good of the rest of men, and to have given to
it melodious utterance for all coming time. Marlowe had
not so large possession in the great faculties and great
feelings of humanity. Then that true pitch of our frame,
in which fun of the higher and finer sort, or of the
broader and heartier sort, but, in whatever sort, true fun
(that merriness of the happy fitting together of our
being) shows itself so readily in liking and in kindly
laughter, and in which, as readily, fellow-feeling,
sorrow-sharing, shows itself in loving tears and tears of
hurt and wrong - was almost wanting in him. From Burns
the fun and fellow-feeling were running over on all sides,
and at all times almost - sad, serious, and merry, all at
once.

Yet feeling, strong and fine, was not wanting in Marlowe. This his 'Tragicall History of Doctor Faustus'
shows, in *Faustus* and in the scholars and others, beyond
all gainsaying. So, too, the episode of *Olympia*, in
'Tamburlaine,' and *Zenocrate*, and better (though there is
too little of her) *Abigail*, the Jew's daughter – these all
show the respect which he could understand and, we may
hope, feel for what in woman is lovely and becoming; and
nothing witnesses more strongly than this that the finer
and better nature was somewhere in this poet, at least at
some times. If he has few women in his plays, and if his
writing is very far from free from a bad taint, which the
times unhappily allowed, he does not riot in the befouling
of that better sex whose goodness is our best possession
and whose badness is the deadliest bane to men.

Of Marlowe's plays, 'Tamburlaine the Great' must have
come in upon the English stage as a new thing; and, in
spite of faults of its author and in spite of its own
faults, it must have come as something wonderful. The
play-goers wondered and applauded much, laughed a little,
and the play was called for, and crowds went to it, for a
hundred nights, before they had had enough of it. So the
author wrote a Second Part, very much of a piece with the
First. That was the earliest English play that, for the
character, and for what was said, and for the way of
saying it, was worth the being recalled to the stage, or
being remembered; and that play was the first work in
which our English blank verse, living, and strong, and
large, was used – as noble, sometimes, as any that came
later.

When Marlowe was stirred with the great thought of
giving to his English fellow-countrymen plays lofty as
the old Greek plays, and in becoming language, the huge
shape of Timour Lenk – Timour the Limper – stalking over
some thousand leagues of the world, this way and that, and
overcoming all the Eastern lands, almost, caught in the
player-poet's eye. That Timour had been, in his flesh
and blood and whatever else helped to his making, a man of
boundless ambition, of very great power over men, of wondrous quickness in gathering hosts, and strength in holding them together, of most uncommon skill in planning, and
downright might in doing in leaguer and field of battle.
Killing, breaking-down, laying waste – the man was, for
hardness of head, hard-heartedness, hardness and heaviness
of hand, worse, if anything, and on a vastly larger scale,
than Horace's Achilles, in ruthless wrong and cruelty:
'Impiger, iracundus, inexorabilis, acer, Jura neg[a]t sibi
nata, nihil non arrog[a]t armis.' Timour Lenk, therefore
– to Englishmen, 'Tamburlaine' – such as he was, and with

crowds of kings becrowned and bedizened with purple and
crimson and satin and velvet, and fettered, withal, walking before and behind him, and sometimes harnessed, by
relays, and under the whip, to his triumphal car, Marlowe
took. This was an heroic figure for a great play of five
acts, for speech of a new sort, on a new scale; and gave
chances for shows upon the stage, to catch and refresh
those who wearied of much speech better than their wonted
talk. His hope and plan the poet sets forth thus, in the
Prologue:

> We'll lead you to the stately tent of war
> Where you shall hear the Scythian Tamburlaine
> Threatening the world in high astounding terms;

and he meant to lead away

> From jigging strains of rhyming mother wits
> And such conceits as clownage keeps in pay.

In this he succeeded, and so well as to make all those of
our own tongue who love work of imagination and verse,
good and fitting, from that time downward, debtors to him.
     In these two plays - the First and Second Parts of
'Tamburlaine the Great' - the love in our hearts, it is
true, is scarcely touched; the higher and finer feelings
are seldom, if they are ever, called out; it would be hard
to find a lofty, noble, or kindly sentiment from the
beginning to the end of them. If one is interested, it is
not that one likes the hero or any single one of the other
men in them. By way of relief to the throng of men, and
those mostly Scythians, Persians, Turks, doing nothing
else than quarrelling, fighting, and bragging, one woman,
Zenocrate, is carried through a play and a-half, and,
though not strongly drawn, lightens the action and makes
all less unkindly. Olympia, taken suddenly into the
Second Part, after Zenocrate's death, and not too suddenly
killed off out of it, is well drawn, though not new, and
helps to the same end. Plautus's 'Captivi,' without a
woman in it, is interesting throughout, for there is
nobleness and faith and trustiness even to death, and the
plot unfolds itself with beautiful exactness. In neither
part of 'Tamburlaine' is there anything that we can call
plot, and the heroic barbarians would be insufferably
tiresome to use, without at least so much of a gentler
element brought in as these women bring.
     For others, such as they are (not much to our liking),
Tamburlaine is strongly drawn, for what the author meant
him, and is kept to his level always; and the generals,

emperors, kings, and the rest are of the same stuff, cut
to slightly different patterns, and of somewhat different
sizes. The tongue that they speak is much the same for
all, and all are so filled, to their very tongue-tips,
with classical mythology (of all things in the world) that
we cannot but wonder after the methods of the schools
where these stalking barbarian slaughterers were made so
glib in this smattering of scholarship. Acheron and
Phlegethon and Styx and Erebus and Tartarus and Tantalus
and the ugly Ferryman, and the Fatal Sisters and Jove and
Janus and Cupid, Apollo, Cynthia, Juno, Bellona, Troy,
Tenedos, Phoebus, Corinna, Lesbia, Boreas, Boötes, Hermes,
prolocutor of the gods, come out of the mouths of any of
them as readily as day and night and rain and sunshine.
Marlowe, if not a very accurately learned man, had taken
his bachelor's and master's degrees in arts, at Cambridge,
and knew enough to put into English, out of Latin, a great
deal that he might better have left where it was when he
found it.

The 'Tragicall History of Doctor Faustus,' of which
Goethe, who owed it nothing, spoke highly, has certainly
not a little in it that ought to live; and Faustus, though
steadily kept down to the level of the vulgar, legendary,
and though not so strong or interesting as Goethe's Faust,
is less hard to like or to forgive than Faust. The up-
heaving, wrenching, twisting, squeezing strength of Goethe
in 'Faust,' the uncouthness, or the rugged homeliness of
words; the loftiness, the floating grace, the witchery of
melody; the pitiable weakness, the hopeless sadness, the
flash of wit, the human heart set down bare before us, and
showing all its working to our eyes; the never-wearying
changefulness of the measure - of all these, little in the
same kind, perhaps, is to be found in Marlowe's 'Faustus';
but there is what will touch the heart and leave it better.
There is enough to show that this author was not all bad,
or always bad.

'Edward the Second' might have been called 'The Tragedie of Piers Gaveston,' and has several characters - as
Gaveston, the Queen, and the King - well discriminated and
well kept up (although the last is often over-drawn); but
as the chief character is one that we do not like to think
of or know about, and there is not one noble scene or
person in the play, it could not be great, nor could it
hold a good place in our liking or our memory. The better
kingliness that comes upon Edward in wretchedness, and in
meeting death, is well done, being done by one who had a
real share of the true insight.

'The Jew of Malta' has some strong character-drawing
and good scenes, and it has, unhappily, some absurd and

preposterous character-drawing and scenes. The Turkish
Admiral and *Abigail*, the Jew's daughter, are admirable, as
far as they go, but are each cut clean out of the play
after a short life in it. 'The Massacre of Paris' has
some pretty sharp and clever work to have gone with stronger and better, but was never filled out to full proportions
of a play. 'The Tragedy of Dido, Queen of Carthage,' shows
some beautiful passages and some very bad things - bad even
for pagans. It cannot, for a moment, stand, as a poem,
beside Virgil's account of Dido's tragedy, and wants a good
deal to make it into a substantial play. The bad parts do
not in any way help, nor were they in any way needed. Not
one of all these that we have run over is without strength
or beauty, more or less.

In these plays, as might be guessed after what we have
said, is no real fun-making of any sort, nor is there a
single character in them capable of the making or enjoying
of fun, or of knowing it when he sees or hears it. There
are, indeed, certain 'situations' which perhaps were meant
to be funny, and most likely were so to the men of the
time, who shouted their lungs out over the kings in harness
and *Tamburlaine's* cry to them: 'Hola, ye pampered jades of
Asia!' Thus - to take an instance out of a stage direction - '*Mycetes*' (whose army is on the ground) '*comes out
alone with his crown in his hand, offering to hide it,*'
and *Tamburlaine*, with another great army there to fight
Mycetes, joins him, asking: 'Is this your crown?' Of unin-
tended funniness is this, where the hitherto shepherd *Tamburlaine*, at the outset of his great march across the
Eastern World, has the Princess *Zenocrate*, daughter of the
Soldan of Egypt, a prisoner, beseeching him as a 'shepherd' (for by his 'seeming' he is 'so mean a man') to
'pity her distressèd plight,' and presently, without the
slightest stay in their talking, he says:

> Lie here, ye weeds that I disdain to wear! [his pas-
>   toral garments]
> This com'plete armor and this curtle-axe
> Are ad'juncts more befitting Tamburlaine;

as if the intermediate process - whatever it might be with
a Scythian shepherd - between the wearing of a garb which
betokened him so mean a man as a keeper of sheep, and the
appearing in full effulgence of a warrior's armor, had
been rehearsed while he stood there talking with the
Soldan's daughter. Other things of this sort might be
found if looked for.

Now, that the bringing in of fun and frolic to offset

sharply the mournful and heart-harrowing of the play
brought wondrous life-likeness into our English tragedy,
others can see easily besides ourselves; and that a new
zest for readers, as well as for seers and hearers, of
plays in our tongue has come with that bringing-in. Our
thoughtful, all-prodding, all-weighing cousin-Germans
were drawn, without a will for it, to English tragedy, and
Frenchmen, too, whose kindred to us and to our tongue is
further off a good deal, were drawn to it against their
will. And, whatever critics may have said about 'unities'
and dignity, all the world likes it better, and will keep
it in a warmer place in the heart, because its gloom is
not all gloomy. Oneness of mood, which must last long
unchanged, as of iron or clay, does not belong to men. In
the glimmer of darkened rooms from which the dead has been
lately borne, will come out a burst of mirthfulness at
unawares, and this from no 'widows of Ephesus,' but from
true mourners. Sometimes the merriness is a fitting and
most touching element in the action and passion. In that
poem truly dramatic, though no drama, and of marvellous
beauty and sadness, 'The Bride of Lammermoor,' the mirth
made by and through old Caleb Balderstone belongs as truly
to the sadness of the tale as the white satin or silken
lining, or the work in bullion thread, belongs to the
black velvet of the pall.

The Greeks and Latins, as we know, unlike our own
greatest writers, held these dark and light things wide
apart, one from the other; keeping sad steadily to sad,
merry to merry. So Frenchmen of the classic rank, whose
tongue is still less than they are either Greek or Roman,
have held, with might and main, to the same rule. Their
French speech often stumbles in trying to march stately
on sublime heights; yet one can never with their leave
smile in one of their tragedies. Any funny thing must
have slipped in in spite of the author (as there will be
sometimes one too sly for him); but can we help smiling
when the Cid, who has killed in a duel the father of his
betrothed, and is now formally pursued by her as the
avenger of blood, makes his way to her in some absence of
the never-absent duenna of Spanish maidens, and proclaims
that to his true love's champion in the lists (whom she
insists upon his doing his best to kill *for his own
glory's sake and to prevent her having to marry her vic-
torious champion, who is hateful - poor fellow!*) he, the
Cid, her lover, will present not his *vie*, his *âme*, his
tête, his *cervelle*, his *poitrine*, or his *poumon*, but his
'estomac ouvert,' 'ravished with the thought' that it is
for her 'honor' that he is thus putting in use his very
best knowledge of anatomy?

Frenchmen, beside Molière, can make fun, and even the
writers of some of their best tragedies; but never, of
their own will, in their tragedies. Marlowe could not, at
any time. But one thing stands out steadfast in our minds
after his scenes and characters all are gone, and that is
the *Verse*. With this the poet sometimes throws a flash of
glory upon a mountain-top, sometimes a golden gladness
over all the heavens; he pours a torrent, splashing and
roaring and glittering, down a cliff's front, or through a
winding glen; he shows a wood waving with green, or standing thick with cool shade; within sight of the many-towned
shore he makes a sea heaving with broad-sailed, deep-
hulled merchant-men, laboring toward some great mart; he
draws a throbbing, boding gloom over earth and sky, or
makes the spring or summer landscape cheery with bird-song
and with the flitting of birds' wings. All comes to us as
it went from him: the angle of reflection to the reader's
eye, as elsewhere in optics, is the same as the angle of
incidence from the author's mind. He can do, in verse,
anything that he knows, and we see all done, and wonder at
the man's strength of bodying and uttering – as great,
when at its best, as in Lucretius, but not so often at its
best as in Lucretius. So Marlowe made Blank Verse almost
what it was ever afterwards.

By the time of Shakspere's best play-writing, and, of
course, long before Milton's time, that measure knew
itself and was known in the realm of English poetry, and
came at call in it; and it wore, always, much the same
outward likeness. In Marlowe's plays we find it learning
to have a life, and to live its own life; we find it growing, and taking shape and character. With him it is most
often dignified, sometimes impressive and even splendid;
now and then, indeed, it is fairly sublime. Often, however, Marlowe's verse is awkward and ungainly, and – alas!
not seldom – laughable or paltry – coming to the ground
with the thought (which it ought to have carried) under-
neath. This one does not like to say of a man strong and
skilful, who has done much good work; but it is only
plainer than most plain things that sometimes he himself,
as one might do who was ashamed or afraid of having wrought
wrought some of his work too well, would with his own hand
mar it after the doing. This fear or shame, though not
often true of any man, might perhaps have been true of
him, for his fellows and comrades were mostly a roystering,
reckless, chaffing, scoffing set. Not a few of them were
nasty, and slippery, and cold-blooded as fishes, and, like
fishes, ready to snatch at and tear, and to gulp down in
gobbets, and batten themselves upon, any unlucky one of
their own kind who chanced at the time to be swimming

weakly or sickly. Among such comrades a man might easily
be shamed for having shown too lofty thought or too good
feeling, or be afraid of showing them. In most ways Marlowe was not better than the rest: there were sad things
enough about his whole life, and they were crowded thick
enough about his death, to make him seem almost the worst
among them.

The want in Marlowe of that finest fashioning and fitting, together from which spring freely forth, ever fresh,
mirth, harmless as happy; sadness needing to be soothed;
quick sorrow with those who are hurt; love, through all
the blood, for what is great and true - the want of this
best making-up, and the want of much growing toward it, or
effort after it, as life among men went on, was likely,
more than scoffing ways of his comrades, or even the
'drink-drowned'-ness of 'spright' (spirit) which Hall
gives him, to make him mar his better work. The 'spright,'
in that state, 'rapt to the threefold loft of heaven-
hight,' as Hall says, might have one head-long downfall at
a time, for it is unsteady, unsafe treading on the clouds,
then; but not a soaring high aloft, and tumbling, and
soaring, and tumbling, between lines following each other
closely. The best genius, from being fully akin to others
of man's kind because it has so much of mankind in it, can
easily go along one or other of the many channels that
lead into its fellows, and look back at itself and its
work from that side. This Marlowe could not; and if it be
he that tries to make us laugh, as in 'Faustus' by a leg
coming off the wizard, and elsewhere by such worse than
clown's play, it is beyond bearing. The likelihood is
that the worst of this is not his; for not only were players and play-writers wont to take and use one another's
thoughts and words, much as fellows of some college-clubs
borrow, without asking, of one another, and wear, shirt-
studs, or neckties, or waistcoats, even, but any of them
almost might write any clownery into any one's play that
was on the boards, and anywhere in it. That borrowing and
using Shakspere did, in a large, free way, and the putting
in of what was meant to be witty or droll, to any one
else's plays, was often done and known to be done; sometimes ordered, of some one or more who happened to have
the time and will.

The history of blank verse in English is but short.
We had had our ten-syllable verse in plenty - in Chaucer
as well as afterward in Dryden or Pope; but everything
with our fathers rhymed; for rhyme had got hold of the ear
of Christendom. Their Latin measures, even, had been
turning into rhyme, for hundreds of years. Happily, just
as it was growing early summer to the thought and fancy

of the English race, the Earl of Surrey, a gallant,
clever, and accomplished knight, and a deft worker in
English rhyming verse, of many sorts, found, when in
Italy, a measure of another sort than any used in England.
Rhythmic it was; dignified, and yet easy; free from all
bondage to rhythm, where rhyming might be a bondage. Of
this great fault glaring example may be found in plays (as
of Racine and Corneille - great writers both) where the
life-likeness is hindered very much by the rhyming of the
speeches, and where a frequent change of speakers makes
the sudden flinging of the rhyme from one to another tiresome and absurd.

Our English poetry, as we find it in Chaucer, is a
supple, lively thing, that would bear cutting and bending
and pulling, like every young language - like Homer's
Greek, where the many vowels, blending sometimes, sometimes sundering; the various alternative endings; the
various inflections for the same verb or noun, make it,
for sweetness of sound, with freedom and strength, the
most perfect vehicle for uttering thought and figure, and
telling and pleading and love-speaking, and for fastening
upon the memory, that ever was in the world. Our English,
though never so free as Greek, and very far less melodious, yet was strong and lively in Chaucer's time, and
freer than now, because it had, side by side, old forms
and new of the same word; could cut off and put on, now
sound a vowel and now keep it still, and had more double
endings than we have. The Italian had much the same qualities, one by one, that we have given to the Greek: its
verse, therefore, had much the same character as the
Greek, and this whether rhyming or unrhyming. All its
verse had kept the double ending, which we have so much
lost, though with the Germans it is still, and may be
forever, easy. In the Italian blank verse the last foot
is that of the old Greek and Latin heroic and trochaic
measures - a long and a doubtful syllable; its rhyming
verse only takes on another grace. It has the double
ending always - perhaps too much; certainly too much for
any but a speech flowing with vowels. Here is a bit (unrhymed) of about the time of Surrey, taken at first
glance:(1)

> Quindi uscian fuor voci canori e dolci
> E di cigni, e di ninfe, e di sirene;
> Di sirene celesti; e n' uscian suoni
> Soavi e chiari, e tanto altro diletto,
> Ch' attonito, godendo ed ammirando,
> Mi fermai ——.   —*Tasso*, 'Aminta.'

Even the eye sees the soft melody of these words; but let
a gentle voice read them to the ear rightly!
This measure Surrey took, without the double ending
but admitting it, and set over, into the first blank verse
that ever was used in English, two books of the 'Aeneid.'
A fair specimen, perhaps, is this:

As when Apollo leaveth Lyciä,

. . . . . .
When that he walkes upon Mount Cynthus' toppe,
His sparklëd tresse represt with garlandes softe
Of tender leaves, and trussëd up with golde,
His quivering darts clattering behind his backe -
So freshe and lustie did Aeneas seme.

Let Surrey, who brought over for us this measure from
Italy, have his credit; and that it was a poet who saw
the worth of it, the spirit and strength of these few
words shall witness: 'His quivering darts clattering
behind his backe' is Virgil's 'tela sonant humeris' (his
weapons sound, on his shoulders). Of course, a little bit
like this above can give no sufficient acquaintance for a
critical analysis: for this a good deal more must be read,
and will be pleasant reading.

Note

1 From thence issued out the sweet and harmonious music
of swans, of nymphs and sirens, celestial sirens; from
thence proceeded sounds so sweet and clear, and so many
other delights, that I stood spellbound with pleasure
and admiration.

45. H. A. JONES

1885

Henry Arthur Jones (1851-1929) was a most successful and
influential dramatic craftsman.
From the 'Nineteenth Century' (January 1885), xvii,
162.

We will take the three greatest and most representative
names of that age, Marlowe, Shakespeare, and Ben Jonson,
and ask how they dealt with religious matters. The comparison is very interesting, as it also incidentally dis-
covers the different bent of each genius and the different
texture of his mind. The essential reverence of these
three writers will scarcely be questioned if reverence is
to be reckoned by the wholesomeness of the feelings
rather than by the squeamishness of the ears. Though even
in the matter of words it may be asked whether the clean
and healthy outspokenness of some of the Elizabethan
writers is not more reverent of everything worth reverence than the putrid leer and imbecile suggestiveness of
some music-hall songs that have been imported into the
modern theatre.

To begin with Christopher Marlowe, 'Son first-born of
the morning, sovereign star!' In Marlowe there is none
of the familiar playful quotation of Scripture so frequent
in Shakespeare, or the broadly comic portraiture of religious hypocrisy unctuously mouthing Holy Writ to its own
ends that Ben Jonson delights in. Marlowe's fiery genius
sets directly about its main ends, and in 'Doctor Faustus'
seizes the heart and core of the Christian doctrine, and
appropriates as much as is necessary for the scheme of his
play. There is no hesitation, no question in Marlowe's
mind as to the perfect right of his art to enter this
region and take full possession of it. Fragments of
Christian dogma are tossed hither and thither in the burning whirlpool with waifs and strays of heathen history and
mythology, while the living heat of the poet's imagination
binds and mats all the strange ingredients into one liquid
flame of terror, and the spectator watches, with harrowing
suspense and breathless inescapable impression of reality,
the damnation of a soul. Omitting the wretched buffoonery
of the comic scenes as possible interpolations or conces-
sions to the groundlings, there is no room left for any
thought of reverence or irreverence. The question of the
comparative truth of the Greek mythology and the creed of
Christendom sinks into a matter of 'words, words, words,'
as we contemplate the awful picture of the death agony of
Faustus. Marlowe compels our acquiescence that that at
least is real, is true. It would be impertinent to defend
the 'Faustus' against any possible charge of irreverence
which the rancid, bilious temperament of superfinical
godliness might bring against it. No poet ever reaches
such inaccessible heights of inspiration without remaining
quite impervious and out of the reach of harm by any
assault from that quarter. It could only be in an out-
burst of bewildered indignation or riotous satire that one

could put the question, whether in the matter of reverence of man's spiritual nature the age that produced Marlowe's 'Faustus' has any need to feel ashamed of itself
when brought to the bar of the age that demanded a version of the same legend brought down to the average
intelligence of a modern burlesque audience.

46. S. BRITTON

1886-7

These are brief extracts from a magazine for 'free-thinkers', edited by G. W. Foote, who also edited 'The Bible
Handbook for Free-Thinkers' (1888). The alignment of Marlowe with Charles Bradlaugh (1833-91), the notorious
Victorian 'atheist', is especially interesting.
    From 'Progress: A Monthly Magazine of Advanced
Thought' (August-December 1886), vi, 412-78; (January
1887), vii, 11-17, 49-54.

Marlowe, like Shelley, came to a violent, sudden and
accidental death in his twenty-ninth year. In almost all
other respects they may be said to have been very dissi-
milar, although the loving student of both will probably
find in the earlier writer indications of that fearless,
wide-eyed spirit of inquiry, of eager prying into the unknown and forbidden, which distinguished Shelley. The
marvellous faculty of stringing common words and simple
ideas into perfect music is common also to both. How
nearly they occasionally approximate in this respect is
not evident to a superficial reader because of the variety
of the instances in which the earlier writer handles
themes giving opportunity for comparison with the later.
Further, they are alike in this - that the reader of their
works finds in the most impersonal of them an intensely
personal element, which enables him to grasp (as far as
his intelligence permits) the inmost essence of their
respective personalities. Know Shakespeare from end to
end and you are little nearer his personality, so perfect
is his objective dramatic power. Study Marlowe's far
smaller and less precious legacy, and you acquire no mean
knowledge of his temperament and intelligence. This is

fortunate, for, save these unwritten records, we know
almost nothing of him. The little that is recorded is
chiefly in the writing of ill-wishers, who if they knew
any good of him did not refer to it. Modern editors, with
the pious desire to whitewash their illustrious subject,
have endeavored to explain away and discredit the contemporary evidence regarding Marlowe. They overlook the
fact, however, that his various accusers, although contradictory as to details, and obviously guided in some cases
by religious or personal malice, are agreed that Marlowe
was a loose liver and an Atheist, and there is much in his
plays and poems to support the soundness of this estimate,
especially as regards the Atheism. An interesting ballad
called The Atheist's Tragedie, found by Mr. J. P. Collier,
which, if not a forgery by that gentleman or some ingenious modern, as is more than possible, is the fullest
statement extant regarding Marlowe.

Lieutenant-Colonel Cunningham, after collating the
vague, prejudiced and contradictory evidence as to Marlowe's end, very sensibly remarks, 'Let any one who is
inclined to place implicit reliance in evidence of this
description take up the works of Peter Pindar, Esq., . . .
and read what is there specifically asserted as the career
of the living William Gifford.' It is not to be supposed
that an avowed Atheist was likely in the days of Elizabeth to fare better at the hands of bigots than in the
days of Victoria. Before too readily assuming Marlowe to
have been a depraved debauchee, we would do well to
remember what monsters of vice Mr. Bradlaugh and other
free-thought leaders of to-day are currently held to be by
the *unco guid* section of society; and that upon the most
trumpery basis fabricated from lies and distortions,...

When we come to the summing-up of the evidence which
exists in Marlowe's works as to his philosophy of life and
attitude towards religion, we find, I think, that there is
absolutely nothing to support the idea that he accepted
Christianity in any form or offered any substitute for it.
A review of his leading characters shows a series of
colossal figures living without religion and generally
defying it, while the course of events exhibits the gods
as powerless to interfere, or interfering only, as in the
case of Faustus, with cruel malignity by the hands of
their infernal subjects whose proceedings their 'good
angel' has been impotent to check. The only exception is
in 'Dido,' where the deities that Marlowe and all his contemporaries knew to be fabulous are active, effectual, and
reverently obeyed controllers of destiny. Did Marlowe
purposely prepare this contrast, or does it exist because,
while he would not pander to a living superstition, he had

no scruple about using the puppets of a dead one as dramatic machinery? The latter is the more likely supposition.
Side by side with the constant flouting at religion is a
curiously persistent belief in 'stars,' and it is not at
all improbable that Marlowe may have held, in common with
many gifted men of his age, that the occult arts veiled
hidden truths and forces. The present-day tendency of
some Freethinkers to take up with spiritism and all its
train of cults favors this view. Such an attitude was
more excusable in his time than in ours, when the staff of
physical science is ready to the hand. Only such paltry
crutches as the black arts afforded were available to the
Elizabethan who threw away the support of religion. The
need of knowledge and Marlowe's craving for it are piti-
fully illustrated in the querulous and incessant demands
of Faustus in his colloquies with Mephistophilis. In the
futile desire to know more, which was *his* sin, Marlowe may
possibly have typified his own mental unrest, and the
doctor's wholly disproportionate punishment may have
shadowed forth the poet's estimate of the scorn and
persecution which surrounded the open-eyed inquirer in
his age. If Marlowe became, as is alleged, a sensualist,
it is not to be wondered at. He had found religion false,
and so turned his eyes from another world to this. Here
he found no firm foundation in science, which was then a
mere farrago of religion-begotten quackery; and nothing
remained but to make the best of the delights of the
little visible world in which he was hedged about by vast
walls built by ignorance, over which no man dare look on
pain of stake and gallows, and above which was only
visible the unattainable heavens. The full force of an
eager nature was thrown into the channels of delight of
sense, and he doubtless tried to make the best of all the
good things of life, concluding with the preacher that
'there is no better thing under the sun than to eat and to
drink and to be merry.' While allowing this, it must be
added that his works do not favor the ill-supported theory
of his abandoned profligacy of character. Their very
existence is proof that a large portion of his short time
of public life was well spent in the production of literature which is obviously the outcome of a clear and strong
head; and their moral tone, so far as there is any, is
sound, if not exalted. In them we trace the hand of a
revolutionary contemner of all established shams, and
perhaps also of one who utterly despaired of any good from
life and mankind. But this very despair and revolt are
the outgrowth of a healthy mind anxious for better things.
Evils and evil-doers are depicted in vivid colors with an
unshrinking touch; not delicately tricked out in

attractive guise to pander to the baser tastes of the
reader or hearer. Where pity and sympathy are asked for
by the author, pity and sympathy are due. We see Bella-
mira die without a regret, but Abigail touches the heart-
strings. Marlowe seems to commend much that the blindly
orthodox do not approve, but from the standpoint of those
who deduce their moral scheme of life from a rational
basis he seldom if ever errs.

47. JAMES RUSSELL LOWELL

1887

James Russell Lowell (1819-91), a genuine Boston mandarin,
succeeded Longfellow as Professor of Belles-lettres at
Harvard in 1855, was editor of the 'Atlantic Monthly'
(1857-61), and served his country abroad in the embassies
at Madrid and London. His most popular publication was
the facile and satiric 'Biglow Papers' (1848, 1867). The
comment on Marlowe is part of the Lowell Institute Lectures, 1887.
   From 'The Old English Dramatists' (1892), 32-6, 39-40,
45-9, 54.

Do not consider such discussions as these *otiose* or *nuga-
tory*. The language we are fortunate enough to share, and
which, I think, Jacob Grimm was right in pronouncing, in
its admirable mixture of Saxon and Latin, its strength and
sonorousness, a better literary medium than any other
modern tongue - this language has not been fashioned to
what it is without much experiment, much failure, and
infinite expenditure of pains and thought. Genius and
pedantry have each done its part towards the result which
seems so easy to us, and yet was so hard to win - the one
by way of example, the other by way of warning. The
purity, the elegance, the decorum, the chastity of our
mother-tongue are a sacred trust in our hands. I am
tired of hearing the foolish talk of an American variety
of it, about our privilege to make it what we will because we are in a majority. A language belongs to those
who know best how to use it, how to bring out all its
resources, how to make it search its coffers round for

the pithy or canorous phrase that suits the need, and
they who can do this have been always in a pitiful min-
ority. Let us be thankful that we too have a right to it,
and have proved our right, but let us set up no claim to
vulgarize it. The English of Abraham Lincoln was so good
not because he learned it in Illinois, but because he
learned it of Shakespeare and Milton and the Bible, the
constant companions of his leisure. And how perfect it
was in its homely dignity, its quiet strength, the
unerring aim with which it struck once nor needed to
strike more! The language is alive here, and will grow.
Let us do all we can with it but debase it. Good taste
may not be necessary to salvation or to success in life,
but it is one of the most powerful factors of civilization. As a people we have a larger share of it and more
widely distributed than I, at least, have found elsewhere,
but as a nation we seem to lack it altogether. Our coin-
age is ruder than that of any country of equal pretensions, our paper money is filthily infectious, and the
engraving on it, mechanically perfect as it is, makes of
every bank-note a missionary of barbarism. This should
make us cautious of trying our hand in the same fashion
on the circulating medium of thought. But it is high
time that I should remember Maître Guillaume of Patelin,
and come back to my sheep.

In coming to speak of Marlowe, I cannot help fearing
that I may fail a little in that equanimity which is the
first condition of all helpful criticism. Generosity
there should be, and enthusiasm there should be, but they
should stop short of extravagance. Praise should not
weaken into eulogy, nor blame fritter itself away into
fault-finding. Goethe tells us that the first thing
needful to the critic, as indeed it is to the wise man
generally, is to see the thing as it really is; this is
the most precious result of all culture, the surest warrant of happiness, or at least of composure. But he also
bids us, in judging any work, seek first to discover its
beauties, and then its blemishes or defects. Now there
are two poets whom I feel that I can never judge without
a favorable bias. One is Spenser, who was the first poet
I ever read as a boy, not drawn to him by any enchantment
of his matter or style, but simply because the first
verse of his great poem was, -

A gentle knight was pricking on the plain,

and I followed gladly, wishful of adventure. Of course I
understood nothing of the allegory, never suspected it,
fortunately for me, and I am surprised to think how much

of the language I understood. At any rate, I grew fond of
him, and whenever I see the little brown folio in which I
read, my heart warms to it as to a friend of my childhood.
With Marlowe it was otherwise. With him I grew acquainted
during the most impressible and receptive period of my
youth. He was the first man of genius I had ever really
known, and he naturally bewitched me. What cared I that
they said he was a deboshed fellow? nay, an atheist? To
me he was the voice of one singing in the desert, of one
who had found the water of life for which I was panting,
and was at rest under the palms. How can he ever become
to me as other poets are? But I shall try to be lenient
in my admiration.

   Christopher Marlowe, the son of a shoemaker, was born
at Canterbury, in February, 1563, was matriculated at
Benet College, Cambridge, in 1580, received his degree of
bachelor there in 1583 and of master in 1587. He came
early to London, and was already known as a dramatist
before the end of his twenty-fourth year. There is some
reason for thinking that he was at one time an actor. He
was killed in a tavern brawl, by a man named Archer, in
1593, at the age of thirty. He was taxed with atheism,
but on inadequate grounds, as it appears to me. That he
was said to have written a tract against the Trinity, for
which a license to print was refused on the ground of
blasphemy, might easily have led to the greater charge.
That he had some opinions of a kind unusual then may be
inferred, perhaps, from a passage in his 'Faust.' Faust
asks Mephistopheles how, being damned, he is out of hell.
And Mephistopheles answers, 'Why, this is hell, nor am I
out of it.' And a little farther on he explains himself
thus:-

   Hell hath no limits, nor is circumscribed
   In one self place; for where we are is hell,
   And where hell is there must we ever be;
   And, to conclude, when all the earth dissolves,
   And every creature shall be purified,
   All places shall be hell that are not heaven.

Milton remembered the first passage I have quoted, and
puts nearly the same words into the mouth of his Lucifer.
If Marlowe was a liberal thinker, it is not strange that
in that intolerant age he should have incurred the stigma
of general unbelief. Men are apt to blacken opinions
which are distasteful to them, and along with them the
character of him who holds them.
   This at least may be said of him without risk of vio-
lating the rule of *ne quid nimis*,(1) that he is one of the

most masculine and fecundating natures in the long line of
British poets. Perhaps his energy was even in excess.
There is in him an Oriental lavishness. He will impover-
ish a province for a simile, and pour the revenues of a
kingdom into the lap of a description. In that delightful
story in the book of Esdras, King Darius, who has just
dismissed all his captains and governors of cities and
satraps, after a royal feast, sends couriers galloping
after them to order them all back again, because he has
found a riddle under his pillow, and wishes their aid in
solving it. Marlowe in like manner calls in help from
every the remotest corner of earth and heaven for what
seems to us as trivial an occasion. I will not say that
he is bombastic, but he constantly pushes grandiosity to
the verge of bombast. His contemporaries thought he
passed it in his 'Tamburlaine.' His imagination flames
and flares, consuming what it should caress, as Jupiter
did Semele. That exquisite phrase of Hamlet, 'the modesty
of nature,' would never have occurred to him. Yet in the
midst of the hurly-burly there will fall a sudden hush,
and we come upon passages calm and pellucid as mountain
tarns filled to the brim with the purest distillations of
heaven. And, again, there are single verses that open
silently as roses, and surprise us with that seemingly
accidental perfection, which there is no use in talking
about because itself says all that is to be said and
more....
     Yes, Drayton was right in classing him with 'the first
poets,' for he was indeed such, and so continues, - that
is, he was that most indefinable thing, an original man,
and therefore as fresh and contemporaneous to-day as he
was three hundred years ago. Most of us are more or less
hampered by our own individuality, nor can shake ourselves
free of that chrysalis of consciousness and give our
'souls a loose,' as Dryden calls it in his vigorous way.
And yet it seems to me that there is something even finer
than that fine madness, and I think I see it in the imper-
turbable sanity of Shakespeare, which made him so much an
artist that his new work still bettered his old. I think
I see it even in the almost irritating calm of Goethe,
which, if it did not quite make him an artist, enabled
him to see what an artist should be, and to come as near
to being one as his nature allowed. Marlowe was certainly
not an artist in the larger sense, but he was cunning in
words and periods and the musical modulation of them. And
even this is a very rare gift. But his mind could never
submit itself to a controlling purpose, and renounce all
other things for the sake of that. His plays, with the
single exception of 'Edward II.,' have no organic unity,

and such unity as is here is more apparent than real.
Passages in them stir us deeply and thrill us to the
marrow, but each play as a whole is ineffectual. Even
his 'Edward II.' is regular only to the eye by a more
orderly arrangement of scenes and acts, and Marlowe evidently felt the drag of this restraint, for we miss the
uncontrollable energy, the eruptive fire, and the feeling
that he was happy in his work....
    There are, properly speaking, no characters in the
plays of Marlowe - but personages and interlocutors. We
do not get to know them, but only to know what they do
and say. The nearest appraoch to a character is Barabas,
in 'The Jew of Malta,' and he is but the incarnation of
the popular hatred of the Jew. There is really nothing
human in him. He seems a bugaboo rather than a man.
Here is his own account of himself:-

[Quotes II, iii, 175-201.]

    Here is nothing left for sympathy. This is the mere
lunacy of distempered imagination. It is shocking, and
not terrible. Shakespeare makes no such mistake with
Shylock. His passions are those of a man, though of a
man depraved by oppression and contumely; and he shows
sentiment, as when he says of the ring that Jessica had
given for a monkey: 'It was my turquoise. I had it of
Leah when I was a bachelor.' And yet, observe the profound humor with which Shakespeare makes him think first
of its dearness as a precious stone and then as a keep-
sake. In letting him exact his pound of flesh, he but
follows the story as he found it in Giraldi Cinthio, and
is careful to let us know that this Jew had good reason,
or thought he had, to hate Christians. At the end, I
think he meant us to pity Shylock, and we do pity him.
And with what a smiling background of love and poetry
does he give relief to the sombre figure of the Jew! In
Marlowe's play there is no respite. And yet it comes
nearer to having a connected plot, in which one event
draws on another, than any other of his plays. I do not
think Milman right in saying that the interest falls off
after the first two acts. I find enough to carry me on
to the end, where the defiant death of Barabas in a cal-
dron of boiling oil he had arranged for another victim
does something to make a man of him. But there is no
controlling reason in the piece. Nothing happens because
it must, but because the author wills it so. The conception of life is purely arbitrary, and as far from nature
as that of an imaginative child. It is curious, however,
that here, too, Marlowe should have pointed the way to

Shakespeare. But there is no resemblance between the Jew of Malta and the Jew of Venice, except that both have daughters whom they love. Nor is the analogy close even here. The love which Barabas professes for his child fails to humanize him to us, because it does not prevent him from making her the abhorrent instrument of his wanton malice in the death of her lover, and because we cannot believe him capable of loving anything but gold and vengeance. There is always something extravagant in the imagination of Marlowe, but here it is the extravagance of absurdity. Generally he gives us an impression of power, of vastness, though it be the vastness of chaos, where elemental forces hurtle blindly one against the other. But they are elemental forces, and not mere stage properties. Even Tamburlaine, if we see in him - as Marlowe, I think, meant that we should see - the embodiment of brute force, without reason and without conscience, ceases to be a blusterer, and becomes, indeed, as he asserts himself, the scourge of God. There is an exultation of strength in this play that seems to add a cubit to our stature. Marlowe had found the way that leads to style, and helped others to find it, but he never arrived there. He had not self-denial enough. He can refuse nothing to his fancy. He fails of his effect by over-emphasis, heaping upon a slender thought a burthen of expression too heavy for it to carry. But it is not with fagots, but with priceless Oriental stuffs, that he breaks their backs.

Marlowe's 'Dr. Faustus' interests us in another way. Here he again shows himself as a precursor. There is no attempt at profound philosophy in this play, and in the conduct of it Marlowe has followed the prose history of Dr. Faustus closely, even in its scenes of mere buffoonery. Disengaged from these, the figure of the protagonist is not without grandeur.... I may be reading into the book what is not there, but I cannot help thinking that Marlowe intended in this to typify the inevitably continuous degradation of a soul that has renounced its ideal, and the drawing on of one vice by another, for they go hand in hand like the Hours. But even in his degradation the pleasures of Faustus are mainly of the mind, or at worst of a sensuous and not sensual kind. No doubt of this Marlowe is unwittingly betraying his own tastes....

Was Marlowe, then, a great poet? For such a title he had hardly range enough of power, hardly reach enough of thought. But surely he had some of the finest qualities that go to the making of a great poet; and his poetic instinct, when he had time to give himself wholly over to its guidance, was unerring. I say when he had time enough for he, too, like his fellows, was forced to make

the daily task bring in the daily bread. We have seen
how fruitful his influence has been, and perhaps his
genius could have no surer warrant than that the charm of
it lingered in the memory of poets, for theirs is the
memory of mankind. If we allow him genius, what need to
ask for more? And perhaps it would be only to him among
the group of dramatists who surrounded Shakespeare that
we should allow it. He was the herald that dropped dead
in announcing the victory in whose fruits he was not to
share.

Note

1 Nothing too much.

48. GEORGE SAINTSBURY

1887

George Saintsbury (1845-1933), Professor of Rhetoric and
English Literature at Edinburgh (1895-1915), abundant
author of literary history and biography, connoisseur of
English prosody and of wine, is not so highly regarded
now as he once was. His observations about Marlowe's life
are conventional and his criticism prejudiced by the
unhappier elements in the tradition.
      From 'A History of Elizabethan Literature' (1887),
76-9.

But the interest of Marlowe's name has nothing to do with
these obscure scandals of three hundred years ago. He is
the undoubted author of some of the masterpieces of English verse; the hardly to be doubted author of others not
much inferior. Except the very greatest names - Shakespere, Milton, Spenser, Dryden, Shelley - no author can be
named who has produced, when the proper historical estimate is applied to him, such work as is to be found in
'Tamburlaine', 'Doctor Faustus', 'The Jew of Malta',
'Edward the Second', in one department; 'Hero and Leander' and the 'Passionate Shepherd' in another. I have but
very little doubt that the powerful, if formless, play of

'Lust's Dominion' is Marlowe's, though it may have been
rewritten, and the translations of Lucan and Ovid and the
minor work which is, more or less probably attributed to
him, swell his tale. Prose he did not write, perhaps
could not have written. For the one characteristic lacking to his genius was measure, and prose without measure,
as numerous examples have shown, is usually rubbish.
Even his dramas show a singular defect in the architect-
ural quality of literary genius. The vast and formless
creations of the writer's boundless fancy completely
master him; his aspirations after the immense too frequently leave him content with the simply unmeasured. In
his best play as a play, 'Edward the Second', the limitations of a historical story impose something like a restraining form on his glowing imagination. But fine as
this play is, it is noteworthy that no one of his greatest
things occurs in it. 'The Massacre at Paris', where he
also has the confinement of reality after a fashion, is
a chaotic thing as a whole, without any great beauty in
parts. The 'Tragedy of Dido' (to be divided between him
and Nash) is the worst thing he ever did. But in the
purely romantic subjects of 'Tamburlaine', 'Faustus', and
'The Jew of Malta', his genius, untrammelled by any limits
of story, showed itself equally unable to contrive such
limits for itself, and able to develop the most marvellous
beauties of detail. Shakespere himself has not surpassed,
which is equivalent to saying that no other writer has
equalled, the famous and wonderful passages in 'Tamburlaine' and 'Faustus', which are familiar to every student
of English literature as examples of the *ne plus ultra* of
the poetic powers, not of the language but of language.
The tragic imagination in its wildest flights has never
summoned up images of pity and terror more imposing, more
moving, that those excited by 'The Jew of Malta'. The
riot of passion and of delight in the beauty of colour and
form which characterises his version of 'Hero and Leander'
has never been approached by any writer. But Marlowe with
the fullest command of the *apeiron* had not, and as far as
I can judge, never would have had, any power of introducing into it the law of the *peras*. It is usual to say that
had he lived, and had his lot been happily cast, we should
have had two Shakesperes. This is not wise. In the first
place, Marlowe was totally destitute of humour - the
characteristic which, united with his tragic and imaginative powers, makes Shakespere as, in a less degree, it
makes Homer, and even, though the humour is grim and
intermittent, Dante. In other words, he was absolutely
destitute of the first requisite of self-criticism. In
the natural course of things, as the sap of his youthful

imagination ceased to mount, and as his craving for immen-
sity hardened itself, he would probably have degenerated
from bombast shot through with genius to bombast pure and
simple, from 'Faustus' to 'Lust's Dominion', and from
'Lust's Dominion' to 'Jeronimo' or 'The Distracted
Emperor'. Apart from the magnificent passages which he
can show, and which are simply intoxicating to any lover
of poetry, his great title to fame is the discovery of
the secret of that 'mighty line' which a seldom-erring
critic of his own day, not too generously given, vouch-
safed to him. Up to his time the blank verse line always,
and the semi-couplet in heroics, or member of the more
complicated stanza usually, were either stiff or nerveless.
Compared with his own work and with the work of his contemporaries and followers who learnt from him, they are
like a dried preparation, like something waiting for the
infusion of blood, for the inflation of living breath.
Marlowe came, and the old wooden versification, the old
lay figure structure of poetic rhythm, was cast once for
all into the lumber-room where only poetasters of the
lowest rank went to seek it. It is impossible to call
Marlowe a great dramatist, and the attempts that have been
made to make him out to be such remind one of the attempts
that have been made to call Molière a great poet. Marlowe
was one of the greatest poets of the world whose work was
cast by accident and caprice into an imperfect mould of
drama; Molière was one of the greatest dramatists of the
world who was obliged by fashion to use a previously per-
fected form of verse. The state of Molière was undoubtedly the more gracious; but the splendour of Marlowe's uncut
diamonds of poetry is the more wonderful.
   The characteristics of this strange and interesting
school may be summed up briefly, but are of the highest
importance in literary history. Unlike their nearest
analogues, the French romantics of fifty years ago, they
were all of academic education, and had even a decided
contempt (despite their Bohemian way of life) for un-
scholarly innovators. They manifested (except in Marlowe's fortuitous and purely genial discovery of the
secret of blank verse) a certain contempt for form, and
never, at least in drama, succeeded in mastering it. But
being all, more or less, men of genius, and having the
keenest sense of poetry, they supplied the dry bones of
the precedent dramatic model with blood and breath, with
vigour and variety, which not merely informed but transformed it. 'David and Bethsaba', 'Doctor Faustus', 'Friar
Bacon and Friar Bungay', are chaotic enough, but they are
of the chaos that precedes cosmic development. The almost
insane bombast that marks the whole school has (as has

been noticed) the character of the shrieks and gesticula-
tions of healthy childhood, and the insensibility to the
really comic which also marks them is of a similar kind.
Every one knows how natural it is to childhood to appreciate bad jokes, how seldom a child sees a good one. Marlowe and his crew, too (the comparison has no doubt often
been used before), were of the brood of Otus and Ephialtes,
who grew so rapidly and in so disorderly a fashion that it
was necessary for the gods to make an end of them. The
universe probably lost little, and it certainly gained
something.

49. HAVELOCK ELLIS

1887

Havelock Ellis (1859-1939) wrote widely and influentially
in literature, psychology, sociology and science. He
founded the Mermaid Series of the best plays of the old
dramatists, of which the Marlowe volume was the first.
    From 'Christopher Marlowe', ed. H. Ellis (1887),
xxxiv-xxxv, xlii, xlvi-xlvii.

For us, however, the wonder of 'Tamburlaine,' and of Marlowe's work generally, lies in the vivid and passionate
blood, in the intensely imaginative form, with which he
has clothed the dry bones of his story. He had no power
of *creative* imagination; Shakespeare borrows his stories,
but he makes it alive with his own soaring passion. With
the exception of 'Edward II.,' which stands alone, Marlowe's dramas are mostly series of scenes held together
by the poetic energy of his own dominating personality.
He is his own hero, and the sanguinary Scythian utters
the deepest secrets of the artist's heart. 'What is
beauty?' he asks himself.

[Quotes 1 'Tamb.', V, ii, 97-110.]

Tamburlaine is a divinely strong and eagerhearted poet,
and these words are the key to his career. He sees for
ever an unattainable loveliness beckoning him across the
world, and how can his ardent blood rest 'attemptless,

faint and destitute?'

[Quotes 1 'Tamb.', II, vii, 21-7.]

the rest is Scythian bathos. Like Shelley, in some prior
state of existence he had loved an Antigone, and he cannot
stay. But like Keats also he has an intense feeling for
the imaginative show and colour of things, of milk-white
steeds laden with the heads of slain men, and

> Besmeared with blood that makes a dainty show,

of naked negroes, of bassoes clothed in crimson silk, of
Turkey carpets beneath the chariot wheels, and of a hundred kings or more with 'so many crowns of burnished
gold.' He is intoxicated with the physical splendours of
imagination, with the vast and mysterious charm of old-
world cities, of Bagdad and Babylon and Samarcand.

> 'And ride in triumph through Persepolis!'
> Is it not brave to be a king, Techelles?
> Usumcasane and Theridamas,
> Is it not passing brave to be a king,
> 'And ride in triumph through Persepolis?'

With this song of radiant joy in the unattainable, young
Kit Marlowe, like another Christopher, sailed to discover
countries yet unknown, to attain the 'sweet fruition' of
his crown....
    In 'Edward II.' Marlowe reached the summit of his art.
    There is little here of that *amour de l'impossible*,
which is, as Mr. Symonds observes, his characteristic
note; his passionate poetry is subdued with severe self-
restraint in a supreme tragic creation. It has long been
a custom among critics to compare 'Edward II.' with
'Richard II.' This is scarcely fair to Shakespeare; the
melodramatic and careless murder of Richard cannot be mentioned in presence of the chastened tragedy and highly-
wrought pathos of Edward's last days; the whole of Shakespeare's play, with its exuberant eloquence, its facile
and diffuse poetry, is distinctly inferior to Marlowe's,
both in organic structure and in dramatic characterisa-
tion. It was not till ten years later that Shakespeare
came near to this severe reticence, these deep and solemn
tragic tones.
    There is, at last, one precious fragment which we
cannot afford to pass by, for it bears Marlowe's intensely
personal impress. Without this fragment of 'Hero and
Leander' we should not have known the full sweetness and

range of his genius. It is the brightest flower of the
English Renaissance, apart from that moral energy of the
Reformation of which Chapman, together with something less
than usual of his elaborate obscurity, afterwards gave it
some faint tincture. It is a free and fresh and eager
song, 'drunk with gladness,' - like Hero who 'stayed not
for her robes,' but straight arose to open the door to her
lover - full of ideal beauty that finds its expression in
the form and colour of things, above all in the bodies of
men and women; for the passion of love, apart from the
passion of beauty, Marlowe failed to grasp. No Elizabethan had so keen a sense of physical loveliness as these
lines reveal: -

[Quotes I, 61-9, 'His body was as straight....']

Shakespeare could not have been younger than Marlowe when
he wrote his 'Venus and Adonis,' which has ever since been
coupled with Marlowe's poem. 'Venus and Adonis' is
oppressive with its unexpanded power; its workmanship is
perhaps more searching and thorough, though so much less
felicitous than that of 'Hero and Leander'; but we turn
away with delight from its massive monotonous energy, its
close and sensual atmosphere, to the free and open air,
the colour and light, the swift and various music of
Marlowe's poem. Shelley has scarcely surpassed the sweet
gravity which the verse of 'our elder Shelley' here
reaches.

50. MARLOWE IN THE LITERARY SOCIETIES (a)

1888

From the proceedings of the Clifton Shakspere Society,
22 May, 1888, in the 'Academy' (13 October 1888), xxxiv,
419-20.

MEETINGS OF SOCIETIES.

CLIFTON SHAKSPERE SOCIETY. - (Saturday, May 22).

J. H. Tucker Esq., in the Chair - Mr. W. Prowse, in a

paper which he read on 'Edward II.,' said that he considered this 'Chronicle' in some respects superior to the
early Shaksperian history-plays, and, with the exception
of some of Shakspere's studies, the finest historical
drama in our language. There are passages in it in which
Marlowe rises to sublime poetic pitch. In the Abdication
scene, Edward opens the debate in a speech of such rich
and varied harmony that in this is to be seen the master's perfect command of his own mighty line. Marlowe's
inferiority to Shakspere is shown in his want of the sense
of humour and in his inability to draw a woman's character. - Miss Emma Phipson sent A few Notes on 'Edward II.,'
in which she said that it seemed to her that, in the
narrow limits to which Marlowe confines himself, he
approaches very closely to Shakspere, if he does not
excel him, in vigour of expression and in boldness of
conception. Marlowe does not trouble himself to depict
the varying moods and inconsistencies of character that
give such reality to Shakspere's personages. He fixed
generally on a single quality, and brings out that quality
with wonderful force. It may be that he had not sufficient skill to analyse more deeply the springs of conduct;
but it was more likely that he deliberately chose to
invest his characters with a singleness of purpose and
definiteness of aim which certainly give to his work a
great charm. None of his characters appear to act from
principle, but solely from impulse; their ideas of right
and wrong are hazy in the extreme. We therefore do not
consider whether, if they were living people, we should
like to have them as friends, as we do many of Shakspere's characters. Marlowe's people do not moralise much
about their actions, and, above all, they do not grow.
They come into the play as counters, ready stamped. Such
as they are in the first act, they continue to the last.
Miss Phipson, after referring to many of the characters
in 'Tamburlaine,' went on to say that she considered
'Edward II.' a very uninteresting production. The repe-
titions are tedious. The last scene, so much admired, is
too horrible to be tragic. The repulsive details, which
may consistently be told in a narrative poem, are out of
place in the dramatic form, which is primarily intended
for acting. In this play there are several illustrations
of Marlowe's knowledge of natural phenomena; and many of
them suggest parallel passages in 'Henry VI.,' and are
interesting in relation to the controversy as to its joint
authorship. - Mr. John Taylor read An Historical Note on
'Edward II.'... A paper by Mr. J. W. Mills on 'Tamburlaine' was read. Mr. Mills chose this play as well exhi-
biting Marlowe's style and power. He said that when we

note the wonderful group of Elizabethan dramatists, we are led to the reflection that in the literature of other nations also dramatic art suddenly reached the zenith of absolute perfection in the hands of two or three contemporaries. The valorous survivors of Marathon, and the heroic seamen who manned the wooden walls of Salamis to rescue Greece and European culture from the gorgeous sensuality of Persian barbarism, might have heard, in the evening of their days, the roll of the thunder of Aeschylus in delightful alternation with the noble eloquence of Sophocles and the tender pathos of the dramatist of love. So in France Corneille, Racine, and Molière arose within the brief space of thirty years; and a like period, in that tranquil epoch of peaceful development succeeding to those sanguinary conflicts that the militant Duchy of Prussia went staggering through, was made illustrious by the birth of Lessing, Goethe, and Schiller. It would, doubtless, in these cases be interesting to inquire what mighty political upheaval among the nations prepared the soil, and what fervent intellectual commotion sowed the seed whence these splendid harvests of literary wealth were gathered into the granary of the world's thought; but as the connexion between 'Tamburlaine' and Shakspere is unquestionable, a close examination of that play is necessary in the study of the literary relations of the Elizabethan dramatists. It is manifest that it was the great success of 'Tamburlaine' which led to the production of the 'Troublesome Raigne of King John.' 'Tamburlaine' marks a great advance in art upon 'Ferrex and Porrex,' or 'Locrine,' and it presents the finality of form for English dramatic writing. In itself, as a spectacle of military bustle and of Oriental gorgeousness, it was in perfect harmony with the taste of the age. Certain episodes of the play, however much they may shock us by their barbarous inhumanity, would exactly hit the tone of thought in a pre-Shaksperian audience, ignorant, uncritical, and, as yet, untrained to the higher pleasures of a refined stage. 'Tamburlaine,' moreover, had some legitimate claims upon popular affection. As a reflex of the spirit of the period, it is all a-blaze with fantastic gems and gold. Again, as in Marlowe's time the most formidable power was neither Spain nor yet the Holy Roman Empire, but the Ottoman Kingdom, passages in 'Tamburlaine' referring to the subjugation of the Turks must have been a delight to an Elizabethan audience. There were also secondary causes which contributed to the success of the play. The ease, fluency, and grace of much of the versification must strike the most careless reader. Sometimes the sentiments are admirable and

beautiful, and their expression most melodious. In this
production of Marlowe's prolific youth, fitful corusca-
tions of genius foreshadowed the highest possibilities of
art. Lines there are, and even passages, quite worthy of
Shakspere. Here and there are some he seems to have
borrowed. That Marlowe may have held atheistical notions
is quite consistent with certain parts of the play; but
there is here no evidence to support the other charge
brought against him of leading a life of gross immorality
and licentiousness. On the contrary, it is extremely
improbable that 'Tamburlaine' could be the work of a man
swayed by libidinous impulses, and holding cheap the
virtue and purity of womanhood. It must be said that the
play abounds in bathos, but from this Shakspere himself
was not entirely free. In the case of 'Tamburlaine,' an
audience would conceive that it was merely that hyperbolical mode of Oriental speech, such as they found in its
more subdued tones even in the Hebrew Scriptures. Anyone
who, with even judgment and attentive mind, reads through
this play, must admire the marvellous ripeness of Marlowe's powers when he was but twenty-two years of age, and
deplore that lofty spirit -

    Still climbing after knowledge infinite,
    And always moving as the restless spheres,

which went down suddenly into darkness, ere yet his sun
had reached the noon. - Mr. Walter Strachan read an
account of The 1886 Pilgrimage to Stratford, recording,
with interesting detail, the doings of a party of the
society who paid a visit to Stratford on May 18. - This
meeting brought to an end the Society's eleventh session.
The plays for next session are 'Merchant of Venice,'
'Friar Bacon and Friar Bungay,' 1 'Henry IV,.' 'London
Prodigal,' 2 'Henry IV.,' 'Edward III.,' 'Henry V.,'
'Every Man in His Humour.' The hon. secretary (Mr. L. M.
Griffiths, 9 Gordon Road, Clifton) will be grateful for
any magazine articles, newspaper scraps, or anything else
to add to the society's library.

51. MARLOWE IN THE LITERARY SOCIETIES (b)

1888

From the proceedings of the Elizabethan Literary Society,
3 October 1888, in the 'Academy' (13 October 1888), xxxiv,
24.

MEETINGS OF SOCIETIES.

ELIZABETHAN LITERARY SOCIETY. -
(*Wednesday, October 3.*)

W. H. Cowsam, Esq., in the chair. - A paper was read on
Marlowe's 'Tamburlaine the Great,' by Mr. Frederick
Rogers. 'It is not often,' said Mr. Rogers, 'that a new
development in literary art is ushered in by the applause
of the common people. But "Tamburlaine the Great" was a
popular as well as an epoch-making play. Popular in the
best, as well as in the worst, sense; popular because it
reflected alike the chivalry and the cruelty of the age
in which it was written; epoch-making because it was the
first play acted in England that was written in blank
verse, and having seen it men could go back to the old
forms no more. But the popular audiences who applauded
"Tamburlaine" were utterly unconscious that the play which
was giving them such keen pleasure was also effecting a
revolution in dramatic and literary art; and the faults of
it, which lie so near the surface for us, were not faults,
but rather merits to them. They would understand the
passion, and in a dim, half unconscious way, would understand the poetry of it; but the "great and thundering
speech" of Tamburlaine would appeal to them most, and
would stir the same emotions and win the same applause
that a noisy and sensational player wins from the gallery
of to-day. It is a young man's play - a young man who
came out of the ranks of the people, and not from among
its leaders, and who, therefore, had within him many
popular sympathies and popular prejudices, which his education at Cambridge might modify but would not entirely
destroy. At the first glance there is much that appears
superficial and childish in the aims of Tamburlaine. Tremendous energy, almost superhuman power, put forth for no
higher purpose that the "sweet fruition of an earthly
crown." But we find also in the play such a picture of

the vicissitudes and misfortunes attending upon royal
power and material splendour as had surely never been
presented in English dramatic literature before. An
epoch-making play indeed, for it showed the men of that
age that all the things they were admiring and worship-
ping - kings, queens, titles, thrones, even nations and
kingdoms - were mere pawns to be moved hither and thither
upon the chessboard of the world by any man whose supreme
genius and determined will had conquered the rules of the
game. A dangerous truth this, if they had been capable of
understanding it, which the stage had never taught them
before. Tamburlaine, notwithstanding his cruel nature,
has a full share of the indomitable spirit which marked
the heroes of the Elizabethan age, and is more an Elizabethan than a mediaeval conqueror. There is an under-
current of contempt for the trumpery trinkets which are
the highest prizes the world can offer, and in the lulls
of warfare he finds time to muse on the great spiritual
realities. He conquers kings, and gives their crowns to
his inferior officers. The pleasure that he values is
that which comes of the exercise of his all-conquering
power. The whole play is full of a profound contempt for
royalty. The tributary kings are mere accessories to the
mighty soldier. They occupy positions very much like
those of supernumeraries in a modern pantomime. A gaoler
who is false to his trust is made a king; kings are harnessed to chariots and made to do the work that slaves
sometimes did in Egypt and Rome, are led about by common
soldiers, beaten with whips, kept in cages, used as
footstools; and the kings of Natolia and Jerusalem are
described as "two spare kings," who are kept as men keep
post horses - to be used when the other kings are tired.
All this, said Colonel Cunningham, is "glorious rant." So
no doubt it is, and it makes us laugh when it is not meant
to; but, in an age when royalty was worshipped, was ever
royalty so satirised before? But Tamburlaine is himself a
king - a king of kings! Yes! but, by virtue of no divine
right ; by his splendid energy and his intellectual power.
With all its imperfections on its head, "Tamburlaine"
remains for us a great English play, for in it are
revealed in all their strange distorted splendour the
romantic hopes and fancies of a poet who was filled with
the spirit of a romantic age. Half a pagan, yet not
blind to the spiritual beauty of the creed of Christ, Kit
Marlowe played with the objects of men's reverence and
worship as children play with toys. Not because he was
without reverence for things worthy of it, but because he
saw that neither the secrets of nature, nor the forces and
motives which govern the actions of men, were in the

keeping of kings or of churches, but were ready to become
the servants of any man who had learned the secrets of
their control. Not for him was any such mighty task, for
he had not learned the initial secret of all - how to
control himself! Like his Tamburlaine, he was a giant in
his aspirations, but a headstrong boy in his actions.'

52. A. C. SWINBURNE

1875, 1896, 1908

Algernon Charles Swinburne (1837-1909), poet and critic,
found in Marlowe a kindred spirit. He could be both per-
ceptive and savage as a critic, though these selections
hardly show these qualities.
   (a) From 'The Works of George Chapman: Poems and Minor
Translations' (1875), lix-lx, lxv-lxvi.

The name of Chapman should always be held great; yet must
it always at first recall the names of greater men. For
one who thinks of him as the author of his best play or
his loftiest lines of gnomic verse a score will at once
remember him as the translator of Homer or the continuator of Marlowe. The most daring enterprise of a life
which was full of daring aspiration and arduous labour
was this of resuming and completing the 'mighty line'
of 'Hero and Leander.' For that poem stands out alone
amid all the wide and wild poetic wealth of its teeming
and turbulent age, as might a small shrine of Parian
sculpture amid the rank splendour of a tropic jungle.
But no metaphor can aptly express the rapture of relief
with which you come upon it amid the poems of Chapman,
and drink once more with your whole heart of that well
of sweet water after the long draughts you have taken
from such brackish and turbid springs as gush up among
the sands and thickets of his verse. Faultless indeed
this lovely fragment is not; it also bears traces of the
Elizabethan barbarism, as though the great queen's ruff
and farthingale had been clapped about the neck and waist
of the Medicean Venus; but for all the strange costume we
can see that the limbs are perfect still. The name of
Marlowe's poem has been often coupled with that of the

'first heir' of Shakespeare's 'invention;' but with all
reverence to the highest name in letters be it said, the
comparison is hardly less absurd than a comparison of
'Tamburlaine' with 'Othello.' With all its overcrowding
beauties of detail, Shakespeare's first poem is on the
whole a model of what a young man of genius should not
write on such a subject; Marlowe's is a model of what he
should. Scarcely the art of Titian at its highest, and
surely not the art of Shakespeare at its dawn, could have
made acceptable such an inversion of natural rule as is
involved in the attempted violation by a passionate woman
of a passionless boy; the part of a Joseph, as no less a
moralist than Henri Beyle has observed in his great work.
on 'Love,' has always a suspicion about it of something
ridiculous and offensive: but only the wretchedest of
artists could wholly fail to give charm to the picture of
such a nuptial night as that of Hero and Leander. The
style of Shakespeare's first essay is, to speak frankly,
for the most part no less vicious than the matter: it is
burdened and bedizened with all the heavy and fantastic
jewellery of Gongora and Marini; it is written throughout
in the style which an Italian scholar knows as that of the
scientisti, and which the duncery of New Grubstreet in its
immeasurable ignorance would probably designate as 'Della-
Cruscan;' nay, there are yet, I believe, in that quarter
rhymesters and libellers to be found who imagine such men
as Guido Cavalcanti and Dante Alighieri to have been
representative members of the famous and farinaceous academy. Not one of the faults chargeable on Shakespeare's
beautiful but faultful poem can justly be charged on the
only not faultless poem of Marlowe. The absence of all
cumbrous jewels and ponderous embroideries from the sweet
and limpid loveliness of its style is not more noticeable
than the absence of such other and possibly such graver
flaws as deform and diminish the undeniable charms of
'Venus and Adonis.' With leave or without leave of a
much lauded critic who could see nothing in the glorified
version or expansion by Marlowe of the little poem of
Musaeus but 'a paraphrase, in every sense of the epithet,
of the most licentious kind,' I must avow that I want and
am well content to want the sense, whatever it be, which
would enable me to discern more offence in that lovely
picture of the union of two lovers in body as in soul than
I can discern in the parting of Romeo and Juliet. And if
it be always a pleasure to read a page of Marlowe, to read
it after a page of Chapman is to the capable student of
high verse 'a pleasure worthy Xerxes the great king.'
Yet there is not a little to be advanced in favour of
Chapman's audacious and arduous undertaking. The poet was

not alive, among all the mighty men then living, who could
worthily have completed the divine fragment of Marlowe.
As well might we look now to find a sculptor who could
worthily restore for us the arms of the Venus of Melos -
'Our Lady of Beauty,' as Heine said when lying at her feet
stricken to death, 'who has no hands, and cannot help us.'
For of narrative poets there were none in that generation
of any note but Drayton and Daniel; and though these might
have more of Marlowe's limpid sweetness and purity of
style they lacked the force and weight of Chapman. Nor is
the continuation by any means altogether such as we might
have expected it to be - a sequel by Marsyas to the song
of Apollo....
     In Marlowe the passion of ideal love for the ultimate
idea of beauty in art or nature found its perfect and
supreme expression, faultless and unforced. The radiant
ardour of his desire, the light and the flame of his
aspiration, diffused and shed through all the forms of
his thought and all the colours of his verse, gave them
such shapeliness and strength of life as is given to the
spirits of the greatest poets alone. He, far rather than
Chaucer or Spenser, whose laurels were first fed by the
dews and sunbeams of Italy and France, whose songs were
full of sweet tradition from oversea, of memories and
notes which 'came mended from their tongues,' - he alone
was the true Apollo of our dawn, the bright and morning
star of the full midsummer day of English poetry at its
highest. Chaucer, Wyatt, and Spenser had left our language as melodious, as fluent, as flexible to all purposes of narrative or lyrical poetry as it could be made
by the grace of genius; the supreme note of its possible
music was reserved for another to strike. Of English
blank verse, one of the few highest forms of verbal
harmony or poetic expression, the genius of Marlowe was
the absolute and divine creator. By mere dint of original and godlike instinct he discovered and called it into
life; and at his untimely and unhappy death, more lamentable to us all than any other on record except Shelley's
he left the marvellous instrument of his invention so
nearly perfect that Shakespeare first and afterwards
Milton came to learn of him before they could vary or
improve on it. In the changes rung by them on the keys
first tuned by Marlowe we trace a remembrance of the
touches of his hand; in his own cadences we catch not a
note of any other man's. This poet, a poor scholar of
humblest parentage, lived to perfect the exquisite metre
invented for narrative by Chaucer, giving it (to my ear
at least) more of weight and depth, of force and full-
ness, than its founder had to give; he invented the

highest and hardest form of English verse, the only
instrument since found possible for our tragic or epic
poetry; he created the modern tragic drama; and at the
age of thirty he went

> Where Orpheus and where Homer are.

Surely there are not more than two or three names in any
literature which can be set above the poet's of whom this
is the least that can in simple truth be said. There is
no record extant of his living likeness; if his country
should ever bear men worthy to raise a statue or monu-
ment to his memory, he should stand before or colour something that will not be expressed or attained, nor pass
into the likeness of any perishable life; but though all
were done that all poets could do,

> Yet should there hover in their restless heads,
> One thought, one grace, one wonder, at the least,
> Which into words no virtue can digest.

No poet ever came nearer than Marlowe to the expression
of this inexpressible beauty, to the incarnation in actual
form of ideal perfection, to the embodiment in mortal
music of immortal harmony; and he it is who has left on
record and on evidence to all time the truth that no poet
can ever come nearer.

(b) The Prologue to 'Doctor Faustus' for William Poel's
production of 1896; text from 'The Tragical History of
Doctor Faustus ... as revived by the Elizabethan Stage
Society', etc., ed. A. H. Bullen (1904).

> Light, as when dawn takes wind and smites the sea,
> Smote England when his day bade Marlowe be.
> No fire so keen had thrilled the clouds of time
> Since Dante's breath made Italy sublime.
> Earth, bright with flowers whose dew shone soft as
>   tears,
> Through Chaucer cast her charm on eyes and ears:
> The lustrous laughter of the love-lit earth
> Rang, leapt, and lightened in his might of mirth.
> Deep moonlight, hallowing all the breathless air,
> Made earth and heaven for Spenser faint and fair.
> But song might bid not heaven and earth be one
> Till Marlowe's voice gave warning of the sun.
> Thought quailed and fluttered as a wounded bird
> Till passion fledged the wing of Marlowe's word.

Faith born of fear bade hope and doubt be dumb
Till Marlowe's pride bade light or darkness come.
Then first our speech was thunder: then our song
Shot lightning through the clouds that wrought us
    wrong.
Blind fear, whose faith feeds hell with fire, became
A moth self-shrivelled in its own blind flame.
We heard in tune with even our seas that roll,
The speech of storm, the thunders of the soul,
Men's passions clothed with all the woes they wrought,
Shone through the fire of man's transfiguring thought.
The thirst of knowledge, quenchless at her springs,
Ambition, fire that clasps the thrones of kings.
Love, light that makes of life one lustrous hour,
And song, the soul's chief crown and throne of power,
The hungering heart of greed and ravenous hate,
Made music high as heaven and deep as fate.
Strange pity, scarce half scornful of her tear,
In Berkeley's vaults bowed down on Edward's bier.
But higher in forceful flight of song than all
The soul of man, its own imperious thrall,
Rose, when his royal spirit of fierce desire
Made life and death for man one flame of fire.
Incarnate man, fast bound as earth and sea
Spake, when his pride would fain set Faustus free.
Eternal beauty, strong as day and night,
Shone, when his word bade Helen back to sight.
Fear when he bowed his soul before her spell,
Thundered and lightened through the vaults of hell.
The music known of all men's tongues that sing,
When Marlowe sang, bade love make heaven of spring;
The music none but English tongues may make,
Our own sole song, spake first when Marlowe spake;
And on his grave, though there no stone may stand,
The flower it shows was laid by Shakespeare's hand.

(c) From 'The Age of Shakespeare' (1908) 1-14.

The first great English poet was the father of English
tragedy and the creator of English blank verse. Chaucer
and Spenser were great writers and great men: they shared
between them every gift which goes to the making of a
poet, in the proper sense of the word, great. Neither
pathos nor humour nor fancy nor invention will suffice
for that: no poet is great as a poet whom no one could
ever pretend to recognise as sublime. Sublimity is the
test of imagination as distinguished from invention or
from fancy: and the first English poet whose powers can

be called sublime was Christopher Marlowe.
The majestic and exquisite excellence of various lines
and passages in Marlowe's first play must be admitted to
relieve, if it cannot be allowed to redeem, the stormy
monotony of Titanic truculence which blusters like a sim-
oom through the noisy course of its ten fierce acts. With
many and heavy faults, there is something of genuine
greatness in 'Tamburlaine the Great'; and for two grave
reasons it must always be remembered with distinction and
mentioned with honour. It is the first poem ever written
in English blank verse, as distinguished from mere rhyme-
less decasyllabics; and it contains one of the noblest
passages, perhaps indeed the noblest in the literature of
the world, ever written by one of the greatest masters of
poetry in loving praise of the glorious delights and sublime submission to the everlasting limits of his art. In
its highest and most distinctive qualities, in unfalter-
ing and infallible command of the right note of music and
the proper tone of colour for the finest touches of poetic
execution, no poet of the most elaborate modern school,
working at ease upon every consummate resource of luxurious learning and leisurely refinement, has ever excelled
the best and most representative work of a man who had
literally no models before him, and probably or evidently
was often, if not always, compelled to write against time
for his living.
    The just and generous judgment passed by Goethe on the
'Faustus' of his English predecessor in tragic treatment
of the same subject is somewhat more than sufficient to
counterbalance the slighting or the sneering references
to that magnificent poem which might have been expected
from the ignorance of Byron or the incompetence of Hallam.
And the particular note of merit observed, the special
point of the praise conferred, by the great German poet
should be no less sufficient to dispose of the vulgar
misconception yet lingering among sciolists and preten-
ders to criticism, which regards a writer than whom no
man was ever born with a finer or a stronger instinct for
perfection of excellence in execution as a mere noble
savage of letters, a rough self-taught sketcher or scrib-
bler of crude and rude genius, whose unhewn blocks of
verse had in them some veins of rare enough metal to be
quarried and polished by Shakespeare. What most impressed
the author of 'Faust' in the work of Marlowe was a quality
the want of which in the author of 'Manfred' is proof
enough to consign his best work to the second or third
class at most. 'How greatly it is all planned!' the
first requisite of all great work, and one of which the
highest genius possible to a greatly gifted barbarian

could by no possibility understand the nature or conceive
the existence. That Goethe 'had thought of translating
it' is perhaps hardly less precious a tribute to its
greatness than the fact that it has been actually and
admirably translated by the matchless translator of Shakespeare - the son of Victor Hugo; whose labours of love may
thus be said to have made another point in common, and
forged as it were another link of union, between Shakespeare and the young master of Shakespeare's youth. Of
all great poems in dramatic form it is perhaps the most
remarkable for absolute singleness of aim and simplicity
of construction; yet is it wholly free from all possible
imputation of monotony or aridity. 'Tamburlaine' is monotonous in the general roll and flow of its stately and
sonorous verse through a noisy wilderness of perpetual
bluster and slaughter; but the unity of tone and purpose
in 'Doctor Faustus' is not unrelieved by change of manner
and variety of incident. The comic scenes, written evidently with as little of labour as of relish, are for the
most part scarcely more than transcripts, thrown into the
form of dialogue, from a popular prose 'History of Doctor
Faustus'; and therefore should be set down as little to
the discredit as to the credit of the poet. Few masterpieces of any age in any language can stand beside this
tragic poem - it has hardly the structure of a play - for
the qualities of terror and splendour, for intensity of
purpose and sublimity of note. In the vision of Helen,
for example, the intense perception of loveliness gives
actual sublimity to the sweetness and radiance of mere
beauty in the passionate and spontaneous selection of
words the most choice and perfect; and in like manner the
sublimity of simplicity in Marlowe's conception and
expression of the agonies endured by Faustus under the
immediate imminence of his doom gives the highest note
of beauty, the quality of absolute fitness and propriety,
to the sheer straightforwardness of speech in which his
agonising horror finds vent ever more and more terrible
from the first to the last equally beautiful and fearful
verse of that tremendous monologue which has no parallel
in all the range of tragedy.
    It is now a commonplace of criticism to observe and
regret the decline of power and interest after the opening
acts of 'The Jew of Malta.' This decline is undeniable,
though even the latter part of the play is not wanting in
rough energy and a coarse kind of interest; but the first
two acts would be sufficient foundation for the durable
fame of a dramatic poet. In the blank verse of Milton
alone, who perhaps was hardly less indebted than Shakespeare was before him to Marlowe as the first English

master of word-music in its grander forms, has the glory
or the melody of passages in the opening soliloquy of
Barabas been possibly surpassed. The figure of the hero
before it degenerates into caricature is as finely touched
as the poetic execution is excellent; and the rude and
rapid sketches of the minor characters show at least some
vigour and vivacity of touch.

In 'Edward the Second' the interest rises and the execution improves as visibly and as greatly with the course
of the advancing story as they decline in 'The Jew of
Malta.' The scene of the king's deposition at Kenilworth
is almost as much finer in tragic effect and poetic quality
quality as it is shorter and less elaborate than the
corresponding scene in Shakespeare's 'King Richard II.'
The terror of the death-scene undoubtedly rises into
horror; but this horror is with skilful simplicity of
treatment preserved from passing into disgust. In pure
poetry, in sublime and splendid imagination, this tragedy
is excelled by 'Doctor Faustus'; in dramatic power and
positive impression of natural effect it is as certainly
the masterpiece of Marlowe. It was almost inevitable, in
the hands of any poet but Shakespeare, that none of the
characters represented should be capable of securing or
even exciting any finer sympathy or more serious interest
than attends on the mere evolution of successive events or
the mere display of emotions (except always in the great
scene of the deposition) rather animal than spiritual in
their expression of rage or tenderness or suffering. The
exact balance of mutual effect, the final note of scenic
harmony between ideal conception and realistic execution,
is not yet struck with perfect accuracy of touch and
security of hand; but on this point also Marlowe has here
come nearer by many degrees to Shakespeare than any of his
other predecessors have ever come near to Marlowe.

Of 'The Massacre at Paris' it is impossible to judge
fairly from the garbled fragment of its genuine text which
is all that has come down to us. To Mr. Collier, among
numberless other obligations, we owe the discovery of a
striking passage excised in the piratical edition which
gives us the only version extant of this unlucky play; and
which, it must be allowed, contains nothing of quite equal
value. This is obviously an occasional and polemical
work, and being as it is overcharged with the anti-
Catholic passion of the time, has a typical quality which
gives it some empirical significance and interest. That
antipapal ardour is indeed the only note of unity in a
rough and ragged chronicle which shambles and stumbles
onward from the death of Queen Jeanne of Navarre to the
murder of the last Valois. It is possible to conjecture

what it would be fruitless to affirm, that it gave a hint
in the next century to Nathaniel Lee for his far superior
and really admirable tragedy on the same subject, issued
ninety-seven years after the death of Marlowe.
   The tragedy of 'Dido, Queen of Carthage,' was probably
completed for the stage after that irreparable and incal-
culable loss to English letters by Thomas Nash, the
worthiest English precursor of Swift in vivid, pure, and
passionate prose, embodying the most terrible and splendid
qualities of a personal and social satirist; a man gifted
also with some fair faculty of elegiac and even lyric
verse, but in no wise qualified to put on the buskin left
behind him by the 'famous gracer of tragedians,' as Marlowe had already been designated by their common friend
Greene from among the worthiest of his fellows. In this
somewhat thin-spun and evidently hasty play a servile
fidelity to the text of Virgil's narrative has naturally
resulted in the failure which might have been expected
from an attempt at once to transcribe what is essentially
inimitable and to reproduce it under the hopelessly alien
conditions of dramatic adaptation. The one really noble
passage in a generally feeble and incomposite piece of
work is, however, uninspired by the unattainable model to
which the dramatists have been only too obsequious in
their subservience.
   It is as nearly certain as anything can be which
depends chiefly upon cumulative and collateral evidence
that the better part of what is best in the serious scenes
of 'King Henry VI.' is mainly the work of Marlowe. That
he is, at any rate, the principal author of the second and
third plays passing under that name among the works of
Shakespeare, but first and imperfectly printed as 'The
Contention between the two Famous Houses of York and Lan-
caster,' can hardly be now a matter of debate among competent judges. The crucial difficulty of criticism in
this matter is to determine, if indeed we should not
rather say to conjecture, the authorship of the humorous
scenes in prose, showing as they generally do a power of
comparatively high and pure comic realism to which nothing
in the acknowledged works of any pre-Shakespearean dramatist is even remotely comparable. Yet, especially in the
original text of these scenes as they stand unpurified by
the ultimate revision of Shakespeare there are tones and
touches which recall rather the clownish horseplay and
homely ribaldry of his predecessors than anything in the
lighter interludes of his very earliest plays. We find
the same sort of thing which we find in their writings,
only better done than they usually do it, rather than such
work as Shakespeare's a little worse done than usual. And

even in the final text of the tragic or metrical scenes
the highest note struck is always, with one magnificent
and unquestionable exception, rather in the key of Marlowe at his best than of Shakespeare while yet in great
measure his disciple.

It is another commonplace of criticism to affirm that
Marlowe had not a touch of comic genius, not a gleam of
wit in him or a twinkle of humour: but it is an indisputable fact that he had. In 'The Massacre at Paris,' the
soliloquy of the soldier lying in wait for the minion of
Henri III. has the same very rough but very real humour
as a passage in the 'Contention' which was cancelled by
the reviser. The same hand is unmistakable in both these
broad and boyish outbreaks of unseemly but undeniable fun:
and if we might wish it rather less indecorous, we must
admit that the tradition which denies all sense of humour
and all instinct of wit to the first great poet of England
is no less unworthy of serious notice or elaborate refuta-
tion than the charges and calumnies of an informer who was
duly hanged the year after Marlowe's death. For if the
same note of humour is struck in an undoubted play of
Marlowe's and in a play of disputed authorship, it is
evident that the rest of the scene in the latter play
must also be Marlowe's. And in that unquestionable case
the superb and savage humour of the terribly comic scenes
which represent with such rough magnificence of realism
the riot of Jack Cade and his ruffians through the ravaged
streets of London must be recognisable as no other man's
than his. It is a pity we have not before us for comparison the comic scenes or burlesque interludes of 'Tamburlaine' which the printer or publisher, as he had the
impudence to avow in his prefatory note, purposely omitted
and left out.

The author of 'A Study of Shakespeare' was therefore
wrong, and utterly wrong, when in a book issued some quarter of a century ago he followed the lead of Mr. Dyce in
assuming that because the author of 'Doctor Faustus' and
'The Jew of Malta' 'was as certainly' - and certainly it
is difficult to deny that whether as a mere transcriber
or as an original dealer in pleasantry he sometimes was -
'one of the least and worst among jesters as he was one of
the best and greatest among poets,' he could not have had
a hand in the admirable comic scenes of 'The Taming of a
Shrew.' For it is now, I should hope, unnecessary to
insist that the able and conscientious editor to whom his
fame and his readers owe so great a debt was over hasty
in assuming and asserting that he was a poet 'to whom, we
have reason to believe, nature had denied even a moderate
talent for the humorous.' The serious or would-be

poetical scenes of the play are as unmistakably the work
of an imitator as are most of the better passages in
'Titus Andronicus' and 'King Edward III.' Greene or
Peele may be responsible for the bad poetry, but there
is no reason to suppose that the great poet whose manner-
isms he imitated with so stupid a servility was incapable
of the good fun.

Had every copy of Marlowe's boyish version or perver-
sion of Ovid's 'Elegies' deservedly perished in the
flames to which it was judicially condemned by the sentence of a brace of prelates, it is possible that an
occasional bookworm, it is certain that no poetical student, would have deplored its destruction, if its demerits - hardly relieved, as his first competent editor has
happily remarked, by the occasional incidence of a fine
and felicitous couplet - could in that case have been
imagined. His translation of the first book of Lucan
alternately rises above the original and falls short of
it; often inferior to the Latin in point and weight of
expressive rhetoric, now and then brightened by a clearer
note of poetry and lifted into a higher mood of verse.
Its terseness, vigour, and purity of style would in any
case have been praiseworthy, but are nothing less than
admirable, if not wonderful, when we consider how close
the translator has on the whole (in spite of occasional
slips into inaccuracy) kept himself to the most rigid
limit of literal representation, phrase by phrase and
often line by line. The really startling force and felicity of occasional verses are worthier of remark than the
inevitable stiffness and heaviness of others, when the
technical difficulty of such a task is duly taken into
account.

One of the most faultless lyrics and one of the love-
liest fragments in the whole range of descriptive and
fanciful poetry would have secured a place for Marlowe
among the memorable men of his epoch, even if his plays
had perished with himself. His 'Passionate Shepherd'
remains ever since unrivalled in its way - a way of pure
fancy and radiant melody without break or lapse. The
untitled fragment, on the other hand, has been very
closely rivalled, perhaps very happily imitated, but only
by the greatest lyric poet of England - by Shelley alone.
Marlowe's poem of 'Hero and Leander,' closing with the
sunrise which closes the night of the lovers' union,
stands alone in its age, and far ahead of the work of any
possible competitor between the death of Spenser and the
dawn of Milton. In clear mastery of narrative and presentation, in melodious ease and simplicity of strength,
it is not less pre-eminent than in the adorable beauty

and impeccable perfection of separate lines or passages.
The place and the value of Christopher Marlowe as a
leader among English poets it would be almost impossible
for historical criticism to over-estimate. To none of
them all, perhaps, have so many of the greatest among them
been so deeply and so directly indebted. Nor was ever any
great writer's influence upon his fellows more utterly and
unmixedly an influence for good. He first, and he alone,
guided Shakespeare into the right way of work; his music,
in which there is no echo of any man's before him, found
its own echo in the more prolonged but hardly more exalted
harmony of Milton's. He is the greatest discoverer, the
most daring and inspired pioneer, in all our poetic
literature. Before him there was neither genuine blank
verse nor genuine tragedy in our language. After his arrival the way was prepared, the paths were made straight,
for Shakespeare.

53. THE MARLOWE COMMEMORATION:
HENRY IRVING AND OTHERS

1891

Henry Irving (1838-1905) was the most conspicuous actor-
producer of his time. His elaborate staging and mannered
acting produced both applause and controversy. On
16 September 1891, he unveiled the Marlowe memorial at
Canterbury.
From the 'Saturday Review' (19 September 1891).

THE MARLOWE COMMEMORATION.

The unveiling of the Memorial to CHRISTOPHER MARLOWE by
Mr. HENRY IRVING was attended by the ceremonial observan-
ces that are proper to so interesting an occasion. The
circumstances were altogether propitious. The Mayor of
Canterbury and a large gathering of the inhabitants of the
city were invited, with a goodly number of the subscribers
to the Memorial, representing literature, art, and the
stage. The conjunction was certainly a very sufficient
answer to certain desponding critics of the movement, now

happily realized in Mr. ONSLOW FORD'S admirable work.
They were met, as Mr. IRVING remarked, to honour a great
memory and to repair a great omission. The meeting was
deservedly successful, as its object was eminently worthy
of recognition. Other great names there are among English
poets - sufficiently numerous, indeed, to inspire the
enthusiasm of extension lecturers and the skill of sculp-
tors for many a year - that may justly claim the like
honour that has been accorded to Marlowe. But of all
those illustrious dead, the greatest is CHRISTOPHER
MARLOWE. He was the first, the only, herald of SHAKE-
SPEARE. He was the father of the great family of English
dramatic poets, and a lyrical poet of the first order
among Elizabethans. He was the first poet, as Mr. IRVING
happily remarked, 'who employed with a master hand the
greatest instrument of our literature.' The blank verse
of 'Faustus' and the 'Jew of Malta,' though prophetic of
SHAKSPEARE, is as individual as that of SHAKSPEARE, or of
JONSON, or of MILTON. The magic of his 'mighty line'
holds us, just as it held JONSON. The productions of
successive masters of blank verse during two centuries
have in no sense weakened our impression of the opulence
of colour and power and music that distinguish the verse
of MARLOWE. This peculiar claim to eminence was rightly
enlarged upon by Mr. IRVING in his eloquent address.
MARLOWE it was who 'first wedded the harmonies of the
great organ of blank verse,' and he it was who 'first cap-
tured the majestic rhythms of our tongue.' The majestic
rhythms of which Mr. IRVING spoke are not only of MAR-
LOWE'S making, but they have remained his to this day.
If his blank verse is something vitally distinct from all
other, the rhymed verse of 'Hero and Leander' is not less
absolutely individual. MARLOWE'S share of this 'Musaean
story' does not differ from CHAPMAN'S more completely than
it differs from all other examples of rhymed heroic verse
in English poetry. But this, of course, is but a truism
to all true ears, though perhaps not altogether superflu-
ous to recall, when to other ears - the ear of the
'Times,' for example - it seems that the versification of
KEAT'S 'Endymion' was directly derived from MARLOWE'S
'Hero and Leander.' Mr. IRVING, however, judiciously
abstained from dealing with such persuasive signs of the
awakened public interest in the poetic works of MARLOWE.
    With regard to the stage writings of the Canterbury
poet Mr. IRVING'S attitude was not less judicious. He was
proud to remember that MARLOWE'S work, like SHAKSPEARE'S,
was written primarily for the stage, and that there is excellent ground for supposing the author of 'Tamburlaine'
to have been himself an actor. But Mr. IRVING did not

promise a revival of 'Edward II.' or the 'Jew of Malta.'
He was very guarded in expressing his opinion of the
dramatic qualities of MARLOWE'S plays, and he was provok-
ingly silent concerning the total banishment of those
plays from the stage. To a student of SHAKESPEARE and an
actor of Mr. IRVING'S eminence, these questions must have
proved tempting. The occasion might be held to warrant if
not a confession of faith in the present times, some can-
did comparative criticism. From MARLOWE to MASSINGER, all
the successful dramatists were poets, and no one so much
as dreamed that matters dramatic would ever be otherwise.
Mr. IRVING did not attempt to show how far it has profited
the stage to be ministered to by dramatists who are not
poets. He was content to leave untouched this delicate
theme. Graceful reference was made by Mr. GOSSE, in
sketching the origin and progress of the MARLOWE Memorial
Fund, to the support the movement received from actors.
They were from the first most helpful and hopeful in the
cause. Mr. IRVING'S speech at Canterbury was the last,
though by no means the least, of his many valuable services, and fitly crowned the successful efforts of the
Committee. Mr. FREDERICK ROGERS, the secretary to the
Fund, and one of the originators of the Memorial, spoke
in appropriate terms of the distinctive qualities of
MARLOWE'S work. He rightly recognized in the poet something more than the precursor of SHAKSPEARE. In his short
career, as Mr. ROGERS observed, MARLOWE inspired a new
spirit into English poetry. His verse is charged with
that 'fine madness' which, as DRAYTON says, 'rightly
should possess the poet's brain.' The ancient theory of
'possession' was justified in him. We do not require to
be told that he was one of the poets who 'never blotted,'
and his verse defies the over-busy toil of those who would
analyse the secret sources of its influence. Few poets
there are whose work is so little suggestive of the Jon-
sonian maxim, 'A good poet's made, as well as born.' Some
dissatisfaction has been expressed with regard to the site
of the MARLOWE Memorial. But the grounds for discontent
seem for us to be entirely unsound. In this matter, as in
the constitution of their Committee, and the choice of
their sculptor, the subscribers are sincerely to be con-
gratulated.

54. UNSIGNED ARTICLE ON 'DOCTOR FAUSTUS'

1893

From 'Temple Bar', xcviii (1893), 515-22.

We are most of us apt to take a somewhat erroneous view of
the Elizabethan drama. It is so obviously Shakespeare who
is the chief representative of that age, that we tend to
overlook the claims of those lesser lights who cluster
round him, less brilliant perhaps, but certainly not in-
significant. Among these none presents a more striking
figure than Christopher Marlowe, in the first place
because, chronologically, his work precedes Shakespeare's,
and thus makes him the earliest dramatist of the Elizabethan age; and secondly, because his genius is of almost
unparalleled, though of unequal, excellence. And when we
remember that 'Tamburlaine the Great,' his first play, was
written in 1587, when the author was only twenty-three,
and that he died in 1593, at the age of twenty-nine, we
feel that we cannot adequately gauge how great the loss to
our national drama has been in his premature death.
    Soon after 'Tamburlaine,' probably in 1588 or 1589,
appeared his second play, 'The Tragical History of Dr.
Faustus.' The merits of this play have as yet received
but scanty recognition, though in technical skill, in
interest of plot and masterly handling, it is scarcely, if
at all, inferior to the better known 'Edward II.,' and is
certainly more advanced than Shakespeare's earlier plays.
The general outlines of the story are well known to English readers, if not through Marlowe, at least through
Goethe. One figure, however, Margaret, which was an invention of Goethe's own, cannot, of course, appear in
Marlowe's 'Faust.' It is well known how highly the later
author thought of Marlowe's work; how he contemplated
translating it into German; how he exclaimed, on hearing
it referred to, 'how grandly is it all planned.' Our only
wonder is that such admiration has not been more universal.
    The reason is partly due to the fact that it is the
edition published in 1616 and other editions of a later
date that have been more commonly reprinted than the
earlier and original edition of 1604. And the later editions may well weary and disgust modern readers, owing to
the predominance of the so-called 'comic interludes,'

about which so much has been said, and so little decided.
   But the state of the case in reality seems clear
enough. Marlowe, we know, founded his play on the prose
history of the 'Damnable Life and deserved Death of Dr.
Faustus,' which was translated into English in 1587.
This work contains the foundation of the comic interludes
which appear in the 1616 edition. But the 1604 edition
omits many of these. We conclude that Marlowe did not
introduce them into the original play, but that they were
added by later hands. And the reason why they were added
appears equally obvious. We know the kind of humour that
found favour in this age; it consisted mainly of horseplay, partly of indecency. Marlowe's 'Faust' was found to
be somewhat lacking in this quality; we may suppose that
the pit was not so full as the manager desired - his obvious course was to insert passages that would be a safe
hit, and he got some playwright to interpolate these incidents, for which there was certainly authority, and the
same authority as the author himself had used, namely, the
prose history of 1587.
   There was, perhaps, another reason for the introduction
of these passages, which we believe has hitherto escaped
observation. It is at any rate noticeable that in almost
all cases they precede a change of scene, and that two or
three characters only appear in them. It seems, therefore, not unlikely that they were inserted to fill up the
interval necessary for this change of scene, and were
acted in front of a drop scene, which would leave a narrow
strip in front of the stage sufficient for the action of
the few characters who appeared.
   If, then, we want a true idea of the play as Marlowe
conceived it, we must turn, not to the edition of 1616
and those subsequent to that date, but to the earlier form
in which it appeared in 1604.
   The curtain is raised to Faust in his study, a
thoroughly dramatic method of introducing him to the
audience, which Goethe also follows. He reviews analy-
tics, medicine, law, but feels that he has grasped the
utmost they can give, and finally opens Jerome's Bible,
in which he reads, 'The reward of sin is death.' 'If
we say that we have no sin we deceive ourselves, and the
truth is not in us. Why then, belike we must sin, and
so consequently die. Ay, we must die an everlasting
death.'
   He may well be puzzled, for he is essentially the
intellectual as opposed to the inspired man; he draws a
logical conclusion - shuts up his Bible, and turns to his
books of magic.
   There could hardly be a more perfect introduction to

the play. We have the whole man as he was before he med-
dled with magic, a perfectly-trained mind, which yet
desires more than mere learning can give it. Marlowe is
fond of this kind of character; Tamburlaine is only
another phase of Faustus. He shares the same boundless
ambition, the same taste for empire, though he tries to
realise his dreams, not by the aid of magic, but of
armies. Like Faustus too, there lies behind his concrete
ambition a desire for something unattainable, something
he can only vaguely indicate.

> Our souls, whose faculties can comprehend
> The wondrous architecture of the world,
> And measure every wandering planet's course,
> Still climbing after knowledge infinite,
> And always moving as the restless spheres
> Will us, to wear ourselves and never rest
> Until we reach the ripest fruit of all.

This intense life, this vivid ambition, is what lends
such an immense interest to Marlowe's heroes. We share
his engrossing sympathy with his main characters, because
we feel how strongly the personal element comes in. Now
in all these figures we have the author himself. There
are no false notes, the character is so strongly and
truthfully sustained throughout the play, that we feel
Marlowe must have known Tamburlaine and Faustus from the
inside, as it were. But this extreme sympathy with the
hero, which is certainly one of Marlowe's chief merits,
carries with it, almost of necessity, one of his most
serious defects. Bound up as he is in the principal
character, he has not enough interest in the minor parts,
and they tend to degenerate into lay figures, put on the
stage merely to fill the scene, or as dummy figures for
the hero to operate upon. There is no following up of
separate threads; one thread is pursued throughout the
play, the others are relentlessly cut in order to trace
its passages more clearly. 'Tamburlaine' is full of such
lay figures; he himself is absolutely the only really
interesting character. In 'Faustus' the nature of the
plot, which Marlowe received ready made, necessitated,
what in his hands became one of the most striking figures
in the whole of English drama. But if Mephistopheles had
not been, by the nature of the play, indissolubly bound up
with Faustus, we suspect that he would have been as much a
lay figure as half of those whose names appear among the
dramatis personae.

This impatience of detail and background is also responsible for the second of Marlowe's defects. He shows a

marked inability to trace change. He can register change, when the change is there, with extreme brilliance and vivid colouring, but his weakness lies in his being either unwilling or unable to trace the process. The effect is the same as a disregard of 'values' in a picture - the absence of gradation not only makes the lines unpleasantly sharp, but positively detracts from the strength of the high lights and deep shadows. Instead of the eye being led up a lane of light to the dazzling streak from which it proceeds, it is suddenly dropped upon a splash of red or orange, that seems comparatively meaningless.

So in Faustus. We appreciate the intense force and truth shown in the first soliloquy in his study and in his last soliloquy just before the end, but we cannot help feeling how much more forcible they would both have been if Marlowe had traced the steps by which, from a learned doctor, he became the devil's due. We see the same in the intermediate scenes. After his compact with Mephistoph-eles, he can pray for deliverance, and incline directly to the advice of the good or bad angel, but he can do nothing more subtle than that; he feels none of the retarding force of old traditions, no remembrances of childhood (for the allusions to childhood and hearing the clock strike ten were not hackneyed in Marlowe's day): he has no long-ing, no regret for the 'days that are no more.' All he feels is a direct passion and a direct pull back, it is all check and checkmate without any manoeuvring; there is no complicated network of feelings and surroundings, such as all those, and especially those who are highly educated and discriminating, must feel about any momentous deci-sions. This fault is particularly characteristic of Mar-lowe. In the 'Jew of Malta' we observe precisely the same defect. Some allowance must, of course, be made for the uniformly contemptible character of Barabas, but in spite of this, one cannot help feeling that a man who killed his daughter, brought on a duel between his two intending sons-in-law, poisoned a servant, a friend, two monks, and an entire nunnery, and finally betrayed Malta, and dies in an unsuccessful attempt to murder Calymath, could have been entirely free from any scruple or misgiving through-out. This fault would probably have disappeared if Mar-lowe had lived; the same defect is painfully apparent in Shakespeare's early plays. But we should remember that Marlowe died before he was thirty, and that his manner of life was not eminently conducive to study and careful writing. No other writer, perhaps, gives us such clear evidence of having thrown his compositions off at white heat, without correction or revision: a speech begun at one tavern would be continued at another, and finished

next day when the author had slept off the fumes of drink.
Marlowe's attempts at humour, as illustrated by these
comic interludes that do appear in the 1604 edition, are
almost always coarse, and never funny. It was reserved
for Shakespeare alone of that age to be funny without
being coarse, and even he is not always successful. And
such humour is exceptionally out of place in Faustus.
The savant of the world, after rejecting all serious
studies as being too elementary for him, sells his soul
to Mephistopheles, in order, apparently, to achieve practical jokes which one would have thought were too elementary for anyone else. He takes away the Pope's dinner,
boxes his ears for crossing himself, throws squibs among
the monks, and gives a wretched horse-dealer a ducking in
a pond. It is for these feats that he sells his soul:
most of us would much rather sell our souls to avoid such.
Mephistopheles, indeed, screens him from detection, but
among all his gifts he cannot impart a sense of humour.

We must of course make some allowance for the spirit
of the times. Marlowe probably had a fair idea of the
kind of joke the mass would appreciate. It is always
difficult for a man to raise his standard of wit above
that of his age.

Genius is, unhappily, too often coupled with bitterness. The very rarity of it makes its possessor feel
lonely and companionless. It was the unusual combination
of genius with geniality that made Shakespeare what he
was, and it is this bitterness that lies deeper than mere
cynicism which makes Faustus so terribly hopeless, so
despairing of salvation, and to which we owe one of the
most striking figures in all drama, namely, Mephistopheles.

Throughout the play Marlowe relies solely on moral, not
on material horror: the atmosphere in which he moves is
all 'air and fire.' This entire absence of material
horror is perhaps the most remarkable feature in the play;
Goethe cannot do without the Brocken scene; Dante makes
each round of the Inferno more physically repulsive than
the last; it is full of revolting descriptions of bodily
torture. We cannot help feeling that when the author aims
at a moral effect, any such allusions is, to a certain
extent, a confession of weakness. But Marlowe will have
none of this. Mephistopheles is the spirit of hopeless
despair, of lost opportunities and bliss forgone. He
gives no descriptions of the tortures that he undergoes
in hell; hell, on the contrary, is everywhere where he is,
he cannot get out of it; it is his own environment.

Hell hath no limits, nor is circumscribed
In one self place, for where we are is hell,
And where hell is there we must ever be.

It is impossible to speak too highly of this awful
pregnant reticence, the utter horror of it lies not in
what is said, so much as what is left unsaid. It is
noticeable that in the original edition, Faustus learns
nothing of hell, except that a great gulf separates it
from God, and that there is no hope evermore for those
who have entered it, while in the later edition, the Evil
Angel spoils the unity and the impressiveness of the last
scene by showing him a vision 'of the dammned souls on
burning forkes,' of 'the live quarters broiling on the
coals.' This must of course be placed in the same cate-
gory as the later comic interludes. The pit and gallery
would no doubt revel in such unsavoury details, the more
realistic the better; and the same reason accounts for
the appearance of the scholars after Faustus' death, who
find his 'limbs all torn asunder by the hand of death.'
These two incidents are entirely parallel to the comic
interludes, though on different lines.
    There is a certain system in the wanderings of Faustus
which we believe has not yet been noticed. As his end
draws nearer, Faustus requires more engrossing pursuits,
which will make him tend to forget his ultimate fate.
Thus at first the very studies which were too tedious for
him, are considered satisfactory; he asks Mephistopheles
a quantity of questions about astronomy, which, as he
says, are 'but freshmen's suppositions.' Then he
travels, and enters upon a course of practical jokes in
a graduated scale, each joke being more emphatically
practical than the preceding, and finally he asks Mephistopheles for a boon 'to glut the longing of his heart's
desire,' his love for the phantom Helen, whom he had
raised to satisfy the scholars. The beauty of this Helen
episode is well known; for melody and perfect rhythm it
ranks with anything in Shakespeare; indeed, in 'Troilus
and Cressida,' Shakespeare has obviously made most of the
opening lines. The subject of the play would naturally
not give many other opportunities for melodious or pretty
lines, but how perfect a master Marlowe really was of the
poetry that appeals more directly to the ear, we can
verify in his 'Hero and Leander' and the Song of the
Passionate Shepherd to his Love.
    In the last scene Marlowe appears at his best, in his
wonderful power of forcibly rendering a momentary scene.
The time for repentance is passed, Faustus dare not bring
his worthless, withered soul to God for fear of the devil,

whose he is; the struggle is over; it only remains to wait
for the inevitable end. He reaches the height of pathos
and the depth of hopelessness. 'Oh, my God!' he cries, 'I
would weep, but the devil draws in my tears; I would lift
my hands, but they hold them, they hold them.'
Art and genius seem to try to rival each other in
Faustus' last soliloquy. The art is perfect - Faustus, in
his dread and terror, praying that this one hour remaining
to him may be lengthened anyhow to 'a year, a month, a
week, a natural day.' By an exquisite touch of nature,'
as F. A. Symonds has remarked, he cries aloud the line,
which Ovid whispered in Corinna's arms:(1)

O lente, lente, currite noctis equi!

The genius is perfect. It is almost impossible to
quote, when all is so marvellous. But there is one passage where Marlowe surpasses himself, where his genius
rises to almost supernatural inspiration; it is in these
three lines:

See where Christ's blood streams in the firmament,
One drop would save my soul - half a drop, ah, my
 Christ!
Ah! rend not my heart for naming of my Christ!

It is the last hopeless cry of one who knows where he
could find safety but knows that it is out of his reach.
 Of Marlowe's life, unfortunately, or fortunately, we
know but little, except a few bare events; of personal
details, nothing. It is conjectured that he 'trailed a
pike in the Low Countries,' for reasons more obscure than
convincing; it is known that he wrote plays, it is conjectured that he was an actor; the manner of his death is
known. We know he was an Atheist, that he wrote a book
against religion which no one would consent to print, and
we find him on more than one occasion hung out to be a
warning and a deterrent to evil-doers. But do we not
learn something of him, which interests us more because it
is so much more personal, in the oft-quoted phrase 'Kynde
Kit Marlowe'?
 As a dramatist, he seems to have achieved an immediate
success, if we may judge from the rapid editions of his
plays that were issued; and the praise showered on him by
those who immediately succeeded him is evidence of the
popularity he enjoyed, not only from the theatre-going
public, but from the critics. In those days it was
exactly Marlowe's style that would be appreciated. Never
has a nation been so full of life, or so eager to learn.

The Reformation and the Renaissance had granted the people
a freedom from a double slavery, from a corrupt system of
religion on the one hand, on the other, from ignorance.
In religion there was no half-heartedness allowed, no
gradations were recognised between a violent Protestant
and a profane pagan: while Sir John Cheke, Colet, Ascham,
on their return from Italy were kindling the spark of the
new intellectual movement, and Elizabeth bemoans that her
Greek is growing rusty. Then came the final impulse for
the love of adventure and life in the discovery of Amer-
ica. 'Where men will not give one doit to relieve a lame
beggar, they will pay ten to see a dead Indian,' says
Trinculo in the 'Tempest.'
   Such are Marlowe's times, and such of necessity are
Marlowe's works, for in those days there were no conventional standards of taste, to which the author must con-
form, and thus obscure his own identity. Exactly the
opposite is seen in the eighteenth century, for almost
any of the writers of that period might have been the
author of any given production, since individuality is
completely dominated by conventional codes of what is
allowable in composition and what is not.
   It is impossible that Marlowe will ever receive just
recognition. He is in the unfortunate position of the
morning star, which invariably gets quenched by the
rising sun. With most English readers it will probably
be Shakespeare first, and the rest nowhere; but we cannot
help thinking that such a verdict is hasty and unfair,
and one against which any reader of Marlowe would give
his unquestioning vote.

Note

1 O run slowly, you horses of the night! (From Ovid,
   'Amores', I, xiii, 40.)

55. W. J. COURTHOPE

1895

William John Courthope (1842-1917) was a civil servant and
literary critic. He was editor of the later volumes in
the (then) standard edition of Pope's works. His

'History' (6 vols) is still widely read, being rich in
generalizations useful in writing undergraduate essays.
From 'A History of English Poetry' (1895-1910), II,
404-5, 420-1.

His plays have of late years been frequently considered
mainly on their technical side, and considering the vast
effect produced on the English poetical drama by Marlowe's adoption of blank verse, this is not unnatural.
As regards his own genius, however, it is not the right
way of judging; for it is plain enough that he made his
technical innovation because blank verse was the only
vehicle of poetical expression adequate to the character
of his thought; we see from 'Tamburlaine' that he regarded eloquence as a means to a practical end; and the
style of his dramas therefore cannot be fully appreciated
without a full comprehension of the intellectual and
imaginative motive which inspired his composition. What
was this? Mr. Symonds says it may be described by the
phrase L'Amour de l'Impossible. In one sense, measuring
the vastness of Marlowe's conceptions and his exaggerated
manner of expression by the limits of actual fact, this
is true; but in another sense, looking to his philosophy,
to his ideas of dramatic creation, and to his view of
rhetoric, it is the exact opposite of the truth. Marlowe
composed on a principle which was simple, direct, and
consistent with itself, but which was distinct from every
principle which had hitherto inspired tragic conception,
though some approach to it had been made in the tragedies
of Seneca. In Marlowe's plays there is no trace of the
hereditary curse of sin, which elevates the tone of
Sophocles and Aeschylus; there is no trace of the doctrine
of physical Necessity, which is the ruling thought of
Seneca; there is but seldom any trace of the conflict between good and evil, conscience and passion, which pre-
vails in the Miracle Plays and Moralities. What we do
find is Seneca's exaltation of the freedom of the human
will, dissociated from the idea of Necessity, and joined
with Machiavelli's principle of the excellence of virtù.
This principle is represented under a great variety of
aspects; sometimes in the energy of a single heroic
character, as in 'Tamburlaine'; sometimes in the pursuit
of unlawful knowledge, as in 'Faustus'; again, in 'The Jew
of Malta,' in the boundless hatred and revenge of Barabas;
in Guise plotting the massacre of the Huguenots out of
cold-blooded policy; and in Mortimer planning the murder
of Edward II. from purely personal ambition. Incidentally,

no doubt, in some of these instances, the indulgence of
unrestrained passion brings ruin in its train; but it is
not so much for the sake of the moral that Marlowe composed his tragedies, as because his imagination delighted
in the exhibition of the vast and tremendous consequences
produced by the determined exercise of will in pursuit of
selfish objects. So far from loving grandiosity and
extravagance for their own sake, the violence of his conceptions springs from a belief of what is possible to the
resolved and daring soul....

His dramas are very ill-constructed. He cares nothing
for the development of plot and concentrates his whole
attention on the exhibition of an abstract principle,
embodied for the moment in a single character. When he
has placed his leading personage in a situation where his
ruling purpose - be it desire of conquest, as in Tamburlaine; revenge, as in Barabas; ambition, as in Mortimer or
Guise - can have full play, he is satisfied. His invention occupies itself with finding means to remove the
obstacles that oppose the achievement of this central
purpose, and up to a certain point his method produces
interesting dramatic situations: the first two acts, for
example, of the 'Jew of Malta' are excellent. But after
a time the action drags through want of complexity; and
then the exhibition of character becomes mechanical and
monotonous.

Again, Marlowe's theory of dramatic action is contrary
to the constitution of human nature: it eliminates the
factor of Conscience. Following Machiavelli in counting
'religion but a childish toy,' and in holding that there
was 'no sin but ignorance,' he exalted 'resolution' as
the highest of human virtues. But this is a principle
better suited for melodrama than for tragedy. If there
is something fascinating in the steady purpose of even a
savage like Tamburlaine, or of a villain like Barabas,
how infinitely inferior in dramatic interest is such a
representation, to the portrayal of that complexity of
motives and circumstance which produces the entanglements
of human conduct! How ill does it compare, for example,
with the situations produced by the *irresolution* of
Hamlet and Macbeth, or by the senile folly of Lear?
Shakespeare was not less keenly alive than Marlowe to the
dramatic value of resolute will as a principle of action:
he has represented it in the character of Iago, working on
the credulous weakness of Othello; but he has constructed
the complex action of his tragedy in such a way that the
spectators are never left for a moment in doubt as to the
moral judgment they ought to pass on the various characters. For the same reason 'Faustus' is Marlowe's greatest

and most interesting play, because in that alone does he give a sustained representation of the state of a human soul torn between the conflicting principles of good and evil.

Once more. The narrowness of Marlowe's conception of Man and Nature is seen in his representations of female character. As his tendency was to make everything in his plays bow before the march of some supreme irresistible will, the weaker feminine element in Nature was necessarily thrust by him into a subordinate position. Marlowe, like Greene, can represent only one type of woman - a being who becomes the devoted, but almost passive, instrument of masculine resolution. Zenocrate, Abigail, Isabel, and (strange to say) Catherine de Medicis, all of them cast in this mould, are the only creations he can show against the endless varieties of female character depicted in the dramas of Shakespeare.

Considering these features in Marlowe's dramas, we cannot fail to be struck with the contrast between his genius and the genius of men like Sidney and Spenser. The two latter reflect the chivalrous element that was still strong in English society, the high principle of honour, the elevation of sentiment, the sense of duty and religion. From all these restraining principles in the conscience of the nation Marlowe cut himself off; and by his exaltation of the Machiavellian principle severed his connection, not only with Puritanism, but with whatever was most lofty and noble in the history of England. On the other hand, his imagination was borne along, as Spenser's and Sidney's never was, on the full stream of a great national movement. His dramas were produced just before, and just after, the defeat of the Spanish Armada - that is to say at the moment when the people were awakening to the full consciousness of greatness in their dangers and their destinies.

56. G. B. SHAW

1896

Bernard Shaw (1856-1950), playwright and critic, in the earlier stages of his career contributed a series of important reviews of contemporary theatre productions to the 'Saturday Review', from 1895 to 1898. The productions

of William Poel (1852-1934) were most influential in the
formation of techniques and attitudes in the modern theatre. For the references to 'Mr. G. B. Shaw', Lamb and
Swinburne, see Introduction pp. 12 and 22, and Nos 27 and 52.
This review, published 11 July 1896, speaks not only for
Shaw but for any surfeited with the kind of comment reproduced in the present collection.
From 'Dramatic Opinions and Essays' (New York, 1909),
36-43.

THE SPACIOUS TIMES

'Doctor Faustus.' By Christopher Marlowe. Acted by
members of the Shakespeare Reading Society at St.
George's Hall, on a stage after the model of the
Fortune Playhouse, 2 July, 1896.

Mr. William Poel, in drawing up an announcement of the
last exploit of the Elizabethan Stage Society, had no
difficulty in citing a number of eminent authorities as
to the superlative merits of Christopher Marlowe. The
dotage of Charles Lamb on the subject of the Elizabethan
dramatists has found many imitators, notably Mr. Swinburne, who expresses in verse what he finds in books as
passionately as a poet expressed what he finds in life.
Among them, it appears, is a Mr. G. B. Shaw, in quoting
whom Mr. Poel was supposed by many persons to be quoting
me. But though I share the gentleman's initials, I do
not share his views. He can admire a fool: I cannot,
even when his folly not only expresses itself in blank
verse, but actually invents that art form for the purpose.
I admit that Marlowe's blank verse has charm of color and
movement; and I know only too well how its romantic march
caught the literary imagination and founded that barren
and horrible worship of blank verse for its own sake which
has since desolated and laid waste the dramatic poetry of
England. But the fellow was a fool for all that. He
often reminds me, in his abysmally inferior way, of
Rossini. Rossini had just the same trick of beginning
with a magnificently impressive exordium, apparently pregnant with the most tragic developments, and presently lap-
sing into arrant triviality. But Rossini lapses amus-
ingly; writes 'Excusez du peu' at the double bar which
separates the sublime from the ridiculous; and is gay,
tuneful and clever in his frivolity. Marlowe, the moment
the exhaustion of the imaginative fit deprives him of the
power of raving, becomes childish in thought, vulgar and

wooden in humor, and stupid in his attempts at invention.
He is the true Elizabethan blank-verse beast, itching to
frighten other people with the superstitious terrors and
cruelties in which he does not himself believe, and wal-
lowing in blood, violence, muscularity of expression and
strenuous animal passion as only literary men do when they
become thoroughly depraved by solitary work, sedentary
cowardice, and starvation of the sympathetic centres.
It is not surprising to learn that Marlowe was stabbed in
a tavern brawl: what would be utterly unbelievable would
be his having succeeded in stabbing any one else. On
paper the whole obscene crew of these blank-verse rhetori-
cians could outdare Lucifer himself: Nature can produce no
murderer cruel enough for Webster, nor any hero bully
enough for Chapman, devout disciples, both of them, of Kit
Marlowe. But you do not believe in their martial ardor as
you believe in the valor of Sidney or Cervantes. One
calls the Elizabethan dramatists imaginative, as one might
say the same of a man in delirium tremens; but even that
flatters them; for whereas the drinker can imagine rats
and snakes and beetles which have some sort of resemblance
to real ones, your typical Elizabethan heroes of the
mighty line, having neither the eyes to see anything real
nor the brains to observe it, could no more conceive a
natural or convincing stage figure than a blind man can
conceive a rainbow or a deaf one the sound of an orchestra.
Such success as they have had is the success which any
fluent braggart and liar may secure in a pothouse. Their
swagger and fustian, and their scraps of Cicero and Aris-
totle, passed for poetry and learning in their own day
because their public was Philistine and ignorant. To-day,
without having by any means lost this advantage, they
enjoy in addition the quaintness of their obsolescence,
and, above all, the splendor of the light reflected on
them from the reputation of Shakespeare. Without that
light they would now be as invisible as they are insuffer-
able. In condemning them indiscriminately, I am only
doing what Time would have done if Shakespeare had not
rescued them. I am quite aware that they did not get
their reputations for nothing; that there were degrees
of badness among them; that Greene was really amusing,
Marston spirited and silly-clever, Cyril Tourneur able to
string together lines of which any couple picked out and
quoted separately might pass as a fragment of a real organic poem, and so on. Even the brutish pedant Jonson was
not heartless, and could turn out prettily affectionate
verses and foolishly affectionate criticisms; whilst the
plausible firm of Beaumont and Fletcher, humbugs as they
were, could produce plays which were, all things

considered, not worse than 'The Lady of Lyons.' But
these distinctions are not worth making now. There is
much variety in a dust-heap, even when the rag-picker is
done with it; but we throw it indiscriminately into the
'destructor' for all that. There is only one use left for
the Elizabethan dramatists, and that is the purification
of Shakespeare's reputation from its spurious elements.
Just as you can cure people of talking patronizingly about
'Mozartian melody' by showing them that the tunes they
imagine to be his distinctive characteristics were the
commonplaces of his time, so it is possible, perhaps, to
cure people of admiring, as distinctively characteristic
of Shakespeare, the false, forced rhetoric, the callous
sensation-mongering in murder and lust, the ghosts and
combats, and the venal expenditure of all the treasures of
his genius on the bedizenment of plays which are, as
wholes, stupid toys. When Sir Henry Irving presently
revives 'Cymbeline' at the Lyceum, the numerous descen-
dants of the learned Shakespearean enthusiast who went
down on his knees and kissed the Ireland forgeries will
see no difference between the great dramatist who changed
Imogen from a mere name in a story to a living woman, and
the manager-showman who exhibited her with the gory trunk
of a newly beheaded man in her arms. But why should we,
the heirs of so many greater ages, with the dramatic
poems of Goethe and Ibsen in our hands, and the music of
a great dynasty of musicians, from Bach to Wagner, in our
ears - why should we waste our time on the rank and file
of the Elizabethans, or encourage foolish modern persons
to imitate them, or talk about Shakespeare as if his moral
platitudes, his jingo claptraps, his tavern pleasantries,
his bombast and drivel, and his incapacity for following
up the scraps of philosophy he stole so aptly, were as
admirable as the mastery of poetic speech, the feeling for
nature, and the knack of character-drawing, fun, and heart
wisdom which he was ready, like a true son of the theatre,
to prostitute to any subject, any occasion, and any theatrical employment? The fact is, we are growing out of
Shakespeare. Byron declined to put up with his reputation
at the beginning of the nineteenth century; and now, at
the beginning of the twentieth, he is nothing but a
household pet. His characters still live; his word pictures of woodland and wayside still give us a Bank-holiday
breath of country air; his verse still charms us; his
sublimities still stir us; the commonplaces and trumperies
of the wisdom which age and experience bring to all of us
are still expressed by him better than by anybody else;
but we have nothing to hope from him and nothing to learn
from him - not even how to write plays, though he does

that so much better than most modern dramatists. And if
this is true of Shakespeare, what is to be said of Kit
Marlowe?
Kit Marlowe, however, did not bore me at St. George's
Hall as he has always bored me when I have tried to read
him without skipping. The more I see of these performances
by the Elizabethan Stage Society, the more I am convinced
that their method of presenting an Elizabethan play is not
only the right method for that particular sort of play,
but that any play performed on a platform amidst the audience gets closer home to its hearers than when it is presented as a picture framed by a proscenium. Also, that
we are less conscious of the artificiality of the stage
when a few well-understood conventions, adroitly handled,
are substituted for attempts at an impossible scenic
verisimilitude. All the old-fashioned tale-of-adventure
plays, with their frequent changes of scene, and all the
new problem plays, with their intense intimacies, should
be done in this way.
The E.S.S. made very free with 'Doctor Faustus.'
Their devils, Baliol and Belcher to wit, were not theatrical devils with huge pasteboard heads, but pictorial
Temptation-of-St.-Anthony devils such as Martin Schon-
gauer drew. The angels were Florentine fifteenth-century
angels, with their draperies sewn into Botticellian folds
and tucks. The Emperor's bodyguard had Maximilianesque
uniforms copied from Holbein. Mephistophilis made his
first appearance as Mr. Joseph Pennell's favorite devil
from the roof of Notre Dame, and, when commanded to
appear as a Franciscan friar, still proclaimed his moder-
nity by wearing an electric bulb in his cowl. The Seven
Deadly Sins were *tout ce qu'il y a de plus fin de siècle,*
(1) the five worst of them being so attractive that they
got rounds of applause on the strength of their appearance alone. In short, Mr. William Poel gave us an artistic rather than a literal presentation of Elizabethan
conditions, the result being, as always happens in such
cases, that the picture of the past was really a picture
of the future. For which result he is, in my judgment, to
be highly praised. The performance was a wonder of artistic discipline in this lawless age. It is true, since the
performers were only three or four instead of fifty times
as skilful as ordinary professional actors, that Mr. Poel
has had to give up all impetuosity and spontaneity of
execution, and to have the work done very slowly and carefully. But it is to be noted that even Marlowe, treated
in this thorough way, is not tedious; whereas Shakespeare,
rattled and rushed and spouted and clattered through in
the ordinary professional manner, all but kills the

audience with tedium. For instance, Mephistophilis was as
joyless and leaden as a devil need be - it was clear that
no stage-manager had ever exhorted him, like a lagging
horse, to get the long speeches over as fast as possible,
old chap - and yet he never for a moment bored us as
Prince Hal and Poins bore us at the Haymarket. The actor
who hurries reminds the spectators of the flight of time,
which it is his business to make them forget. Twenty
years ago the symphonies of Beethoven used to be rushed
through in London with the sole object of shortening the
agony of the audience. They were then highly unpopular.
When Richter arrived he took the opposite point of view,
playing them so as to prolong the delight of the audience;
and Mottl dwells more lovingly on Wagner than Richter does
on Beethoven. The result is that Beethoven and Wagner are
now popular. Mr. Poel has proved that the same result
will be attained as soon as blank-verse plays are produced under the control of managers who like them, instead of openly and shamelessly treating them as inflic-
tions to be curtailed to the utmost. The representation
at St. George's Hall went without a hitch from beginning
to end, a miracle of diligent preparedness. Mr. Manner-
ing, as Faustus, had the longest and the hardest task;
and he performed it conscientiously, punctually, and well.
The others did no less with what they had to do. The
relief of seeing actors come on the stage with the simplicity and abnegation of children, instead of bounding
on to an enthusiastic reception with the 'Here I am again'
expression of the popular favorites of the ordinary stage,
is hardly to be described. Our professional actors are
now looked at by the public from behind the scenes; and
they accept that situation and glory in it for the sake
of the 'personal popularity' it involves. What a gigantic
reform Mr. Poel will make if his Elizabethan Stage should
lead to such a novelty as a theatre to which people go to
see the play instead of to see the cast!

Note

1 All those most in the style of our time.

Select Bibliography

The following is a select list of books and articles containing material, or discussions of material, relevant to the study of Marlowe's reputation up to 1900.

BAKELESS, JOHN, 'The Tragical History of Christopher Marlowe', Cambridge, Mass., 1942, 2 vols.
BOAS, FREDERICK, 'Christopher Marlowe: a Biographical and Critical Study', Oxford, 1940.
BROOKE, C. F. TUCKER, The Reputation of Christopher Marlowe, 'Transactions of the Connecticut Academy of Arts and Sciences' xxv (1922), 347-408. Indispensable.
BROWN, J. R., Marlowe and the Actors, 'Tulane Drama Review', viii (1964), 155-73.
CHALMERS, A. D. (ed.), 'The General Biographical Dictionary', 1815.
LEE, SIDNEY, article on Marlowe in the 'Dictionary of National Biography', 1893. Essential for the state of Marlowe scholarship at the time.
O'NEILL, JUDITH (ed.), 'Critics on Marlowe', 1969. Of 123 pages of selections, 27 are devoted to critics before 1930.
RIBNER, IRVING, Marlowe and the Critics, 'Tulane Drama Review', viii (1964), 211-24. Important.
SEYLER, DOROTHY U. The Critical Reputation of Christopher Marlowe, 1800-99. State University of New York at Albany dissertation. See 'Dissertation Abstracts International', I, xxx, 3435A-36A.

Index

Index references are grouped as follows: I Authors of critical comment reproduced; II Marlowe: summary comment; life and opinions; plays and poems; III General, including other authors, actors, publishers, etc.

I AUTHORS OF CRITICAL COMMENT